ONE GOAL,
ONE HORSE

Ricky George

Pen Press Publishers Ltd
London

ONE GOAL, ONE HORSE

Ricky George

First published in Great Britain by
Pen Press Publishers Ltd
39-41, North Road
Islington
London N7 9DP

ISBN 1 900796 44 9

A catalogue record of this book is available
from the British Library

Cover photograph of Earth Summit © Trevor Meek

Dedicated to

Vicky and Ella

Acknowledgements

Thanks go to Val Winfield my long suffering secretary of sixteen years duration, for her help in preparing the manuscript and putting up with my incompetence. To Jeff Zemmel for reminding me of the events *he* was involved in. To Keith Dodd for giving me the idea for the title. To Motty, obviously, who along with Ronnie Radford, Billy Meadows and Ken Nicholas became my greatest friends through football. And most of all to Patricia, Daniel, Adam and Rebecca for their encouragement, love and support.

One Goal, One Horse
Author's Note

I had a varied and exciting football career. At the age of fifteen, I joined Tottenham Hotspur in June of 1961, just after the club had won the "Double". I spent four years at White Hart Lane before being released on a free transfer to experience life at clubs such as Watford, Bournemouth, and Oxford United. Latterly, I returned to my home town club, Barnet, where I spent the greater part of my career, appearing nearly three hundred times. For a short spell in the early seventies, I was transferred to Hereford United, where I took part in an historic FA Cup victory over Newcastle United. The goal I scored in that match, which turned out to be the winner, gave a headline to the career which otherwise would have been one of happy, local memories, albeit interesting and exciting to me, but not of interest to anyone else, on the surface.

Whilst still playing part-time, I worked for Adidas, the German Sports shoe manufacturer, before going into business on my own in 1975.

The Adidas experience was memorable as I was dealing with International players of both England and Scotland. There are several stories.

In 1993, I took part in an operation to save Barnet Football Club from extinction. This turned from glory and elation into bitterness and litigation, ending in great disappointment and severe financial loss for me. The story is remarkable, stranger than fiction.

My business career has been a tale of great success and huge failure, in at times, spectacular circumstances.

In 1992, I had the good fortune to be offered a sixth share in a racehorse, Earth Summit. The Horse cost five thousand eight hundred guineas in total, and after winning the 1998 Grand National, took his career earnings to in excess of £300 000. My winnings from the National came at another critical, financial period in my life.

Through it all, I have had the support of my family, in particular my wife of thirty years, Patricia, who is the finest example of a friend I shall ever know.

This book is dedicated to her, our three children and the memory of my Mother, May Victoria George, who taught me the meaning of true love and who is the inspiration behind my desire to write.

Foreword
by John Motson

I first met Ricky George in 1964, across the counter in the old Barnet Press newspaper office where I was a junior reporter. He had just been released from Tottenham to go to Watford, a move that marked the start of a fairly chequered footballing career.

But the moment that changed both our lives was in 1972. I was a junior member of the 'Match of the Day' commentary team sent to cover an FA Cup third-round replay between non-league Hereford United and the mighty Newcastle. The match that Newcastle were expected to win easily became what I still consider to be the greatest cup shock of my time, as Rick's winning goal clinched the match for the underdogs. That evening the game, accompanied by my commentary, got national prominence on 'Match of the Day' and played a major part in changing the course of my career.

From what had previously been a trial position, I was offered a new contract as a regular member of the 'Match of the Day' team, and I've been there ever since. Now in my thirtieth year with the programme, I am delighted that Ricky George has chosen this moment to write his memoirs.

Our paths crossed again some twenty-five years later when Ricky bought a share in the steeplechaser Earth Summit. I must say, rather red-faced now, that I actually turned down a share in the horse but suggested to the partnership that Mr George might be interested. He was, and the rest is history, as Earth Summit went on to win the 1998 Grand National. Although I hadn't taken the opportunity of a share in the horse, Ricky and I had a sizeable joint bet on the winner!

We still have a Christmas reunion after all these years to celebrate the anniversary of Hereford's win, an event that had such a great influence on both our lives. Our friendship has endured throughout and I've always had the warmest regard for a guy who is notoriously unreliable, but which makes him even more fun.

There are many adjectives that could be applied to Ricky George: lucky and courageous are only two of them. But if I had to sum him up in one sentence it would be this: he is one of the most generously spirited people I have ever met.

'Motty'

Introduction

On a chilly February night in 1998, I was walking home along Barnet High Street with Keith Dodd, a close friend, someone I had known for over thirty years. We had been out for one of those rare evenings, a few pints in the Monken Holt and a Chinese in the spectacularly empty Golden Bird Restaurant. It was rare because these days we only see each other in couples or in Florida, where we both have holiday homes. This, in spite of the fact that we live barely 200 yards apart.

It had been a good night and we had discussed everything from business to the cost of our wives' preoccupation with the game of golf. I had enjoyed it and we'd had some laughs, our voices echoing noisily around the Golden Bird.

As we walked briskly northwards up the Old Great North Road that runs right through the centre of Barnet and on to Hatfield, Keith brought up one subject that had not been aired.

'By the way,' he began, 'every time I open the newspaper there's something about you in it, it's either that blinking goal or that bloomin' horse of yours.'

We both laughed. 'That sums my life up, doesn't it?' I said. 'One goal, one horse.'

'There you are, mate,' Keith was still laughing as we parted and he walked on, 'you've got the title for your book now.'

I am amazed, even today, at the amount of coverage Hereford United's FA Cup victory over Newcastle in 1972 still commands, particularly on BBC TV. Ronnie Radford's wonderful equaliser is still regarded as one of the great goals of all time. My strike was far less impressive but its impact created the history. As the winner, it gave me a precious memory from what would have been an enjoyable but, outside of Barnet, a largely anonymous football career. From Tottenham Hotspur where it began in 1961 to my home town team where it finished in 1977, there are dozens of stories I

1

have yearned to impart. But to whom? Barnet supporters may be interested in some. In 1993, for example, sixteen years after playing my last professional match, I found myself embroiled in a bitter and acrimonious battle for control of the club. That is a book in itself.

Keith's amusing jibe was to prove dramatically prophetic. The 'bloomin' horse', a handsome brown gelding by the name of Earth Summit, had won the Coral Welsh National at the end of December. That event, and my association with the animal, had lead to a great deal of publicity concerning the comparisons between great sporting moments in one's life. The Martell Grand National, the world's greatest steeplechase, had been Earth Summit's target since 1994 when, as a novice, he cantered away with the Scottish National at Ayr.

Could the incredible happen? How much luck is anyone entitled to? Who wins the lottery twice?

On April 4th 1998, the bloomin' horse won the Grand National by eleven lengths and a distance. The incredible had happened.

In the twenty-six years between the two great events there has been plenty to keep my adrenaline racing. It is not all football and racing related, in fact some business experiences I have had have been positively terrifying.

I think it adds up to a book and, having been handed the title on a plate, I would never have forgiven myself if I hadn't written it.

As for its merits, I'll let you decide.

Chapter One
Knave or Legend?

In February 1996, my friend and business partner Jeffrey Zemmel and I had a very early morning meeting at the Regents Park Marriot Hotel. So early, in fact, that I was back home just before 9am.

As I walked into the kitchen my mobile phone rang; it was my wife Patricia.

'Where are you?' she asked.

'I'm in the kitchen,' I replied.

'No, don't mess around honey, please, I'm serious.'

I laughed and went upstairs to the bedroom where she was phoning me from. She wasn't laughing. One of our closest friends, Tish Hannington, had just called to say there was a big headline and article about me in the *Daily Mirror*. I went straight out and bought a copy. There was a recent photo and a banner headline that read 'FA Cup Legend in £4 Million Fashion Fraud Quiz.' The article referred to the fact that I had been interviewed, along with several other people (about thirty in fact), over an alleged fraud on the designer footwear and apparel giant, Timberland. I called Jeff Zemmel and read him the article.

'It's an outrageous slur,' he commented, 'there's no way you're a legend, how dare they?'

A couple of weeks earlier, two officers from Surrey Police had called at Jeff's home, politely explaining that they were investigating an alleged fraud. He was invited to attend an interview at Woking Police Station. They asked him if I would give them a call on the same subject.

About six months before that, we had been involved in putting together a deal, worth $6 million, to purchase shoes from Timberland UK. The goods should have gone to South Africa but at the last minute the buyers backed out. We had no choice other than to sell them domestically. One of our

3

customers based in the East End sold a quantity into SavaCentre, the giant outlet owned by Sainsburys supermarkets. When Timberland heard that their shoes were being offered cheaply in a supermarket, they claimed the goods had been stolen and called the police. Incredibly, a warrant was granted and both SavaCentre and our East End wholesaler were descended upon. Thousands of pairs of shoes were seized and impounded, and other warehouses and outlets were raided simultaneously. In the space of twenty-four hours the Surrey Police retrieved nearly seventy-five percent of merchandise for a company which no longer had title to it. It was a classic case of the bigger the plaintiff the stronger the action. I was outraged.

Though I was interviewed, after eighteen months of investigation the matter was dropped. The majority of the footwear turned out to be of second quality and was returned to Timberland. A compensation figure was agreed and that was the end of it.

I decided against issuing proceedings for libellous use of the word 'legend'.

Chapter Two
The Horse

I always wake just before seven in the mornings. Today was no different and I was in a strange bed. In room number two of the Park Hotel in Aintree, Patricia was sleeping in the tiny bed next to mine. I looked at her and smiled to myself, thinking of her words to me a few months before, just prior to the Welsh Grand National. She had been standing at the sink in our kitchen at home in Barnet. It was Boxing Day and she was looking gorgeous in a little black, fluffy woollen top, black leather trousers and yellow marigolds. I was watching her washing up and mulling over what time we would leave to go to Chepstow the following day.

I had been on about it all over Christmas, much to her annoyance.

Without turning round, she said, in that wonderfully dismissive way of hers, 'If Earth Summit wins tomorrow, I'll...' She made me a promise so erotic that I couldn't possibly print it; suffice to say it contained enough graphic detail to provoke a split-second thought that I might possibly nobble all our four-legged Superstar's opponents in the three-mile, five-furlong steeplechase.

I didn't need to because on that day 'Digger', as he is known at the yard, ran his rivals into the bottomless Chepstow ground. Jumping the last fully fifteen lengths in front, he saw off a determined challenge by the diminutive grey, Dom Samurai, to win the Coral Welsh National by one-and-a-half lengths, at the incredible odds of 25/1. My returns that day included, belatedly, one in kind from Patricia.

I looked away from my sleeping beauty and pulled back the curtains a fraction. To my delight I saw it was raining, heavily. '*Yes!*' I whispered loudly, punching the air. She stirred, turned over and without opening her eyes, murmured, 'No, honey, I'm too tired.'

It was Grand National day, 1998. Even now, I find it hard to believe that after thirty-four years of trying to find the winner of the world's greatest steeplechase, we actually owned a horse that would go to post along with thirty-seven others that very afternoon.

The *Racing Post* and *Sporting Life* had been pushed through the door and I tried to settle back quietly on my bed and read all about our chances. It was impossible to concentrate. What, with respect to all the hacks, could anyone tell me that I didn't already know about Earth Summit?

Apart from any other reason to choose a horse to follow in the Grand National, there are two very obvious abilities the animal must possess. To jump and to stay the distance, four and a half miles. As there are very few races of four miles and beyond in the racing calendar, it is impossible to assess the latter in the majority of runners. Of those horses who had competed in the great race before, one, Rough Quest, was a previous winner. He was a danger if reproducing his best form. Of the others, the grey, Suny Bay, had finished second last year. Following my basic principals for National success, both had rock solid credentials.

I made them the dangers to Earth Summit.

There were no big headlines concerning our chances on the morning of the race. Rough Quest was well fancied, as was Suny Bay, even with top weight of twelve stone. The real clue, however, lay in the betting.

Nowhere could you get better than 10/1 for Earth Summit. Ladbrokes went 9/1, as did Corals. Over the preceding weeks, we had been backed from 33s, steadily, down through 25s, 20s and 16s; even 12/1 was no longer available.

Someone was backing our horse, and I wasn't sure it was the owners.

The Summit partnership consists of six men, five in early middle age. The youngest by some way is Mike Bailey, a local housing officer from the Wirral in Cheshire. Michael, as his mum calls him, is a racing anorak. A Liverpool lad and single, he spends his free time at the races. He is quiet, shy even and very knowledgeable on matters of the Turf. As far as I know, he doesn't bet.

Gordon Perry describes himself as 'something in the city, doing a bit of this and a bit of that'. He is an ex-army officer, also single, who loves his racing every bit as much as Mike Bailey does. Gordon is the epitome of the perfect English gentleman, polite, genteel and a touch shy, until a few post-race whiskies have been downed in earnest. Gordon does bet but I have no idea of his maximum stake. He is always nervous before a race, but sensitive and emotional, a genuine chap. Peter Earl is an accountant. Apart from being a five-handicap golfer, he is, by some way, the best looking of the partnership. He has an appealing charm to go with all that and before I give the impression that he and I are in any way 'friends', I will add that he is very happily married to the lovely Jo. As an accountant, I have no doubt that he is a sensible punter, but that is none of my business. Peter Earl is one of the few people you meet in life who retain their charm when completely pissed.

Nigel Payne heads the Summit partnership. A school friend of Peter's, Nigel's many qualities do not include boyish good looks and golf proficiency. Not that he is unattractive to women. Liz Payne, another lovely lady, clearly adores her husband and I have heard rumours that one Kathy Twiston-Davies has, on the odd occasion, pinched several inches of the fleshy posterior whilst threading her way through the throng at the Hollow Bottom in Guiting Power.

Whether or not this last piece of Cotswolds smut has any basis in fact one can only speculate. What is not in dispute is the popularity of this essential sportsman. He originally qualified as a solicitor after leaving Lancing College, but the free spirit that lives within a man like Nigel Payne took him by the hand and led him into a world far more suitable. He went to work for Ladbrokes. In 1976 he became press officer at Aintree, a job for which he was so eminently qualified, he is still there today, twenty-odd years on. His lifelong ambition has been to have a runner in the Grand National. Apart from his family, Nigel has two loves in life, Arsenal Football Club and Earth Summit. What a year 1998 was for him.

Early in 1992, he decided to put together a small group to purchase a four-year-old gelding by probably the best specialist National Hunt stallion ever to stand in Britain.

Celtic Cone won nine flat races and five hurdle races in a four-year career between 1969 and 1973, before retiring to stud at Robin and Scarlet Knipe's stud in Herefordshire. His wins were all tests of stamina. The Queen Alexandra stakes, over two-and-three-quarter miles at Ascot, is the longest race in the flat calendar and one of the longest handicaps; the Ascot stakes is over two-and-a-half miles. Both fell to the son of Celtic Ash.

Nigel, through his work in the media, had come to know a guy called Bob Sims who runs a very successful company that buys media space for clients. Bob, apart from being a lifelong National Hunt enthusiast, is also a lifelong friend of mine. We met at the age of ten when representing Barnet Boys Under Eleven football team. Having attended East Barnet Grammar School together, Bob and I share some memories that are not all soccer related.

Nigel and Bob were looking for a sixth partner. I received a call from the Media Shop on September 30th, 1992.

Bob Sims has an endearing way of addressing old friends.

'Hello Wanker,' came the familiar dulcet tone. He got straight to the point. 'Now look, Motson says you might be cunt enough to take the final share in this horse I'm involved in.' His reference to our mutual friend, BBC's greatly loved John 'Motty' Motson, was because John had actually turned down the opportunity to take the final share.

Bob gave me brief details and told me the financial outlay. Earth Summit, named after the momentous event that took place in Brazil in 1992, had cost 5800 guineas at the Doncaster Sales. My share would cost me about £1200 because the other five had already incurred some fees at Nigel Twiston-Davies' Grange Hill stables. Bob, typically frank, went on, 'If you've got any brains, George, you'll wait until tomorrow when he runs in his bumper at Cheltenham.' A bumper is a National Hunt flat race.

The following day, I found myself in William Hill's betting shop in Barnet High Street.

Earth Summit is easily distinguishable by his three white socks and two blazes of white, one between his eyes and one between his nostrils. He is not very big, slightly less than sixteen hands, and has a fairly short stride.

Throughout the two-mile race of twenty-odd runners, he was never out of the front five. Shaken up a couple of times to keep his place, he kept on up the Cheltenham hill to finish second, a length and a half behind the winner, Amtrak Express.

I called Sims immediately. He didn't disappoint. 'I take it you're in, George, make sure that cheque goes off, you unreliable bastard.' I was still smiling as I wrote it.

Thus, via the reluctance of my old mate Motty and the

charming auspices of my old mate Sims, I became part owner of Earth Summit, equine superstar.

Earth Summit's mother is a mare called Win Green Hill and she is owned by trainer and breeder Jim Old. Win Green Hill is by National Trust, a tough stayer on the flat, winning nine races from twenty-eight starts in four seasons. The mare won a novice chase at Devon and Exeter and the family has produced a number of point-to-point winners, showing some jumping ability in recent generations. However, the most significant ancestor of Earth Summit's female line was a mare called Yesterling who was foaled in 1889. Yesterling was an ancestor of Anglo and Red Alligator, winners of the Grand National in 1966 and 1968 respectively.

In the year Earth Summit was foaled, 1988, Celtic Shot won the Champion Hurdle, the biggest success so far for the sire, Celtic Cone. The handsome stallion also sired Celtic Chief, third in the Champion hurdle the same year, and Ryde Again who won the Daily Express Hurdle at Ascot. Stan's Pride was another high-class hurdler by Celtic Cone, whose progeny also include the classy chaser Combs Ditch, and Laundryman, who won five novice chases in 1990-91. Other noteworthy sons of Celtic Cone were Celtic Ryde and Celtic Isle, and most recently, Go Ballistic, who beat subsequent 1998 Gold Cup second, Strong Promise at Wincanton, and was in fact favourite at 7-1 in the 1997 National, in which he pulled up three out.

In the February 1988 edition of *Pacemaker International*, around the time of Earth Summit's birth, Charles Lewis wrote of Celtic Cone:

'A particularly game performer, he had the ability to quicken at the end of a gruelling race and possessed almost the perfect credentials for a breeder seeking a potential jump stallion.'

Well spotted, Jim Old.

Earth Summit, though lighter in his coat than his father, has inherited the other distinguishing features of Celtic Cone, namely the three white socks and white blaze.

Later on in the same 1988 article, Lewis, writing about Combs Ditch and Stan's Pride, stated: 'Both horses were at their best with plenty of give in the ground as indeed are many of Celtic Cone's stock.'

I looked out of the window again. It was still raining.

9

Those backing Earth Summit to win the 1998 Martell Grand National were the wonderful mass of people known as the Great British Public.

Not many will take the trouble to go as far back as 1889 to trace the bloodline of a thoroughbred racehorse before investing a few quid. Many will, however, have taken serious note of the form of an animal who has appeared over thirty times on a racecourse.

Regular students of form will know that Celtic Cone's progeny appreciated soft ground. All will know that Earth Summit's track record clearly shows a liking for long distances. He is not the fastest horse in Nigel Twiston-Davies' yard, but I venture to say he is close to being the most popular. This is partly due to his wonderful temperament, which is greatly due to his courage and character.

Of his thirty-three races prior to the 1998 Martell Grand National, our hero had won eight times, finished second on six occasions, and third once. He unseated Carl Llewellyn at Worcester in a novice hurdle as long ago as 1993 and fell once, at the second last at Cheltenham, when looking all over the winner of the Compass Group Handicap Chase in December 1994.

In April 1994, ridden by David Bridgwater, the Stakis Scottish Grand National, over four miles and one furlong at Ayr, was taken in phenomenal style. Not only was Earth Summit still a novice at six years old, he won, easing up by fourteen lengths on *good* ground. Those who backed him that day enjoyed odds of 16/1.

The big one was always the target, but after Tom Jenks rode him to a hard-fought win in very heavy ground in the Edward Hanmer Memorial Chase at Haydock in January 1995, a leg injury was sustained that put 'Digger' out for the rest of the season. Nigel Payne telephoned me to say, 'Unbearably bad news, we'll miss the Grand National.' That phrase, that I often remind him of, was a gross overstatement compared to what happened nearly a year later.

Having run second to the brilliant Master Oats in a rescheduled Coral Welsh National at Newbury on New Year's Eve, we were well fancied to take the Greenalls National trial at Haydock on February 24th 1996. Tom Jenks had taken over again from David Bridgwater, who had ridden at Newbury.

10

Going well, turning out on the second circuit, the gelding broke down with what could have been a fatal injury. The suspensory ligament which literally holds the hoof to the leg was nearly in two. Prompt action by the Haydock vet saved him, but his prognosis was that Earth Summit would never run again. Unbearably bad news.

Once again, a tilt at Aintree's historic race had been foiled by injury. I can imagine how Nigel Payne felt about it; after all, we all knew we had a horse that was tailor-made for an endurance test and that had always been Nigel's goal.

The main concern of all the owners, though, was that our hero would survive. If he never ran again, he owed us nothing. Seven victories, including a Scottish National and nearly £100 000 in prize money is more return than anyone could possibly have dreamt of when we got together in 1992.

The fact that Earth Summit survived his injury at all is remarkable. That he set foot on a racecourse again is a tribute to the loving care and attention he received over the next twenty-one months, plus his own amazing constitution. The credit goes to the brilliant Nigel Twiston-Davies and his team, in particular Marcella Bayliss, his lass, the one who had looked after 'Digger' night and day since they both arrived at Grange Hill in 1992.

Nigel Payne, great communicator that he is, kept us informed as to the wellbeing of the horse, remaining, as always, optimistic about his chances of returning to the turf.

I tried to remain philosophical about it all, not daring to wish for too much.

Then, on 19th November 1997, we all gathered at Haydock to witness an emotional return to the scene of the gelding's appalling injury. We held our breath for the three miles as Tom Jenks gently eased his mount back into the fold. Running against the class of Suny Bay, General Wolfe and See More Business, Earth Summit stayed up with the field until he weakened on the second circuit to finish fifth of ten starters. As six anxious owners plus the trainer's wife stood like expectant fathers while Tom talked us through the race and Marcella checked him over, the great horse stood, looking as fresh as a daisy. 'He jumped very well, I'm very pleased with him,' was Jenks' happy summing up. The gelding was pronounced sound.

'Thank fuck for that,' said Kathy Twiston-Davies.

Chapter Three
The Grand National

I disagree with those who call this great race a lottery, although curiously enough the first winner, back in 1839 was named just that, Lottery.

All racing is a gamble, and the definition of lottery being anything that can be described as 'chance' can apply as well to the sport of kings. Up to a point.

Picking six random numbers out of forty nine and hoping to get not one right but all six, is indeed a game of 'chance'. If the average amount of runners in a horse race is, let's say, ten, you have a ten to one 'chance' of picking the winner. With ninety-nine percent of races containing horses that have run before, punters have the opportunity to consider the merits of a horse before laying their money down. While it is not an exact science, there is some skill involved in the final choice or choices of the average regular racing person. However, if you are someone who bets only when the Derby comes around or The Grand National, you may just pick a name that takes your fancy without bothering to look at the previous form. Then you are taking part in a lottery.

Any race of thirty runners or more all carrying different weights is, on the surface, a very difficult event in which to choose the winner. On the surface.

The conditions of entry for The Grand National in 1998 was as follows:

'For seven-year-olds and older which, before February 9th have run three times collectively in steeplechases or hurdle races in Great Britain or Ireland or have won a steeplechase or hurdle race in Great Britain or Ireland, and provided that the handicapper is prepared to allot them a rating of 110 or more.'

In this year's race Suny Bay was allotted top weight with a

rating of 170. Out of thirty-nine declared overnight to run, thirty-one horses were allotted bottom weight of ten stone with ratings of 142. No horse can carry more than twelve stone or less than ten in the race; however, not one of the thirty-one bottom weights were officially rated as high as ten stone. Dun Belle, had she been allowed, would have carried nine stone twelve, so was two pounds out of the handicap. Had Decyborg been allowed to carry his official weight, he would have been an incredible sixty pounds lighter than Suny Bay at seven stone ten pounds.

These statistics, which may be tedious to read, give some real clues to the form student. The handicapper arrives at his figures on the basis of recent form. Suny Bay, second last year and a winner three times in 1997, including a brilliant Hennessey Gold Cup at Newbury in November, was regarded as the best horse in the race by the handicapper. Decyborg, a winner four times in 1997, twice over fences and twice over hurdles, was rated the worst horse in the race by the handicapper. Suny Bay's wins were all in the highest class, accumulating prize money of £128 000. Decyborg's spoils amounted to £11 300.

So, for the purposes of this story, let us assume that all those horses out of the handicap proper (ten stone) were most unlikely to win this year's race. After all, only six bottom weights had won in fifty-one years, one of those being the 100/1 outsider, Foinavon, in 1967.

At the other end of the scale, only one horse had carried twelve stone to victory since 1945, the magnificent Red Rum, in 1974. Odds were against Suny Bay, super horse that he is.

Thirty-seven went to post, Avro Anson and Stormtracker withdrew because of the ground. We've established thirty couldn't win (Stormtracker would have carried bottom weight, fourteen pounds out of the handicap), and Suny Bay had a huge task.

For the form student, that leaves six to choose from.

Second in the weights was Rough Quest, a winner of the race in 1996.

The banner headline that screamed up at me from the Grand National edition of the *Racing Post* said, 'I think we can win it again.' It was Rough Quest's jockey, Mick Fitzgerald, predicting a repeat of two years before. On that great day for him he told the world through Des Lynam that the winning feeling was 'better than sex'.

13

There have only been seven horses win the race more than once in its 160 year history, and only two this century, Reynoldstown and Red Rum. In addition, only eight horses carrying over eleven stone three have won in the last fifty years and the same number, eight, have triumphed over the age of eleven in the same period. Rough Quest, at twelve years old, was set to carry eleven stone four pounds. The weight of history was stacked against him.

Nevertheless, on the morning of the race, Rough Quest was clear favourite at six to one.

His form since 1996 had been indifferent and he had sustained an injury at Kempton in the King George VI chase. Also, although he had won on soft going, it was becoming increasingly clear that Aintree was going to be heavy. Major doubts for the early favourite.

One pound below at eleven three was Martin Pipe's talented but eccentric eight year old, Challenger Du Luc. The gelding's owner, David Johnson, described his horse as an 'enigma'. Hardly a comment to inspire confidence when backing a horse to win a race that requires, at the very least, a game performer, one that will keep going whatever. Also, Challenger Du Luc had never won a race beyond three miles and was not proven over that much shorter distance than the one he would face today. At odds of eleven to one, Challenger Du Luc did not make much appeal.

Scotton Banks, a winner over the course in March 1996, had twelve wins and over £120 000 of prize money to his credit, but the Le Moss gelding had not won for two years and was unfancied at odds of 28/1.

David Nicholson's Banjo, a class performer with eight wins and £186 000 to his name had raced three times against Earth Summit since our horse's comeback in November. In the Welsh Grand National on heavy going, he had finished thirty-five lengths adrift and was not certain to stay in today's testing conditions.

The only other horse in the handicap proper besides Earth Summit was Jenny Pitman's Nahthen Lad. This nine-year-old, set to carry two pounds less than us, was one I made a big danger after his third at Haydock in the Peter Marsh in January. However, he disappointed in his next two outings and, having shared the lead with Earth Summit for a long way in the Greenalls National trial on 28th February, they both finished a long way down the field behind the little grey Dom Samurai. The main factor against Nahthen Lad's chances, however, was the lack of form of the Pitman yard, just three chase wins from forty-seven runners.

In contrast, Nigel Twiston-Davies' Grange Hill Farm stable was still in cracking form, having had fourteen placed horses, including five wins in the two weeks leading up to the big Martell showpiece.

Even though our hero had also disappointed in his two races since the Welsh National triumph, we were reminded that he had still only run five times since the twenty-one month lay-off and it was entirely probable that the herculean effort he put in at Chepstow to win the Coral-sponsored three-mile, five-furlong slog had taken a great deal out of him. He had been off the track since February before coming to Aintree and Marcella had informed us that he was 'absolutely on the button'.

So simple then, to pick the winner of the world's greatest steeplechase with the added benefit of that other priceless form guide, hindsight.

In anyone's terms, Earth Summit had an outstanding chance. Proven over long distances, a brilliant jumper, a mudlark, happy in the most extreme conditions, game and genuine, even though some doubters may question the fitting of blinkers. The only quirk in his character that I know of is that he doesn't like right-handed tracks. When Liverpool hotelier William Lynn organised the Grand Liverpool Steeplechase in 1839, the Aintree circuit was already a left-handed course.

QED or, as Kathy Twiston-Davies might put it, 'Thank fuck for that'.

A lottery then? No, in my opinion, but a wonderful spectacle that has captured the public's imagination for nearly 160 years. The names of the fences are so well known: Becher's Brook out in the country, number six on the first circuit and twenty-two on the second, named after Captain Becher who fell from his mount Conrad in the first ever race. In those days, the brook was formidable, eight feet wide, requiring a prodigious leap to clear it. Today, although dramatically reduced in size, the landing side of the fence is nearly two feet lower than the take-off side, providing those wonderful pictures of the horses reaching out for the ground. From Becher's, after the canal turn, the next brook is number nine and twenty-five, named Valentine's after a horse of the same name who cleared it spectacularly in the 1840 race after looking like pulling up before it.

In those days, what is now the water jump in front of the stands, number sixteen and jumped only once, was a five foot high stone wall – a horrendous obstacle that was removed from the race in 1841, only to be reintroduced two years later. It was finally removed forever in 1844. In 1847 the race was named the Grand National for the first time and won by an Irish horse named Matthew This victory, also the first success for the Emerald Isle, encouraged more owners from over the Irish sea to take part in the great race.

The water jump and the chair are the only obstacles jumped once in the race. The chair, right in front of the stands and number fifteen, is where the judge used to sit as the runners flew over in the olden days. It is a narrow structure, five foot two inches high and three foot thick, with a ditch on the take-off side six foot wide. These days the chair is regarded as the most treacherous of the thirty obstacles.

The fence after Becher's Brook is regarded as a straightforward obstacle with no great distinguishing features. This is number seven on the first circuit and twenty-three second time round. As innocuous a part of the race as this fence has been, it was the scene of the biggest pile-up in Grand National history in 1967.

Ever since that amazing day, the seventh/23rd obstacle has been known as the Foinavon fence – more of which later.

I was playing for Oxford United at the time, and, like most of the 1967 Grand National field, my football career was in free-fall.

Chapter Four
Tottenham Hotspur

It all began so promisingly, when I left school on my fifteenth birthday. I graduated from the Wood Green and District under fifteen team to represent Hertfordshire Schools against Middlesex, Surrey and Suffolk. The game against Suffolk was played on Ipswich Town's ground. We won 6-2 and I scored twice.

For nearly two years I had been attending White Hart Lane twice a week to train with other schoolboy hopefuls. I was confident of becoming a Spurs player. The match at Ipswich was watched by Bill Nicholson and his assistant manager, the late Harry Evans. After the game they both approached me and the great man told me I would be a Tottenham apprentice as soon as I turned fifteen.

In the summer of 1961, the Spurs were on top of the world. The 'double' had been won for the first time in the 20th century and the first team contained no fewer than eight international players.

Tottenham Hotspur. Just hearing the name sent shivers down my spine when I was a little boy. 'Hotspur' – a word utterly unique, conjuring up all kinds of heroic childhood images, like 'Roy of the Rovers'. Where did that name come from?

In the 1880s, much of the land in the Tottenham area was owned by The Northumberland family, direct descendants of the 14th century Earl of Northumberland, head of the Percy family. In 1399, King Richard II was deposed by his brother Henry. The Percy family remained loyal to Richard and continued the fight to overthrow Henry. The Earl's teenage son, Sir Henry Percy was a courageous and fiery leader of the rebel forces. His brave exploits on the field of battle led to the nickname 'Harry Hotspur'. Presumably the 'Hotspur' referred to the use of his spurs to kick his horse into action.

William Shakespeare immortalised him in both *Richard II* and *Henry IV*.

Legend has it that two brothers named Casey, living in the area in the 1880s, were instrumental in forming a cricket club to play on Tottenham marshes. They were both studying 15th century history and discovered the ancestor of the Northumberlands, slain at Shrewsbury in 1403, and his wonderful name. They called the cricket club the Hotspur CC.

As with so many football club origins, the cricketers had nothing to do in the winter, so they formed Hotspur FC under a gas lamp in Tottenham High Road in August 1882. In 1885 Tottenham was added to the title and a year later they set up headquarters at 748, High Road. The building, known as 'the Red House', is still part of the club offices and stands like a sentry in front of the present super stadium, which has been the permanent home since 1899.

Around this time, Tottenham adopted the colours of white shirts and blue shorts as a tribute to Preston North End, who had just won the 'Double'. They achieved this feat without conceding defeat in the league or a goal in the cup. Preston were known as 'The Invincibles'.

The ground was never officially named and for many years was known simply as the High Road Ground. White Hart Lane is actually a few hundred yards from the ground but the train station that bears its name was probably the reason why around the time of the First World War, Tottenham Hotspur's stadium became popularly known as White Hart Lane.

My brother, father, grandfather and several uncles had all been Spurs supporters forever and I was taken there at the age of eight to sample the atmosphere.

The date: February 12th, 1955 – my initiation into the world of 'the Lillywhites'.

Blackpool were the visitors: Stanley Matthews, Stan Mortensen, Bill Perry and practically all of the famous side that won the FA Cup in 1953. I will never forget the thrill I felt as the Spurs took the field. The roar of 48 000 people was awesome as I saw up close for the first time Len Duquemin, Johnny Brooks, George Robb and Danny Blanchflower.

George Robb was a left-winger and an amateur. He was a teacher at Christ Church College in Finchley. Johnny Brooks was related to my brother Michael's best friend, Michael Sadler – a cousin! Brooks was a real hero, blond, good-looking, with a devastating body swerve. Len Duquemin, 'the Duke', was an old-fashioned centre forward born to carry a number nine on his broad back; I could almost smell the linament glistening on his thighs. Danny Blanchflower, recently signed from Aston Villa, was destined to become one of the legends of White Hart Lane.

Tottenham Hotspur: a fantasy in the world of an eight-year-old. Seven short years later, I was part of it.

With a name like Hotspur, the club just had to become famous. At the turn of the century they were the only major club in North London, with Woolwich Arsenal, as they were then, still playing on Plumstead common in South-East London.

The Football league consisted of clubs in the North of England. Tottenham competed in the Southern League, not being considered good enough for Football League status. However, in 1901, the Spurs won the FA Cup for the first time, beating Sheffield United 3-1 at Burnden Park, in a replay after a 2-2 draw at Crystal Palace, watched by an incredible 110 000 people. Tottenham Hotspur were the first southern club to win the cup for eighteen years and remain the only non-league club to have won it since the formation of the Football League in 1888.

In 1921, now in the Football League, Spurs won it again, this time at Stamford Bridge in front of 73 000, beating Wolverhampton Wanderers, 1-0. Tottenham were still the only southern professional club to have lifted the trophy. The last side from the south of England to hold the cup were the Old Etonians, in 1882.

The legend had begun, the Spurs would always be famous.

Some people think that the great support began after the 60-61 'Double' year. In fact, there were some enormous crowds at White Hart Lane through the intervening years and the team they called the 'push and run' team played to average attendances of nearly 60 000 in their glory seasons of 1949-50 and 50-51. The second division was won with record points, followed immediately by a first League Championship for Arthur Rowe's exciting squad of players that included both Alf Ramsey and Bill Nicholson.

The mid-50s saw the squad gradually change as players grew old and moved on, making way for Blanchflower, Jones, Mackay, Smith and White. Bill Nicholson fashioned a side

19

that would surpass anything Tottenham had achieved before, with a playing style that at times was so simple it took your breath away.

If I had been awestruck watching from the terraces, then imagine the thrill of going behind the scenes of number 748, High Road, N17. There was nothing grand about the entrance in those days, nothing like Highbury's famous marble halls. The players' entrance was just a small door, but it led you under the old West Stand to the corridor which held the doors to the dressing rooms and whose cold stone floor led down a flight of steps before climbing another flight upwards to the hallowed surface, the pitch.

The West Stand was a masterpiece of architecture, replacing the small wooden stand that the club had brought from its previous ground at Northumberland Park. It was opened in 1909 to celebrate promotion, after only one season in the Football League, to division one. The designer was Archibald Leitch and the stand was a larger version of those he had designed four years earlier at both Stamford Bridge and Craven Cottage. There was seating for 5000 and room for 4000 in the covered paddock in front. For nearly twelve years the West Stand stood proudly surveying the three uncovered sides of White Hart Lane until, in 1921, to celebrate the FA Cup success, the Paxton Road End was covered. Two years later an almost identical stand was built at the Park Lane End.

As at Craven Cottage and Stamford Bridge, the West Stand had a large, mock-Tudor gable. In 1910 the famous ball and cockerel symbol was added to the top of the gable. In 1936 Leitch was once more commissioned to build the huge East Stand. The ball and cockerel remained on the West Stand until floodlights were installed in 1953 when it was moved to the other side to take its place in history. I read in Simon Inglis' wonderful book, *The Football Grounds Of Great Britain*, that the ball may actually be a time capsule, containing mementoes from 1910 and before.

As an eight-year-old, the sight of the East Stand rising up to the sky to my left was awesome. As a fifteen-year-old apprentice professional, I climbed to the very top of it to help decorate the press box in the summer. I have touched the 'time capsule'.

On my second day as a Spurs player I was taken back to

White Hart Lane from the training ground at Cheshunt for treatment on an injured knee. There was only Cecil Poynton, the first team trainer and myself on the coach back down the A10. Once at the ground, I was put on the treatment table with a small infra-red lamp trained on my knee. Cecil put a towel over the rest of the bottom half of my anatomy and left the room.

I suddenly became aware of another presence in the treatment room. On the bed opposite me I could see only a beefy leg and the back page of the *Daily Mirror*. As I sat quietly, contemplating for the thousandth time exactly where I was, I was conscious of the fact that the newspaper was slowly being lowered. I watched, fascinated to see what mystery lay behind the erect tabloid.

Eventually, the top of a dyed blond head revealed itself, followed by two beady and suspicious eyes. The man looked at me, burped loudly and raised the journal back above eye level.

I laughed, nervously, and this time the paper was lowered completely.

'What are you fucking laughing at?' Before I could answer, mercifully, Cecil came back at that very moment.

I was about to be introduced to the infamous David 'Monty' Sunshine.

Coming from middle-class Barnet, I was a little, just a little, unprepared for the diverse group of people I would encounter at a professional football club.

'This is Ricky George, Monty,' Cecil said.

'What is he, a fucking pop singer?' Monty chuckled, and burped again.

'This is David Sunshine,' Cecil explained. 'We call him Monty, Monty minces, he can't see a fucking thing.'

'I can fucking see you, Cecil, you old twat.'

Cecil laughed and left the treatment room, shaking his head. A second or so later he popped his head back in and said to Monty, 'Turn left when you come out, you won't hit anything' and left again, laughing.

'Bollocks,' came the reply from behind the *Daily Mirror*.

So this was it, the cream of professional football, the hallowed inner circle. This was a whole new experience for me. At fifteen I was invited into the privileged world of my heroes, which until now I could only gaze and wonder at, dream about. I hadn't quite expected to meet a Monty Sunshine but in many ways he and his attitude were typical of the characters that exist beneath the glamour of the first team.

There was nothing unkind or cruel about the banter. The backroom staff were a group of old players who had done and seen it all. They had been pros before the war and had their careers cut short because of it. They had played in the days when the players were second-class citizens are far as the clubs were concerned, earning a pittance when the stadiums were full every week. Inevitably, these men brought a certain amount of cynicism to the environment of the club. This created an atmosphere that rubbed off on everyone, particularly those who did not make the first team and had very little chance of ever doing so. So it was a little bit like the Army. The worst trait you could have was sensitivity and thin skin. I'm afraid I possessed a little too much of both.

David Sunshine had been signed by Spurs from Essex Schools Football. He was short and stocky with practically no neck, which was why one of his other nicknames was giraffe. The blond hair, I was told, was bleached, by his hairdresser girlfriend.

He had suffered a broken leg the previous season so I didn't see him on a football pitch for some time. I recall him limping and it may be that his leg never fully recovered. Eventually, he returned to match fitness and I played a few games in the youth team with him.

There are three games that remain in my memory to this day.

The first was a South-East Counties league match against Brentford one Saturday morning. We were at home at the magnificent Cheshunt training ground, which is now a Marks and Spencers. Monty was left back and, as I have pointed out, his eyesight was not the best (hence Monty Mince Pies).

Brentford kicked the game off and the ball was chipped out to the right-winger at just above head height. As the whistle blew, Monty started his run from left back to get tight to the winger quickly. He was quite quick and was at full pace when the ball arrived in the air to the unsuspecting Brentford outside right. To Monty's dodgy eyes the ball must have been a blur because he hit the poor guy on the run; without halting his stride he headed the back of the player's head, rendering him unconscious. There was nothing intentional about it, but it was a sickening sight. Monty played on, never felt a thing.

The Brentford player was taken to hospital, suffering from concussion.

The second was away to Chelsea Youth in a cup match. It was a Wednesday night at Stamford Bridge. For some inexplicable reason our youth team manager, Sid Tickeridge, played Monty up front. Chelsea had some team: Ron Harris, John Hollins, Peter Houseman, John Boyle, all destined to have great careers at the top.

This was the Doc's era: Tommy Docherty had fashioned a style at the Bridge that combined steel with skill. Chelsea's defenders took no prisoners, as I had experienced several times. But none of them had experienced a forward like Monty before. My recollection of that night is the sight of him going from defender to defender and kicking each one of them in turn, whether the ball was there or not. It was as if he had a rough idea of where the ball was travelling and, like a bull rushing from one matador to the next, Monty almost had smoke coming out of his nostrils. He left a trail of Chelsea players in his wake, ruefully examining their shins and ankles.

The tactic worked and, though we'd gone behind early on, Monty unsettled them to such an extent that we grabbed an equaliser near the end to earn a replay at White Hart Lane.

The third match, and by far the funniest, was on a very wet Saturday afternoon away to Portsmouth. The game was played on a muddy, slippery pitch with a pronounced slope going from end to end. We were getting hammered 5-2 and had lost our goalkeeper, Roy Brown, two goals before with an injury. Centre half Ben Embery went in goal. A long clearance from Pompey down the slope reached Ben, who was standing on the edge of the penalty area. The ball shot straight between his legs as he went down to collect it.

The ball was now on its way to our goal as Ben held his head in horror. Suddenly, charging around from left back appeared Monty, arriving at pace to clear the ball away from the goal. 'At least it won't be six,' we all thought. But no, Monty lashed at the ball with his right foot, missed it completely and fell, face first into the muddy goal mouth. He struggled up onto his hands and knees and crawled after the ball, trying to head it away from the goal-line, which by now it had nearly reached. Every time he aimed his head at the ball he missed. He looked like one of those French pigs burrowing for truffles.

Finally, Monty and the ball ended up in the back of our net. It took Ben Embery several seconds to untangle him from the netting.

We trudged off, soaking wet, muddy and dejected. A 6-2 reverse at Portsmouth would not go down well in the corridors of power at N17.

As we were silently pulling off our kit, Roy Low, a superbly skilled and unusual character, said to Monty, 'What were you doing there, Mont, when you were crawling along the line?' Monty ignored the question. 'Only I thought you might have been looking for the ball,' continued Lowy. A few of us started to laugh, then it spread and in seconds we were all in utter hysterics. Dear old Sid Tickeridge was bemused. He was unique amongst football people, as he never swore. 'I've heard of smiling in defeat, lads, but this is going too far.' We were crying, desperately trying to stop.

All except Monty. He limped into the showers. 'Bollocks, you cunts.'

The daily routine at White Hart Lane was something like this. The first team squad were out first, doing a bit of running, jogging and sprinting on the track around the pitch. While they were doing that, the reserves would be playing six or seven a side in the gymnasium, affectionately called the car park, which it was built over and which it now is again. The third group out was a mixture of Youth and 'A' team players. We would run until the gym was free. That time could vary between forty-five minutes and an hour and a half, depending on the day of the week or whether the first team squad had decided to stay in there kicking lumps out of each other.

The 'A' team is something that doesn't exist today. It was a third team and contained an interesting group of players. With the odd exception they were all full-time professionals. Their ages could range between seventeen and thirty something. These guys had been thought good enough to be retained year after year without ever getting anywhere near to a first team place. When injuries occurred, one or two might get an occasional outing in the reserves but even that was rare, such was the depth of talent available. If you add to this equation the fact that then, as now, the policy was to buy established players from other clubs, the odds against an apprentice making it all the way to the first team at Tottenham in 1962 were lengthy, to say the least. Of the group of players I spent my three years with, only one made it to the first team for any significant spell. His name was Philip Beal and he was an accomplished defender.

The team I played for on Saturdays at that time was the youth team, who competed in the South-East Counties League against the youth teams of all the other clubs in the south east of England. The 'A' team played in the old Eastern counties league against the first teams of clubs like March Town, Newmarket Town, Lowestoft and Great Yarmouth. The man in charge of the 'A' team on Saturdays was also in charge of us on a daily basis.

To say there was a cynical core running through the back room at White Hart Lane in those days is not to seek an excuse for my failure to make the grade. I did get something of a shock, however, when it became clear to me that I was not a star. Before signing those forms I thought everyone loved me. Once behind those big gates in Tottenham High Road, I was just another flash little git who needed kicking into shape, literally.

The back room staff and all players bar the first team were just accessories. I won't say our matches weren't important because winning games was what we were being employed to do. The only people that really mattered, though, were those who performed week in, week out in front of 50 000 spectators. It is worth noting that of the squad of thirteen or fourteen that won the double, only four were home-grown. Those four – Peter Baker, Ron Henry, Tony Marchi and Terry Dyson – were in their late twenties, having been at the club for years.

Those players who stayed for years, in some cases their entire careers, and never got within shouting distance of the first team inevitably developed an attitude, as a group. The most significant thing about them all was that they were good players; some of them, had they gone to other clubs, would have succeeded. In fact, when a few I recall were finally released in their twilight years, they went on to play several hundred games for clubs in lower divisions.

I think it would be fair to say that the man in charge of us during the week didn't like me. Joe, as I will call him, thought I needed toughening up. I was still only fifteen but as I was told more than once, I was now in a man's world. He had never seen me play before I arrived full-time and formed an opinion that was never to alter. His method of toughening me up, a combination of rough treatment in the gym and humiliation in front of my contemporaries, which in some circles would be regarded as just mickey-taking, drained every last drop of confidence I had.

Believe it or not, there were times when I dreaded going in. I never told anyone and it is to my eternal regret that I allowed it to have the effect it did.

The humiliation thing took two forms. Describing it now, thirty-seven years later, may well make pathetic reading, but here goes.

I wore my hair long in those days in a sort of Elvis style which had evolved from a Johnny Haynes quiff. I was from Barnet and, that word being the rhyming slang for hair, I was called 'Barnet George' or more kindly 'Bonehead'. These nicknames were thought up by Joe, as were other charming descriptions of other boys. When I look back and remember how it all affected me I shudder to think how I would have felt being called 'the Yid' or 'Sooty'. I will leave that to your imagination.

My hair was mentioned at some point every day and I was called, variously, a poof, a pansy or a Barnet softie. I think the fact that I came from an area that had long been regarded as middle-class didn't help either; Joe obviously thought I came from a privileged background. I wasn't an out-and-out cockney but I didn't speak with a plum in my mouth either. One of my mother's big concerns was that we should speak correctly, so I didn't swear at that time, though it seemed to be a way of life in football clubs. My general demeanour just didn't go down well with Joe and maybe it was just his way of waking me up to the real world. And maybe I *was* just too damn sensitive.

The worst of it though, and on reflection the most important, was that he clearly didn't rate me as a player. I was never praised, only criticised and in a manner that cut deeply into my own opinion of myself.

On Saturdays, when we played South-East Counties games, we were out of Joe's control. He always went with the 'A' team. An ex-player, a very nice man called Sid Tickeridge, managed the youth team but we only saw him

26

Saturdays. I had some good games and scored a few goals. On Monday mornings, however, the news of a goal by R George would be greeted with something like 'Fucking hell! They must have been bad for him to score, what'd you do, Barnet, keep it in your trousers Friday night?' And other pearls of wisdom.

The worst of all worlds was when, towards the end of my sixteenth year, I was selected to play for the 'A' team. What this usually meant was that Sid Tickeridge had suggested in his report to Bill Nick that I should be moved up to gain more experience. Joe had no choice and had to include me in his squad of twelve. There were no substitutes so on some occasions I would travel up the Great Cambridge Road and the old A11 to Sudbury or somewhere and carry the skip as twelfth man. When I did play I discovered another form of intimidation. Some of the defenders you would meet in that league were expert at frightening the life out of a flash kid wearing a Spurs shirt. Too often, in front of my biggest critic, I allowed that to happen and after one such experience we were all out on the track at White Hart Lane the following Monday morning.

The boss made one of his rare appearances at a training session. The squad of twenty or so were standing around stretching and waiting to start. As Bill approached silence fell. He glanced in my direction and then addressed Joe. 'How did Barnet do?'

'No, no good at all,' he replied. The look on Bill's face spoke volumes; I was obviously a huge disappointment.

To say I was finished there and then would be too dramatic but it certainly didn't help my cause.

That summer, for the second time, the youth team went to Holland for a tournament that included Ajax, Feyenoord, Munich 1860, Nimes, Rapid Wien and Chelsea. For the second year running we reached the final. I played in all the games and Bill flew over for the finals both times. The previous year's match had been against the national youth side of Israel. I scored our goal in a 1-1 draw but we lost on penalties. In 1963 we played Chelsea in the final. In front of nearly 20 000 spectators we lost a thrilling match by three goals to two. Chelsea's team included Ron Harris, John Hollins, Peter Houseman, John Boyle and Peter Osgood. I loved those trips, they were happiest of my three years at Tottenham.

I signed full professional forms for the club shortly after our return from Holland, on my seventeenth birthday.

I was now earning twelve pounds a week. The day in the life of a young professional differed greatly from a day in the life of an apprentice. Here's how.

Apprentice: arrive 9.30am, train 10 o'clock to 12-12.30 approx. Lunch somewhere in Tottenham High Road, the White Hart pub, the Hotspur Cafe or George's Cafe, where the players would sometimes congregate in the mornings to delight in a coffee and one of George's 'fag ash rolls'. 2pm: change into work clothes, clean either dressing rooms, treatment room, bathrooms or sweep the gym. 4-4.30pm: change, shower, play snooker or go home. Sometimes, at the end of the day, the huge, communal bath would be filled with cold water. A candidate would be selected and thrown in fully clothed. All good harmless fun. I used to be terrified.

Full Professional: arrive 9.30am, train 10 o'clock to 12-12.30 approx. Lunch: Mondays, Park Royal dogs, Tuesdays, Dagenham, Thursdays Stamford Bridge, Fridays, Park Royal, again. I don't know what on earth we did Wednesdays, there were no dog meetings. We couldn't go horse racing, it was too far and no-one had a car.

You may think this a slight exaggeration. It isn't.

Such antics could be regarded as a complete waste of a young life and not conducive to building the right character, but I gained some valuable experience at those long-forgotten venues. I learned the way the odds worked, the jargon associated with the sport of gambling, and how to lose your wages.

As an apprentice I never cleaned one pair of football boots, not even my own. They were the property of the club anyway, I was just borrowing them. I cleaned plenty of toilets, though, under the watchful eye of Joe. Occasionally Cecil Poynton, the first team trainer, would send one of us down to the 'snobs', the cobblers in Park Lane, to get a boot mended or have a new patch put on. 'Barnet, pop these down to the snobs and get them to put a patch over this bit that's worn away. They're Greaves' boots, he always wears them out on that bit, bloody nuisance.' The great James P was wearing out bits of his boots scoring hat-tricks for the first team and England. Bloody nuisance.

No story of Tottenham Hotspur in the 60s is worth its salt

without mention of the greatest goalscorer of modern times. It was in the November of 1961 when Bill Nick ended Jimmy's exile in Milan and added him to an already glorious team. He was still only twenty-one when he returned to London and I remember his first team debut, at home to Blackpool, as if it were yesterday. For twenty minutes or so the expectancy of the enormous crowd was overwhelming. When Jimmy went anywhere near the ball the roar was incredible. For that first twenty minutes he hardly touched it. Then Spurs got a throw in near the corner flag at the Park Lane end. Mackay threw it to Smith, who back-headed into the penalty area. With the ball at shoulder height, Greaves left the ground, and with his body nearly vertical, scissor kicked the ball, on the volley, into the back of the Blackpool net. The old stands shook with the deafening noise that engulfed White Hart Lane. He scored twice more in a fabulous 5-2 victory.

The first to congratulate Jim was Dave Mackay. Even if you didn't know that, you might have guessed it had you been a regular watcher in those days. As Greaves was a goalscorer supreme, so Mackay was a footballer supreme. Which means, in my opinion, that he had everything in his play and personality that you would want to possess if you were seeking to create the perfect specimen. If that sounds over the top, then permit me to quote no less a judge than Greaves himself. Jimmy, as a TV pundit and commentator of many years standing, has said on air that in his opinion, Dave Mackay was the greatest player ever to wear a Tottenham shirt. I believe that would be the view of all who were able to witness the man on a regular basis during his ten years at White Hart Lane. Bill Nicholson, who signed the Scot from Hearts in 1959, is quoted as saying that the club changed from the moment Mackay arrived, such was the personality of the man.

One of few precious memories for me of my time at Tottenham was being on Dave's side in the six-a-sides that were part of pre-season training. Bill would mix the teams up so that a couple of first teamers would be with youth and 'A' players. Mackay would be constantly talking, encouraging, applauding. 'Ricky, Ricky, here, son'. I passed the ball ten yards to his feet. 'Great ball, son, well played.' He made you feel ten feet tall, he inspired you, urged you to follow his example. And that is how he played, week in, week out.

After the European Cup semi-final defeat against Benfica

in 1962, Dave was on the treatment table the following morning looking drained from his exertions during a match that extracted every emotion imaginable from those who witnessed it. I had never seen the great man look so sad.

There is no mystery to the great success of that wonderful Spurs team. The double side, without Greaves, were a team of vast experience, each player a master of his art in his own position: Bill Brown, the Scottish International goalkeeper with lightning reflexes; Baker and Henry, the two full-backs steeped in the great Tottenham tradition of passing; Danny Blanchflower, already in his thirties, the intelligent, skilful craftsman, linking defence with attack. The softly spoken Irishman, sadly no longer with us, was a great captain of both club and country.

Big Maurice Norman was a centre half in the classical mould. His giant stature could have made him a physical player but he was far from that. He tackled hard and fair and it was 'Monty's' dark head that appeared first when the ball was in the air.

Cliff Jones, right or left wing, was another player to whom you could apply the title 'great'. The Welsh international, no more than five foot six, could beat a man six or seven ways. With right and left feet he could go inside, outside or down the middle. With the type of pace and speed of thought possessed by so few, Cliffy would create havoc whenever he had the ball. He scored dozens of goals for club and country, many of those with his head as his perfect balance and agility enabled him to jump higher than anyone else I've ever seen. Once in the air, he could hang for a split second before timing the contact perfectly, directing the ball where he wanted it to go – in the opponents' net.

Cliff Jones was also a kind, friendly and unassuming guy. He had time for everyone, a true hero.

Cliffy's great pal at Tottenham was the man they called 'the Ghost'. John White was the youngest of the double team, a superbly skilled player, so skilled I've seen him sit on the treatment table with his legs dangling over the side keeping an orange in the air with both feet. Not pacy like Jones, 'Chalky', as Mackay would call him, could caress a football as if it were a precious jewel. The 'ghost' monicker came from his ability to lose his marker and pop up in yards of space to receive a pass. He would then hold the ball until exactly the right moment and release with delicate accuracy to a team-mate, usually in an attacking position. The link between Blanchflower and White was almost telepathic.

'The Ghost' was tragically killed by lightning on Crews Hill Golf course, Enfield in 1964. He was twenty-five years old.

Terry Dyson, the son of a jockey, played on the left wing during the double year and scored in the FA Cup final against Leicester. One of the few who came through the ranks at Tottenham, 'Dice' was and still is an infectious character. Five-foot-four, he played every game as if it were his last, like a pocket Mackay. Naturally left-footed, Terry Dyson competed with another Welsh International, Terry Medwin for the wide position during the golden years. Either one could beat a man and score goals, complementing the ability around them.

Completing the team of '61 were two more famous names. Les Allen had come to White Hart Lane from Chelsea in exchange for an earlier hero of mine, Johnny Brooks. He was one of those players born to score goals. As his son Clive would do twenty years later, Les found the net with ease on a regular basis. It is an ability too often taken for granted by spectators. It's goals that win games and Allen took great advantage of the supply from White, Blanchflower, Jones, *et al.*

As did Bobby. Everyone at Tottenham in those days was called by their first name. From Bill Nick down, you knew who was being spoken about. Bobby was Bobby Smith, a centre forward signed from Chelsea in 1956. While a great player, he was a man you couldn't imagine playing in another position. He wasn't tall but on the pitch he was fearsome. His burly, awkward appearance would completely fool opponents, who could not imagine his terrific skill. Bobby formed devastating goal-scoring partnerships with Les and Jimmy, for England with the latter.

So there they were. The history-makers. Then you added Mackay. Then Greaves, a year later. In 1962 they won the FA Cup again, beating Burnley 3-1. In 1963 the European Cup Winners Cup came to White Hart Lane, the first European trophy to grace a British boardroom. A home-grown youngster had been added by now, a centre forward by the name of Frank Saul. He and Jimmy shared four goals in a scintillating 5-1 defeat of Atletico Madrid in Rotterdam.

During the 1950s when I first went to watch Spurs there was a player who flitted in and out of the first team but always seemed to score goals. He was a powerfully-built, fair-haired individual from Hackney. His name was Alf Stokes.

Alfie was a colourful character, on and off the pitch. On it, apart from his goals, he would always try something different. His favourite was the back-heel. Sometimes he would shape to back-heel the ball and just wave his foot over it, completely fooling his opponent. The crowd used to love it.

His reputation off the pitch was that of a sharp East End boy with a quick wit and an eye for a deal. The players earned a pittance in those days (at least compared to today's top performers), so Alfie might supplement his income with the odd parcel of shirts or ties he had 'come across'. He was also famous at the London dog tracks and rumour had it that, when playing away, he would get injured fifteen or twenty minutes from the end of a game so that he could get to Clapton Dogs for the first race.

Whether or not that was true, I cannot say, but what I do know is that between 1952 and 1959, Alf Stokes made eighty-nine first team appearances and scored an incredible sixty-two goals.

One morning during my third year at White Hart Lane, Bill Nick took me to one side and said, in that intense manner of his, 'You remind me of a player we had here once, I called him a soccer spiv. His name was Alf Stokes, and when I became manager I got rid of him.'

In 1964 he got rid of me.

I can't remember much about my final season. What I do remember very well was the day sometime after Easter of the 1963-64 season when I was called into Bill's office. I followed Bobby Smith in to see the manager.

He was sitting behind his desk looking very unhappy. The last time I had been in there was less than a year before to sign the contract that would make me a pro.

For the first time in four seasons Spurs had not won anything. The club had transfer listed the first of the Double legends at a knockdown £5000. I don't think Bobby had taken it very well and Bill looked as though he was about to cry.

He didn't mince his words. 'At the end of the current season the club have decided to grant you a free transfer.' That was it. There were no words of comfort, regretful statements or even a bit of advice to end what had been a four-year association with this famous club. For my part, I took the news without saying a word, stupidly not having the presence of mind to at least ask for an explanation.

I have thought long and hard about it all since and it was as if I had been punished for not fulfilling the promise I must have shown to Bill as a schoolboy. How could I have come out of that office feeling more sorry for him than for myself?

As I walked out of the ground, I bumped into Eddie Baily, who was now assistant manager. 'Has he given you a free?' he asked. I nodded. 'I think you should go to South Africa, there are plenty of opportunities out there these days.' I nodded again and walked on.

'Well, that was good advice,' I thought. 'Mm, South Africa, maybe I'll go there tomorrow.'

Chapter Five
Growing Up?

Unknown to me, my parents went to visit Bill Nicholson, by appointment. Baily was there as well and repeated his advice about South Africa. Bill told my folks that the view was that I didn't have the right attitude to succeed at a club like Tottenham. He was being kind to them.

On reflection, Bill Nick was absolutely right. The way to deal with people like Joe was to dig in, grit your teeth and fight back. That was what they wanted to see, a man with strong moral fibre, strength of character and plain, old-fashioned guts!

I had gone the opposite way. I had sulked, withdrawn into myself, feeling hard done by and wronged. I became the type of player a manager detests most. If I wasn't going to stand up for myself in these circumstances, how would I be when the chips were down when it mattered most, on the pitch?

I know all this now, I am fifty-three years old.

There were positive things to be taken from my time at White Hart Lane. I had been privileged to observe truly great players at close quarters, something I would benefit from in later life. In spite of my wimpish attitude I did grow up a little and the skin on my back grew a tiny bit thicker. But whatever the failings in my own character, I was determined never ever to humiliate someone in an attempt to get the best out of them.

I also became a racing enthusiast.

Having been introduced to the little establishments we call betting shops, I couldn't wait to visit a proper horse race meeting. The nearest track was the long defunct Alexandra Palace; the 'Frying Pan', as the circuit was called, was situated in the valley, way below the front facade of the huge Victorian structure from which, on a clear day, you can see right across London to the docks.

On summer evenings it would attract thousands. All the top jockeys rode there and I recall Lester Piggot, Scobie

Breasley, Frankie Durr and Ron Hutchinson all being cheered home up the short straight in front of a very old grandstand.

It was after one Monday night meeting in the summer of 1962 that I gained some valuable experience in the art of lovemaking with an older woman. I shared this unforgettable event with Bob Sims ('Hello, Wanker'), Rick Salter, Peter Hunt and the entire midfield of Minchenden Grammar School's First Eleven. The lady in question was an extremely attractive thirty-year-old, who went out at night equipped with a ground sheet and a large supply of Durex.

Some days after, I noticed a growing irritation around my penis and testicles. Having scratched myself red raw, I decided to consult the trainer at Spurs. Joe was in seventh heaven when he realised that I had contracted 'crabs'. Crabs, I am ashamed to say, were literally that, tiny lice crawling around in the pubic hair, getting right under the skin and spreading unless 'burnt out' immediately.

Joe, Cecil Poynton, Jack Coxford and Andy Thompson, the white-coated backroom staff at White Hart Lane, came daily to witness the 'treatment' I received to cure this sexually transmitted disease.

The 'treatment' was liberal doses of Whitfield ointment applied to the affected areas. It was a white, strong-smelling substance which Joe delightedly daubed on my private parts and surrounding areas while I stood on the bench in the dressing room in front of all my contemporaries. The pain was indescribable. Try to imagine the most tender part of your body, red raw and itching, having acid administered to it.

I got loads of sympathy. 'That'll fucking teach you, you randy little git. You'll know all about it if it gets in your fucking hair, serves you fucking right.'

For months afterwards, every time I walked in the ground Cecil would say, 'You haven't been with crab Annie again, have you?'

What fun. At least I was able to prescribe the treatment to my mates. I think Sims kept his as a memento.

I learned to drive when I was still sixteen and in the summer of 1963, Frankie Saul sold me a motor car. It was a maroon Hillman Super Minx convertible, vintage 1947. I agreed to pay Frank £20 for the car, and its appearance in the car park at White Hart Lane caused a great deal of amusement. It really was an interesting piece of machinery, looking for all

35

the world like a larger version of the little red car so loved by Enid Blyton's famous character, Noddy.

I took the most incredible risk by driving the car home from Tottenham. It was untaxed, uninsured and I was under age, still holding only a provisional licence.

On that occasion I avoided bumping into Mr Plod.

My parents were horrified. A quick check showed the car up to be seriously unroadworthy. A friend came round and fixed the brakes, lights, horn and steering. He couldn't do anything, though, about the bits that flew off when cornering. But I was shrewd, I only ever paid Frank £10.

The August bank holiday weekend that year promised to be a hot one. Patricia, who I was already dating by this time, went to Paris with her two best friends, Janet Gregory and Jan Dennis. My best friend, Rick Salter and I decided to go away as well, though we weren't sure where because, although we had our little maroon car that now went 'parp parp, parp parp', we didn't have enough money.

On the Friday evening we pooled resources and invested £5, 10 shillings (£5.50) in a win yankee at Nottingham races. The bet was placed on four favourites, all at relatively short odds. We awoke Saturday morning to find that all four had obliged, and picked up something like £60 between us, which was a small fortune. It was enough to take us away for the bank holiday and remains my one and only win yankee success in thirty-six years.

Rick was a year older than me and held a full driving licence. At midday we boarded the Minx and with the hood down pointed her south-west, towards Bristol. Our intended destination was Plymouth in Devon, but Bristol was a convenient staging post as the Saturday evening greyhound meeting was due off at 7.45.

We stopped briefly in a betting shop in Wantage or somewhere to back a horse ridden by Duncan Keith and trained by Walter Nightingall in the 2.30 at Sandown. The colt led all the way and hacked up over seven furlongs at odds of 7/4.

At Eastville Stadium in Bristol we scooped the forecast three times. Fish and chips and a few pints in a Bristol hostelry and we were on our way, aiming to be in Plymouth by dawn. We had had an amazing run of luck which was about to be endorsed, in spectacular fashion.

At some point during the night I took over the wheel while

36

Rick got some sleep. Although I had no experience of night driving, the roads were quiet and the route straightforward. I have no idea to this day where we were or what time it was, but I was suddenly woken by a jolting, bumping movement. As my eyes opened I saw a sign saying 'Dual Carriageway Ahead' right in front of my eyes. I ducked instinctively and we smashed into the sign and careered back across the road, ending up on the grass verge on the opposite side – the left hand lane, the correct one.

During my slumber while in charge of the wheel and the safety of my friend, I had drifted across the single carriageway, across the oncoming traffic lane and on to a very uneven grass verge which undoubtedly saved our lives.

I stopped the car and, shaking like a leaf, climbed out. Rick, realising what had happened, got out and lay in the road, laughing hysterically. All he could think to say was 'You cunt, George!' How right he was.

The little maroon car had a nasty bump on her face that would have made Big Ears cry. The impact had buckled the crank shaft pulley and torn the fan belt. Without a fan belt the radiator would overheat. We were in the middle of nowhere in the middle of the night.

We made it to Plymouth by stopping every few miles to fill the radiator, arriving around 9am. It was Sunday of August bank holiday and the temperature was soaring. We found a disused car dump and began clambering over and around hundreds of wrecks to see if we could find a replacement crank shaft pulley.

After two or so hours of fruitless search, tired and filthy we found a beach full of women. There is no finer sight to two exhausted teenagers miles from home than the sight of the opposite sex in swimsuits.

Fortified, we parked the Minx with her bonnet down and stretched out on the sand.

It was late afternoon when we woke. The beach was nearly deserted.

Having cleaned up in a public loo, we went into the town looking for action. Sunburnt and starving, we found a pub by Plymouth harbour full of evil looking men and women and proceeded to get blind drunk.

Several hours later I drove through the main street of Plymouth with Rick throwing up over the side of the car. A policeman stepped out into our path and held up his hand. I drove straight under his arm without hesitating for a second, not daring to look back. Somewhere in the back streets a few minutes later a Royal Navy night patrol van pulled us over and out got Mr Plod putting on his hat. We were in serious trouble. I was a learner driver (we had the L-plates displayed) and my instructor was being sick. We were both drunk and I had just ignored an officer of the law, nearly knocking him down in the process.

'I think we'll lock you up for the night,' said the policeman. As drunk as I was, I thought of my parents, Bill, Nick, Joe and, oh my God, Patricia! I started to plead with him, telling about our misfortune and how sorry we were. Incredibly, he took pity and told me to drive a safe distance and sleep it off. What a great bloke, I will never forget him.

We awoke on bank holiday Monday with splitting headaches, a disgusting smell of vomit and a flat tyre. I was amazed to find Frank Saul had sold me a car with no spare.

We patched the Minx up as best we could in the circumstances and, stopping every few miles to refill the radiator, made for home.

There was one more stop, though, which we just had to make: the bank holiday race meeting at Devon and Exeter, high in the beautiful Haldon Hills.

There was quite a bit of cash left from our yankee and other coups so, like the shrewd judges we obviously were, we backed six consecutive losers, the even money favourite unshipping his jockey at the last when twenty lengths in front.

As the little maroon car chugged happily away from the pretty racecourse, Big Ears suggested we pick up two female hitchhikers en route. They were the ugliest women Noddy had ever seen but Big Ears, being a randy bastard, climbed in the back with one of them. After about a hundred yards he shouted to Noddy to stop the car.

'Get your horrible hands off my lovely cock!' yelled Big Ears in terror.

The ugly girls got out and we limped back to Barnet potless, penniless and skint.

So I was into the two Gs, Gambling and Girls. Bloody right: I was a professional footballer.

I was also totally in love with the girl who would become

my wife, and if that seems a contradiction in terms, remember I was only seventeen.

I had a brilliant childhood, growing up in a tiny council house in New Barnet, and I sampled the pleasures of life at a very early age. At the bottom of the road was Pymmes Brook, the tributary that runs all the way from Hadley Woods to Edmonton. Hadley Woods were two hundred and fifty yards from my house and from the age of seven I spent my summers fishing in Jack's Lake, playing football in Victoria Park and, when I was slightly older, being a voyeur.

There was a wonderful, natural bowl in the woods where we would ride our bikes furiously down one hill and freewheel up the other, just like today's man-made skate parks. Close by were several heavily wooded areas very popular with courting couples. When I was about nine or ten, my friend Colin Levy and myself were caught watching a boy only about three years older than ourselves making love standing up with a fourteen-year-old beauty called Rosemary. We were spotted by her, looking over his shoulder as she leant against the tree with her legs up around his waist. Instead of being angry, she told him to carry on and us to continue watching. We did, and I fantasised for months after about her until one memorable, glorious night, when I finally discovered what coming was.

After that, I couldn't wait to experience the real thing. I was approaching my thirteenth birthday; the lucky girl was fifteen and vastly experienced. I just about got my zip undone.

I cannot name her as she still lives in Barnet, whereas Rosemary moved away many years ago.

Barnet, of course, became my favourite amateur team. It didn't matter if you were Spurs or Arsenal, we were all Barnet supporters and my love affair with Underhill began at the age of seven.

I always wanted to play for Barnet like my big brother but Tottenham came along first.

My big brother Michael, nearly four years my senior, was a good all-round sportsman. He was my first hero and also the first major influence in my desire to be a footballer. It was Michael who would take me every Sunday on winter afternoons to join in with his friends in five-a-side, six-a-side and sometimes eleven-a-side matches. Being so much younger and smaller meant that I had to be quick and skilful to stay in the game. Michael and his lifelong friend, the goalkeeper Michael Sadler, both got in the youth team that Barnet FC ran in those days.

I wasn't to know, when Tottenham released me shortly before my eighteenth birthday, that I would one day be playing for a now professional Barnet FC as a married man by the age of twenty-two.

Chapter Six
Division Three

I didn't go to South Africa. I went to Watford on a month's trial.

The manager was another Bill – McGarry – also a Yorkshireman like Nicholson. He had a different style to the Spurs boss, a wicked and at times unkind sense of humour but as a younger manager of a smaller club, he was very ambitious.

My trial lasted two games: an away match at Queens Park Rangers and then a Wednesday night home game against Millwall were good enough for McGarry to give me a year's contract.

I had trained hard and focused on performing well in the reserve matches which would determine my immediate future. After those first two games I was not surprised to be taken on, as pleased as I was. My confidence was high for the first time in three years and after a few short weeks at my new club, I found myself within touching distance of first team football.

Watford's first team, having missed out on promotion to the old second division the season before, had started badly. McGarry, offered the vacant manager's job at Ipswich Town, packed his bags and left. Two weeks later I made my league debut.

Sammy Chung and the legendary Watford trainer Pat Molloy were put in temporary charge of affairs. The super-fit Chung gave me the news that I had been selected to play at outside right away at Port Vale.

It was a mild September night. The huge pitch at Vale Park was immaculate and I loved every minute of the nil-nil draw.

In the Watford team that night was a twenty-eight-year-old full-back by the name of Ken Nicholas. Ken was already a veteran of over 200 first team games for the club and he lived less than 100 yards from me in East Barnet. He was to become a great friend and mentor.

I had no car at this time; the Super Minx was long gone and I could not afford to buy a proper vehicle. My wages were £16 a week and £25 in the first team. So I became Ken Nicholas' chauffeur. We would leave East Barnet at eight every morning and drive straight to Harwoods Road, Watford, where he and another player, Tony Gregory, owned a small sports shop. It was at the establishment known as Gregory and Nicholas that I first learned the basic principals of business...and a few other things as well.

Ken was one of several great characters that I met or heard about during my spell at Vicarage Road. He had played for England Schoolboys with Bobby Charlton and joined Arsenal straight from school. Having joined Watford, he followed the legendary Cliff Holton from Highbury to be part of the side that gained promotion from division four in 1959-60. This period in the club's history is still referred to as 'The Holton era'. He was, and still is, one of the funniest guys I have ever met. If his winger was giving him a hard time he used to reach down as if to pick up the ball whilst in play. It used to fool some players but in one match it fooled the referee and he gave a penalty. Through my friendship with Ken I was introduced to some very interesting people, not least the ex-Watford goalkeeper, the late Dave Underwood. There's more about Dave and Ken later in the book.

I stayed in the first team for matches at home to Exeter City and away at Bournemouth. I did quite well and seemed set for a long run under the joint stewardship of Chung and Molloy. The club had advertised for a new manager and, shortly before a first round FA Cup tie away at Reading, appointed Ken Furphy as player-manager from Workington Town.

His first match in charge was at Reading. The game was almost a local derby and a ferocious match in front of 12 000 finished in a comprehensive 3-1 win for the home side. The new boss made seven changes, including myself. As he was a right full-back, he dropped Nicholas in favour of himself.

I experienced none of the intimidation or attempts at 'character building' that had blighted my time at Tottenham, and I continued to train and play in the reserves. Mr Furphy was a passionate and enthusiastic manager and, relatively young himself, started to weed out older players and bring in new faces.

I had absolutely no problems with him and caused him no great distress. Maybe for a while he forgot about me. It must have been sometime in March that season when I suddenly and unexpectedly found myself selected for the first team. It was a home game in the league against Barnsley on a Tuesday night. The first half went okay as I went past the full-back several times and drew some generous applause from the Watford supporters. In the second half my performance could best be described as anonymous.

The following day, or the day after, Mr Furphy called me into his office. 'Your old boss was here to see you play the other night,' he confided.

'Really?' I said, wondering what was coming.

'He says you haven't changed, in the game one minute and out of it the next.'

'Really?' I said again. Furphy looked worried, as if he wanted to say a lot more.

'Is that all, boss?' I said, all too casually. Furphy sighed and shook his head.

A few weeks later I got the dreaded news: another free transfer. What the hell was going on with this career of mine? My friends and family could not believe it. I was not yet nineteen but, despite having been considered at some point good enough for league football, I was now not regarded as being worthy of another contract at £16 a week.

Almost immediately I received a telephone call from Reg Flewin, the manager of Bournemouth. He was very keen for me to go and see him, unable to understand how I came to be available.

I arranged to go down to Dean Court with my old Tottenham colleague, Roger Smith. On a beautiful May day we arrived at the prettiest of all football league grounds and the delightful Mr Flewin offered me a year's contract *plus* a signing-on fee that would enable me to buy a brand new Austin Mini.

And so I signed for Bournemouth and Boscombe Athletic.

I still cannot fully appreciate what went wrong at Watford. Maybe I just wasn't Furphy's type of player. If I had not been good enough then I guess at some stage someone would surely have sat me down and broken the news. This never happened and the amazing thing is that, nearly six years later, when I was playing for Barnet, the same Ken Furphy expressed an interest in taking me back to Vicarage Road. I declined and went to Hereford United. Living away from home was a good thing in retrospect: my parents could get a bit of peace, Patricia could get a bit of peace, Ken Nicholas could get on with building his business and I learned to live with strangers.

Reg Flewin was a good man. Kind and considerate. If I couldn't play for him, then who could I play for?

I disillusioned him early on. We played away at Salisbury in a pre-season friendly. Patricia came down for the weekend and I asked if I could be excused travelling back on the coach to Bournemouth after the game so that I could be with her. He was furious and refused. I did not understand that then and we had a row.

But soon I settled into a way of life in digs and played reserve team football. The first team did not do very well and during November of that year, Reg took ill. The team affairs were taken over by the two trainers, Arthur Cuncliffe and John Kirk, and as at Watford, these understudies put me straight in the side. We played Oxford United away on a crisp Wednesday night and for forty-five minutes I had a blinder. At half-time a blanket of fog enveloped the Manor ground and the game was abandoned. I had not been given the opportunity to fade and so received rave notices the following day in the Bournemouth papers. Even one of the nationals gave a short report entitled 'Bright Boy Ricky Dimmed by Fog'. Wow!

The following Saturday we played Peterborough United at home. We lost 3-2, much to the disappointment of all concerned, and before the next match, away at Exeter City, Arthur Cuncliffe took me to one side. 'It's not all over, son, but you're dropped.' I went with the team as substitute but in those early days of subs you only came on if someone was injured.

I got back in the side away at Scunthorpe United one freezing, snowy December Saturday and got kicked from pillar to post all afternoon in a 1-0 defeat. At this stage, I must confess, I wasn't really enjoying my vocation and I guess this feeling, combined with the general malaise in my attitude, was leading inexorably to another free transfer.

The late Freddie Cox was appointed manager of Bournemouth that same month, an event that coincided with a serious bout of tonsillitis that struck me down at home in Barnet one weekend. After a match, wherever we had played I would jump in the car and zoom home in time to spend a few hours with Patricia. This particular weekend laid me low enough to have to spend all of Christmas at home.

During my absence Freddie set about the task of saving Bournemouth from relegation. He had been a winger in his playing days, having excelled for both Arsenal and Spurs. I never saw him play but I was told he was fast and aggressive, a real handful at only five-foot-six.

It was his second spell in charge at Dean Court, having settled in the area some years before. He had business interests in the town and I imagine he was looking forward some years hence to a quiet retirement. Bournemouth, though a beautiful, resort has a reputation of being full of elderly retired folk. Nothing could be further from the truth; part of its great charm is that it has something for every generation.

The brand of football that Freddie chose to play to ensure the club's survival in the third division had even the good-natured residents of Boscombe resorting to acts of vandalism. After one excruciating nil-nil draw towards the end of that season, I saw half a dozen or so seat cushions thrown onto the pitch in protest.

Ironically, the little winger picked a team that had no place for wide players. If Alf Ramsey's team would be called 'the wingless wonders', that was nothing compared to Freddie's ultra-defensive system which only allowed one or two players at the most into the opponents' half.

Can you remember which position I played in those days?

To be fair to Freddie, he did avoid relegation and his tactics were years ahead of their time. His opinion of a third or fourth division player was that he needed to be able to kick, run, trap and head the ball at pace, while also possessing endless stamina. I know many who would agree with him today.

There certainly didn't seem to be any place for me in this set-up but, having recovered from illness, I was welcomed back and took my place in the reserves once more.

I had been in various lodgings since arriving on the South

coast, but by now I was living with an older player and his very young family. Ken and Barbara Hodgson were Geordies. He had been a Newcastle United player at one time and Reg Flewin had signed him from Scunthorpe the previous season.

Ken and I had got on well and he was another with a great sense of humour. I slept on their sofa in the lounge. On my first night he brought me in a huge pile of 'Roy of the Rovers' comics, all in sequence, going back years. I'm still trying to get through them.

I was nineteen, Ken and Barbara were twenty-four. They had two little girls, Sharon, three, and Gaynor, nine months. They had a beautiful golden Labrador called Towan and lived in a club bungalow at Bear Cross, just outside Poole. These delightful people became my family for six months.

Ken was a practical joker and one of his favourites was to put a sheet over his head and jump out at me as I passed a doorway or a cupboard. One day, thinking he had heard my car pull up, he rushed into his bedroom to await my entrance. Barbara, not seeing, opened the door to the gas man who, passing the bedroom door, got the fright of his life.

Though Ken did not share my passion for horses, at the end of the week when money was tight, I was given the empties to take back to the Off Licence and permission to use that as 'playing up money'. If ever a two shilling win double would oblige, I would repay him and Barbara by taking them out to the pub for a couple of celebratory drinks.

After training on the day before Good Friday 1966, Freddie called the entire playing staff into one dressing room. 'There are two first team matches and one reserve match this Easter,' he advised us. 'No-one, but no-one is to leave Bournemouth this weekend.'

I went straight out to the car park, jumped in the green mini and zoomed up the A30. I arrived in North London in time to meet Patricia from the tube at Woodside Park.

The following morning, Good Friday, we drove down to Camber sands to join our wonderful group of friends in a caravan, where they were spending Easter. As far as I was concerned, I would not be required for any first team game, only the reserve match at Dean Court on the Monday night.

On the Monday, just after midday, we left for the drive along the south coast to Bournemouth. It was a journey of nearly three hours. We came in through Boscombe and past Kings

46

Park, within sight of the football ground. I was surprised to see a lot of cars and activity outside the stadium; after all, the kick-off was not until 7.30 and it was only five to three.

Poor, slow-witted, undedicated fool! Of course the kick-off was at three, it was a bank holiday.

I rushed into the players' entrance, leaving Pat to park the car. Freddie was standing by the dressing room door with Ken Hodgson. 'This is on your head!' he roared at Ken and then at me, 'Get changed and see me afterwards!'

We beat Bristol Rovers 3-2. I scored one and made one.

'Thank God you played well,' Ken whispered to me after the game.

Freddie had calmed down by the time I got into his office. I had played well and that undoubtedly helped, though I was still fined £20 for being late. If he had known that I had driven from Bournemouth to London to Camber and back to Bournemouth, it would have been far, far worse.

Patricia was waiting in the car, reading. I put the mini in first gear and drove back to Camber.

The season was coming to its end and as always the rumours started circulating with regard to the retained list.

Ken Hodgson and I played in a reserve match away at Reading on a Wednesday night. It was the last match of the season and Reading needed to beat us to win the Combination Division Two championship. They played several regular first teamers and, in front of 7000 noisy fans, beat us 3-2 in one of the most brutal matches I have ever played in. After the match our dressing room looked like a military hospital. Five players required stitches in either head or leg wounds. There must have been a serious bonus offered to the Reading players that night.

My parents had driven down with Patricia to witness the battle. After the game we had a drink together in the players' lounge. I told them the retained list was due the following day and I had heard that I was to be given a new contract. Pat gave me a little wry smile that said 'We'll see'.

Ken, Barbara, the two girls and the dog brought my letter in the next morning. Ken had opened his and was retained for another season on the same terms. There was silence as I lay propped up on the sofa, fumbling with the envelope. As I read the contents of my third free in as many years, Barbara's eyes filled with tears. Sharon, seeing her mummy crying,

47

started to cry as well. Soon baby Gaynor was crying too. I was close to tears by this time and Ken was looking sadly at Towan, who cocked his head on one side and went with the mood. The Hodgsons were such a great, supportive family and the time I spent with them was far and away the happiest of my season by the seaside. I loved them all and have never forgotten them.

At least this time I went to see Freddie Cox for an explanation. He said, 'I think you'd be happier living back in London near your girlfriend'. Had I been that obvious? Most decidedly, yes.

'We had discussed getting married and moving into a house down here, boss,' I ventured, pathetically. We hadn't. My girlfriend was having a great time working for Rothmans Carreras in Baker Street and I had as much chance of persuading her to give that up, marry me and move to Bournemouth as I had of rejoining Spurs.

Freddie was positive. 'I'll tell you what: go back home, discuss it again and give me a ring when you're absolutely certain that's what you both want to do.' Shrewd old bugger, he could read me like a book.

Ken Nicholas was on the phone immediately. He was now playing for Guildford City in the Southern League. At that time non-league clubs like Guildford were paying almost as much part-time as the third and fourth division outfits. Ken's shop was doing well and he advised me to go part-time and learn the business. Very sound advice from a very good friend.

I ignored it and accepted the offer of a month's trial at Oxford United.

Before that took place, Pat and I had arranged to go on holiday to Spain with two dear friends, Jan Gregory and Dennis Sullivan. I had part exchanged the green mini for a grey mini-van, registration number UPR 190.

For a change I had little or no money, so took a summer job for about three weeks at Barnet General Hospital, working as an orderly in the food stores. My working companions were an elderly man from Newcastle, who was a racing buff and historian, and a disabled man in his early thirties. The younger man, whose name was Roger, spoke four languages fluently. In our tea breaks I brushed up on the French I had been quite good at in my schooldays, learned the crude basics of German and Italian and heard all about the exploits of Charlie Smirke, Harry Wragg and Gordon Richards.

Roger was schizophrenic and his condition was strictly controlled by drugs. At that time he was living in a hostel in Elstree where he was monitored and cared for. Today he lives on his own in a council flat in Barnet. He is luckier than most of his fellow sufferers as he is just about able to look after himself. He rings me once a week on average.

When I had saved some money, Pat, Jan, Dennis and I drove in the mini-van to Estartit on the Costa Brava. Correction, I drove to Estartit. The Air car ferry that carried us and UPR 190 to Le Touquet in Northern France took less than twenty minutes to complete the journey from Lydd Airport in Kent. Once on French soil we took the N7, the Rue Nationale, through central France, stopping only to refill and take light refreshment. We travelled from nine at night until eleven the following morning, by which time we had reached Toulouse, no more than 300 miles from the Spanish border.

By this time I was totally exhausted and Dennis took over the wheel. We were in traffic in the centre of the French city which is home to the Airbus Industry. Dennis' eyes fell upon a pair of legs that moved provocatively along the pavement to his right. A Renault Sixteen stopped in front of us as we crawled towards it. 'Dennis!' I shouted. He stood on the brake, but it was the accelerator. We smashed into the back of the Renault at twenty miles an hour and rising.

It was midday and boiling hot in the South of France in June. It was also Saturday and we had a mini-van with a smashed-in face and a broken distributor cap.

Apart from wanting to kill Dennis, we desperately needed to find a garage to help replace the broken part. It was not easy and after several abortive attempts at making enquiries of passers-by, we slumped onto a table outside a cafe, feeling thoroughly miserable. The police had taken ages to complete the details of the accident and seemed determined to take as many photographs as possible. These were our first holiday snaps.

Then, out of the blue, he arrived. A young guy, maybe only seventeen or eighteen, stopped by our table and asked in perfect English if he could help us. He was good-looking so the girls immediately perked up. We explained what had happened and I took him over the road to where the mini-van was stranded to show him our problem.

He disappeared for about forty-five minutes, returning with

a new distributor cap which he then proceeded to fit before our astonished eyes. It took an age to remove the damaged piece as the impact had caused some buckling, but miraculously, when he stood up and suggested I try to start the engine, it fired first go. All four of us hugged him in turn as, embarrassed by our gratitude, he accepted the money for the new cap but not a penny more. He stood and waved until we were out of sight.

We stayed in a funny little hotel just inside the Spanish border and arrived on the Costa Brava later that third day. Estartit is a natural harbour and the beach curves all the way round and out again towards the open sea for some distance. Even in 1966 there was development taking place up and down the coast, the first stop for the millions of British holiday makers who would invade Spain in the years to come.

We deliberately went to the quietest part of the beach. The four of us lay in the hot sun, the main port of Estartit to our left and the gleaming Mediterranean to our right.

At some point during the afternoon we heard someone calling to us from the balcony of a new block of apartments directly behind us. Turning around, we saw a small man with a large smile on his face holding an equally large bottle of champagne in his hand. He was beckoning to us to join him. There was no-one else on this part of the beach so we accepted the invitation.

The apartment block was still in its final stages of completion and as yet was not occupied. The lift worked and we went up to the third floor to be greeted by our host. His manner was so friendly and welcoming that we felt at ease immediately. The champagne was poured before any introductions were made and, grinning broadly, we all toasted each other.

Our host was Count Tullio De Fillipis. He was Italian but introduced himself in French as the owner of the apartment block(s). A little later we were introduced to his partners, a Spaniard by the name of Conrades and a Venezuelan called Walter.

We chatted in halting French for a while, eventually explaining who we were and where we came from. The Count, upon hearing we had just arrived, immediately placed an apartment at our disposal for the duration of our holiday. If this sounds far fetched, I can only tell you every word is as it happened.

For the next twelve days we lived, rent free, in a beautiful new flat overlooking the beach. At night we went into Estartit and ate at the Eden Restaurant, which the Count insisted upon paying for, and during the day we slept on the beach.

I think it would be fair to say that had our party consisted of just Dennis and myself, we may not have received such generosity from a complete stranger. However, no favour was asked of us and at the end of our holiday all we could do was thank this lovely little guy from the bottom of our hearts. We stayed in touch with Count Tullio for many years after. Patricia and I went to Rome on our honeymoon and met his family. The only way we could reciprocate his generosity was to invite his fifteen-year-old son, Marcello, to stay with us for a spell while he learnt English.

We had experienced extreme kindness and generosity of spirit from two complete strangers, in completely different circumstances. These events combined to make our summer of '66 a glorious memory.

Footnote: Dennis and I had taken £20 each away for our fortnight's holiday. We had some style in those days.

Dennis and Jan did not stay together; each married different partners years later. Jan is happily married to Chris Lehman and they live in London with Josh, Max and Georgina. Dennis lives in Toronto, Canada with Marie-Beth and their children, Oliver and Marie-Louise.

That first holiday we shared was unforgettable for many reasons. It made me realise how spontaneous acts of kindness can bring so much happiness. It also gave Patricia and me the precious gift of Jan and Dennis as lifelong friends.

The champagne was nice as well.

Chapter Seven
1966, Dreaming Spires, Foinavon and All That

We returned home from our wonderful holiday in Spain in time for the World Cup Final. I was due to begin my month's trial with Oxford United the week following England's historic victory over West Germany.

On that never-to-be-forgotten day, I sat in Pat's parents' lounge and watched the game alone. Her family were not football people and I think they were busying themselves in the garden while Patricia made the most of whatever sunshine there was.

I don't know why, but I remember not being as ecstatic about it all as I should have been.

Many times I have said that the excitement one experiences as a kid watching football is never repeated once you start to play the game for a living. It was certainly that way for me; any great excitement I derived from the game thereafter would be as a result of something that I was participating in.

Upon signing professional forms for a club in those days, you were handed a tiny book about the size of a playing card. This was a book of rules. Today, nearly forty years on, the rules make interesting and amusing reading. For example:

Rule 11: Dancing after Wednesday nights is strictly forbidden.

Rule 12: Smoking on match days is strictly LIMITED.

Rule 13: Gambling for high stakes is strictly forbidden. (Tell that to Kevin Keegan!)

Rule 14: Players who wish to stay overnight after matches, or visit their homes (?), must make their request to the manager in time for the necessary arrangements to be made.

Rule 17: Players are instructed that they must not under any condition DISPUTE OR AGREE WITH DECISIONS MADE BY THE REFEREE. They must at all times be respectful and observe rulings of official at once.

Rule 18: The directors wish to point out the honourable place your club has been given in the game, and request that every player assists in building up professional football generally.

(Extracts from my *Players Book of Rules* at Oxford United, 1966-67)

To my shame, apart from smoking, I guess I broke all the rules at one time or another. And while we may smile at the quaintness of it all now, how poignant is Rule 18? How privileged we all were (and are) to represent the game – a responsibility to set an example that sadly too few of my contemporaries took seriously.

Pre-season training at Oxford was tough and there were a lot of road runs, I recall. Ron Atkinson was skipper of a relatively young football league club. As Headington United they had been elected to the Football League some six years before. I noticed the perspiration squelching out of big Ron's shoes as he toiled around the streets near the Manor ground.

My trial was similar to the month two years before at Watford. I worked hard and was very fit by the time I played my first match. After two games and barely one week of the season, I was in the first team away at Swansea Town. It was a typical late August Saturday. The sun was shining on the Vetch field. The pitch had that luscious early season sheen and with 9000 people inside, the stadium looked full.

On this day I had the privilege of sharing the same stage with a legend of Welsh football, Ivor Allchurch. What I noticed about him was his control of the ball and how he was able to hold it for as long as he wished. He held off all challenges until the time was right to release the ball. His passing drew bursts of warm applause from the home fans, but it was to be our day. The Swans squandered too many chances and we gradually took control. Allchurch faded in the heat and we pushed forward. I had drifted over to the right wing to escape the attentions of Roy Evans, the right back. With a bit of space I went past the left back on the outside and crossed to the far post where Tony Buck volleyed home. There were fifteen minutes to go.

There used to be a big clock on the stand opposite the main stand at the Vetch in those days. As Swansea pressed for an equaliser, I found myself glancing up at the clock as the minutes ticked by. With the ninety minutes nearly up, Roy

Evans looked at the clock and pleaded with it to stop. The whistle went and we shook hands. 'Well played kid,' he said as we walked off.

Some years later, while driving to a match at Hereford, Roy Evans and his Swansea team-mate, Brian Purcell, were killed in a car crash. I can still see him looking at that clock. At that time it was all that mattered.

The following Saturday I made my home debut against Middlesbrough, one of the favourites to gain promotion to the old second division. This game was to be my very best for Oxford United and although we drew nil-nil, I received nine out of ten in *The People* newspaper the following day.

The following Saturday we were away at Shrewsbury. The Shrews used to play their home games at 6.30 on Saturday evenings. As we stepped off the coach in the Gay Meadow car park, three very familiar figures appeared, strolling casually towards us. Patricia, Janet and Dennis had driven up to watch the match. They were eating fish and chips and with huge grins on their faces proceeded to embrace me in front of the entire team and the manager. They knew I was acutely embarrassed but they just kept smiling. I refused the chips and hurried into the changing rooms. Apart from missing an open goal, I played quite well that night. We drew 1-1.

Next Saturday we drew again, at home to Colchester, and then I was dropped.

If I had been bright I would have seen a familiar pattern developing. But no chance, I was loving every minute of being in Oxford, in or out of the side, so what? Easy come, easy go.

We played away at Walsall one night in the reserves. I scored the greatest solo goal of my life. We were completely outplaying the home team and leading 2-0. Receiving the ball on the right, I went inside the full-back and began weaving my way into the penalty area. I cannot remember how many players I went by, only that it seemed like twenty. I found myself facing a stranded goalkeeper and slotted the ball into the back of the net as he rushed at me. *The Oxford Times* reported the goal, quoting Lord Macaulay, a former Prime Minister: 'Even the ranks of Tuscany scarce forbear to cheer'.

I didn't get back in the first team until an FA Cup first round replay away at Bedford Town, then of the Southern League. Without warning, 'Tosher Turner', as the manager was affectionately known, stuck me in after a 2-2 draw at home. Here was another unwanted experience, being the wrong side of a 'giant killing'. In front of 11 000 passionate home fans, Bedford dumped us out of the cup with a late free kick taken by former Oxford player Danny Paton.

The coach journey back to Oxford was miserable, an indication of the effect a cup defeat inflicted by a team from the non league can have. Not surprisingly, I lost my place once more.

Oxford was conveniently situated for a racing enthusiast. Newbury and Cheltenham were close by and at the local greyhound track you could either play up the afternoon's winnings or chase the losses.

I became a passionate fan of National Hunt racing. My favourite jockey was Josh Gifford who rode many great horses for the legendary trainer, Captain Ryan Price. Many's the time I stood with my Oxford team-mates in the Newbury enclosure cheering home a winner for the Gifford/Ryan Price partnership. All the big races were run on Saturdays of course, so we put our bets on in the local bookie's opposite the ground. Ben was his name and occasionally, when we were skint at the end of the week, he would give us credit.

At this time I shared a cottage in the country with three other players, Colin Clarke, John Evanson and the goalkeeper, Brian Sherrat. Clarky was a Glaswegian and had previously been at Arsenal. He was a tall, elegant left-half in the Jim Baxter mould. He loved to beat a man – nutmegging was his favourite – and deliver a thirty-yard pass, posing with his leg still off the ground as the ball found its target. One day, during a fuil-scale practice match, he did exactly that, exaggerating the final act so much that we laughed. The manager sent him off for showing too much style!

Colin Clarke was my gambling companion and was one who took advantage of Ben the bookie's credit facilities. On one occasion, losing a few quid too many, he approached the counter in Ben's shop. Shoving a £5-win betting slip across it, he looked at Ben and in his broad Glaswegian spelt out 'S-L-A-T-E'. To which Ben replied, in the same vein, 'B-O-L-L-O-C-K-S'.

On Grand National day 1967, we were playing Brentford reserves at home. For weeks I had been looking forward to the great race. Even though it would be run while we were playing it had become nearly an obsession with me since two years before when a horse called Jay Trump came over from America amidst a great deal of publicity with the National as his specific target. Jay Trump had been my first winner of the race in the year when it seemed increasingly likely that Aintree would be no more.

In 1966, had I followed Jay Trump's trainer, Fred Winter, I would have been celebrating a 50-1 winner as Anglo raced away from the favourite, Freddie, who, carrying my money, finished runner-up for the second year running.

1967 was to be my hero's year, I was sure of it. Again, there was speculation concerning the future of the race and it seemed that every year would be its last. Champion jockey Josh Gifford was riding a ten-year-old trained by Ryan Price called Honey End. The horse started at favourite at odds of 15/2. I waited until the day of the race and, having saved £20, I obtained 8/1. I didn't back the horse with Ben because I was so certain of him winning and I did not wish to take £160 from a small guy whom we all liked.

At some point during the game the result of the race was given to my opposing full-back, a giant Scotsman by the name of Hamish Macdonald. I wasn't that keen on Hamish, he had kicked me a few times in the past and wasn't a chatty sort of bloke. I saw him glower as he asked the guy on the bench to repeat the name of the winning horse. I saw a golden chance to chat him up, you know, get friendly so that he wouldn't kick me so hard next time.

'Who won the National?' I said casually.

He looked at me as if deciding whether I was worth the time of day. 'Foinavon,' he grunted and looked away. I was speechless. Surely he was wrong, surely someone was winding him up? This horse Foinavon had not entered calculations; how could he beat Honey End?

My anxiety made me bolder so I asked him again: 'Are you sure?'

He looked at me with utter contempt and raised his eyes as if to say, 'Do you think I would make that up?'

He was obviously a punter so I tried again. 'I backed the favourite'.

'So did I,' he growled in pure Glaswegian. My heart sank, now I knew it was true. This man was a punter like me, we had a lot in common. I waited for the next time the ball was miles away from us.

'Jesus, what price was Foinavon?'

Hamish stopped, looked at me again with that same loathing and stuck his big ugly face one inch from mine. *'Who fucking cares? Piss off!'*

Foinavon returned 100/1 on the book and an incredible 444/1 on the tote if anyone at all had ventured to lay money on this nine-year-old no-hoper. For all that, Foinavon's name remains etched indelibly into Grand National history. An early faller, Popham Down, ran across the field of runners at the 23rd fence and caused absolute chaos as horses fell, refused or were brought down. John Buckingham, some way behind the main group of horses on Foinavon, picked a clear path on the outside of the mayhem and jumped the fence to go clear. He was the only runner to clear the obstacle at the first attempt. Honey End and others either had to go back and jump the fence or remount and jump it to continue in the race. In the end, Foinavon stayed in front long enough to hold off the favourite by fifteen lengths, having been nearly 200 yards in front at one stage. The 23rd fence on the Grand National course is now called the Foinavon fence.

On Easter Friday, soon after the big race, I found myself back in the first team once more, at home to Leyton Orient. Big Cliff Holton, coming to the end of his career, was centre-forward for the Os and, seeing him for the first time close up, I was in awe of his size. I had a good first half kicking up the slope at the Manor ground. Ron Atkinson gave me great encouragement at half-time by telling the rest of the team to get the ball to me as often as possible.

Ten minutes into the second period, my confidence sky high, I jumped for a ball just on the halfway line in front of the stands. Atkinson was going for the same ball and I didn't call to let him know I was behind him. Instead of heading the ball, I headed the back of his head which felt like an iron bar. I went down holding my left eye to find that within seconds I was covered in blood. The cut over the eye required five stitches and heralded the end of my time in the city of dreaming spires.

The following day the first team played the return at Orient. I was back in the reserves on the Monday, black eye, stitches and all, at home to Notts County.

'Tosher' Turner never spoke to me again. I received the standard free transfer letter one morning, packed my bags and went home to Barnet.

Chapter Eight
Whoops-a-Daisy

Anyone who had the pleasure to meet and know Dave Underwood will appreciate this chapter, which is dedicated to him.

Ken Nicholas called me one day in 1966 to repeat his advice of the previous year. He was now playing for Hastings United in the Southern league first division. He had joined the Sussex club from Guildford for one reason and one reason only: Dave Underwood.

Dave was a goalkeeper. He looked like an old-time prize fighter. His face bore the scars of many courageous feats in crowded goal mouths and the oft broken nose added to the character in the face. Had Dave gone to Hollywood he would probably have gained many parts in movies just because of that face. He did make an appearance once in an episode of 'Till Death Do Us Part', the classic 60s Johnny Speight comedy starring Warren Mitchell and Dandy Nicholls. The co-stars of that famous series were Una Stubbs and Anthony Booth, father of Cherie Blair.

Dave had become manager of Hastings United. After a career that had taken him from Kingsbury Town to Edgware Town, Queens Park Rangers, Watford (three times), Liverpool and Fulham, the big guy had gone into management under a chairman with London underworld connections, not dissimilar to Al Capone.

That first season he gathered a lot of old pros around him: Ken Nick and Tony Gregory from his days at Watford; Ray Brady, Keith Rutter and Peter Angell from QPR; Bobby Smith (ex-Spurs) from Brighton, Billy Meadows (ex-Arsenal) from Dunstable. They won promotion at the first attempt.

After that first season, Dave stepped down as manager and Keith Rutter took his place. He carried on playing for a while and it was at this time that I finally took the hint and dropped out of League Football.

For the record, I had been six years at Football League level. During that time I received four free transfers in succession. I was twenty-one years old.

I joined Hastings for £18 a week, more than my basic at Oxford. It was part-time and nobody trained at Hastings. My first training session was at Southall's ground in West London. I think there were about five of us that turned up. Dave was one and although I had met him a couple of years before, I was struck by this big man, nearly forty and vastly experienced, who just seemed intent on enjoying himself.

Dave Underwood's form of mickey-taking was totally without malice. Not many people could get away with some of the strokes he pulled, but if you had even a modicum of humour inside you, you would just have to laugh.

Watford's first £5000 deal was to sell Dave to Liverpool in December 1953. While at Anfield he nearly caused the chairman to die of heart failure. The team were staying in a hotel somewhere and Dave decided to dress up. He put on his big dark overcoat back to front, a stocking over his face and a trilby on his head. He then travelled down in the hotel elevator to the ground floor. As the doors opened, Dave leapt out yelling 'Boo!' at the top of his voice. The Liverpool chairman was waiting to enter and fainted on the spot.

I think it was soon after this incident that Liverpool sold him back to Watford.

While playing at Vicarage Road with Ken Nicholas in 'the Holton Era', Dave would often go down as if seriously injured when the defence were taking a bit of a hammering. Play would be stopped as the trainer, Pat Molloy, rushed on to attend to his goalkeeper. As Pat knelt down close to the big man, Dave would whisper, 'Give us a fag, Pat.' For a minute or so there would be 'treatment' administered and then the game would continue. The break in play quite often resulted in the opponents' momentum being broken.

Dave's favourite expression was 'Whoops-a-daisy' and because of a pronounced lisp, his voice was unmistakable. Therefore his favourite became 'Whoopth-a-daithy'.

As a result of his relationship at Fulham with Johnny Haynes in particular, Dave was introduced to a 'showbiz set' during that time. In the Hastings spell there would be various games played on Sundays which both Ken and I were invited to play in. Some famous names like Michael Craig, Tommy Steele, Marty Feldman and Roy Castle would turn out for a team called 'Gerry's'. This was the team founded by actor Gerald Campion who played 'Billy Bunter' in the TV series years ago in the 50s. Also in the side were the author and playwright Willis Hall and the odd world-class footballer like Haynes himself.

It was totally due to Dave that I finally got to play alongside my childhood idol in these games which, although meaningless, were nevertheless keenly contested. John Haynes could only play football one way and I was determined not to look a fool in front of him. Consequently, I would turn in some energetic performances for 'Gerry's'.

Ken and I were always late for the games on Sundays, usually because we were waiting for the girls to decide whether to bother coming or not. One game was arranged against the inmates of Ford open prison in Sussex. Dave told us the game was due to kick off at 2 pm. At five minutes to two, we rushed breathlessly into an empty visitors' dressing room. Fifteen minutes later in strolled Dave with the rest of the team. He looked at us, broke into the familiar wicked grin and said, 'Whoopth a Daithy, I've thuthed [sussed] you two, alwayth late. Kick-off'th at free.'

In my first game for Hastings United I scored three goals in a 5-1 win over Queens Park Rangers reserves. The following Wednesday, when I arrived at the ground for a game, Dave was standing under the main stand surrounded by a group of people, players and others. As I approached he called out, 'Here comth two-goal Ricky!'

As I joined the group Dave said again, 'All right, Two-goal?'

I corrected him. 'Three, Dave.'

He could not contain his delight. 'Whoopth a Daithy!'

Being at Hastings gave him another glorious opportunity to get someone going. We were all at a game in Watford one night and somebody called out, 'Where you playing now, Dave?'

'Hastings United, you know 1067 and all that.'

The guy paused and thought for a second, then jumped straight in. 'Don't you mean 1066?'

We all chorused together: '*Whoops-a-daithy!*'

Dave didn't stay long at Hastings and during the one

season I spent there, he departed to do other things. He was always around though and it seemed wherever there was a football occasion you would find the big man holding court. For a while he was employed by ITV to grab soccer players out of the bath for a post-match interview in the early days of 'The Big Match'.

So I continued to see a lot of him for one reason or another. During Hereford's cup run in 1972 our fourth round replay at West Ham was played on a Monday afternoon. The crowds were so great that we were forced to abandon the team coach and pile into a police van just to get to the ground. As we arrived at Upton Park there were thousands milling around the players' entrance, which is protected by a waist-high fence. Forcing our way into that small area, the first person I saw standing in the doorway was Dave Underwood. A huge grin on his face, he looked at me and Billy Meadows: 'Alwayth late.' I was so nervous but seeing him standing there gave me a great feeling of comfort.

I had arranged tickets for most family and friends but I still had to meet Ken Nicholas outside that same entrance. There were barely twenty minutes to go before kick-off and I had Ken's ticket with me. Dave was like a massive guardian angel. 'See if you can find Ken and give him this.' I thrust the ticket in his hand.

Ken remembers the episode. 'I was about ten deep in amongst thousands trying to attract the attention of players, officials, anyone. It was absolute chaos. Suddenly I saw Dave. He was holding a ticket in the air, shouting, "Anyone seen Ken Nicholas? Ticket for Ken Nicholas!"

'I started jumping up and down, yelling at the top of my voice, "Dave, *Dave!*" After a few seconds of this, he turned away and went back inside. I was apoplectic, screaming at the top of my voice. Then he re-appeared, wicked grin on his face. He had seen me immediately and done his usual "Whoopth-a-daithy, Ken." He was killing himself laughing as he gave me the ticket.'

In later years Dave became chairman of Barnet Football Club. He was never different though, no matter what the circumstances, and my relationship with him remained the same as those of hundreds of others who encountered him, both in and out of football.

Towards the end of my own career I was included, via the

auspices of Dave Underwood, in several big charity football matches. One such game was for the 'Goal-diggers' charity and it was played at Dam Park Stadium, Ayr. The fixture was 'Old Scotland versus Old England'.

When I tell you that our team consisted of Gordon Banks, George Cohen, George Eastham, Roger Hunt and Bobby Charlton, you will understand what that occasion meant to me. It was 1975 and those players were still relatively fit. The game was played in front of 10 000 people on a beautiful September day. As we arrived at the ground Bobby looked at the pitch and rubbed his hands together, saying almost to himself, 'Pitch looks great'. I realised that this man, like Johnny Haynes just wanted to play football, like any kid, anywhere in the world.

Our opponents' team read as famously as our own: Bobby Shearer, Eric Caldow, Billy McNeil, Bertie Auld, Jackie Mudie, Jim Baxter.

I was still only twenty-nine and playing regularly so I was able to get in the game a lot on what was quite a warm day. At one stage Bertie Auld, one of Celtic's famous Lisbon Lions, grabbed hold of me and, pausing for breath, whispered, 'Slow down for fuck's sake!' I took that as a great compliment.

But the greatest compliment of all came from Charlton himself. I had managed to go past an ageing Bobby Shearer and, hearing a shout from Bobby, squared the ball back to the edge of the penalty area. He was in full flow and met the ball perfectly as he always did, cracking an unstoppable shot high into the Scotland net, left foot. As the applause rang around the stadium, he looked across at me, put a hand up in acknowledgement and said, 'Good ball'. We won the game by six goals to four. I had turned out for England in a team that consisted of five world cup winners. Was I lucky, or what?

I have big Dave to thank for that glorious memory and for so many others. A couple of pages in a book does scant justice to the life of a man whose personality touched so many. I am sure there were those who perhaps did not appreciate some of his antics but I maintain that if you had a sense of humour, he could never offend you.

Dave and Sheila Underwood suffered a most appalling tragedy in 1979 when their only child, Dave Junior, died after a minor operation. He was a carbon copy of his dad, a great guy aiming to live life to the full. Young Dave was twenty-eight years old.

Even though he bore this terrible loss well to the outside world, Dave's heart was broken. I saw him many times in the ensuing years and the sadness was forever in his eyes.

Big Dave Underwood died on the 25th of January 1989 in Durban, South Africa, where young Dave had spent some years playing football. His memorial service, held at Great Missenden in Bucks some months later, was attended by dozens of people: famous footballers, old footballers, TV personalities and those who will remember him as a mentor, confidante and a never-to-be-forgotten human being.

Chapter Nine
Bill the Shoot

One of the guys at that first training session with Dave Underwood was a centre-forward by the name of Billy Meadows. I had never seen him before and had not heard of him.

The other players called him 'Bill the Shoot' and I soon found out why. We were at home to Weymouth on the first Saturday of the new season, 1967-68. It was pouring with rain and the ball was whipping off the lush, grassy pitch.

About ten minutes into the game, Bill received a pass about ten yards into the Weymouth half. He turned and, seeing there was no-one within tackling distance, pushed the ball forward a couple of times. I was in yards of space on the left wing and called to Bill to pass it wide. He had taken three strides to a spot about twenty-five yards from the Weymouth goal. Ignoring me and everyone else, Bill pulled back his left foot and struck. The next thing I saw was the shower of water that fell from the back of the net as the ball crashed into it. Running over, I joined the others as we congratulated him on a superb goal. 'I don't miss 'em from there,' he said with a touch of arrogance.

As we lined up for the restart, Ken Nicholas called to me from left back. 'Don't expect a pass from him anywhere near goal, he loves a shot.' You could say that again.

William Mark Meadows had started his career at Arsenal. Playing wing-half in an 'A' team game one night, he scored eight goals in a 13-0 victory over Dunstable Town. George Swindon, the Arsenal manager at the time, dropped him for being greedy! He didn't make the grade at Highbury and went into non-league immediately. By the time I met up with him at Hastings, he had played for a few clubs, one of which was Dunstable. Dave Underwood had had a short spell there prior to becoming manager at Hastings and took Bill with him.

It was Dave, of course, who had given him his nickname. I cannot think of anything more appropriate. At every club he scored goals, lots of them and they were great goals most of the time. He wasn't tall, about five nine, had no pace and a right foot that he used principally to stand on. Through years of challenging big ugly centre-halves and goalkeepers, he had broken his nose half a dozen times. An early cartilage operation had left him with a slight limp and his front teeth were missing.

I have to say that in eighteen years and over 600 games I never witnessed a better striker of a ball, or a better header.

The season at Hastings was dire. After a very few games most of the previous year's successful team drifted away. Bill and I, living a couple of miles from each other in North London, travelled to games together, home and away. Big Dave had gone and Ken Nicholas, now into his thirties, had more or less retired.

Some weeks before the end of the season it was clear we would be relegated. On the very last day we were away at Cambridge United, still a Southern League club and already champions. We were losing 3-0 with no more than ten minutes to go. Our right full-back was a little Scotsman called George Duncan. From about the halfway line he swung in a high cross towards the Cambridge penalty area. The ball evaded everyone and was coming to the end of its flight on the left-hand corner of the box. Bill's eyes had followed the path of the cross and, like all natural scorers, he was in the right place at the right time. The ball was at knee-height as he connected on the volley. It scorched into the roof of the Cambridge net with such ferocity I thought it would remove the entire structure. The goalkeeper was still looking out towards where he thought the ball was as it bounced back past him. There were around 4000 Cambridge fans saluting their team's successful season. The applause lasted nearly a minute.

Within a week the entire squad at Hastings were given free transfers.

One of the top sides in the Southern League Premier that year were my home town team, Barnet. When they came down to Hastings earlier in the season they had comprehensively beaten us by two goals to nil.

The manner of the victory was most impressive. Unlike the majority of Southern League teams, Barnet chose to win their matches by playing pure football. The team was skippered by a midfield player named Gerry Ward.

Gerry was another whose career started at a famous club. In this case he had become the youngest player ever to represent Arsenal in a first division fixture. He was still young when he was sold cheaply to Leyton Orient and from there he went to Cambridge City. Barnet signed him at the start of the '67-'68 season. He was a delightfully skilled footballer. Neat control and superb passing ability with either foot and an intelligent football brain combined to make him a thoroughbred amongst non-league players. He was surrounded by a lot of good players who had been at the club since the amateur days.

Barnet Football Club had existed since 1888 as one of the most famous amateur clubs in the country. As former members of the Athenian league they had won the FA Amateur Cup in 1946, beating Bishop Auckland three goals to two at Stamford Bridge in front of   56 000 people. In 1948 they reached the final again, only to lose to Leytonstone.

I became a supporter at an early age and when, in 1959, Barnet reached the Amateur Cup Final again, I stood with my schoolfriend Johnny Danter amongst 70 000 at Wembley to witness a 3-2 defeat by Crook Town.

Under the guidance of manager Dexter Adams, the club turned Professional at the start of the 1966-67 season, winning promotion at the first attempt.

I was now approaching my 22nd birthday. In the seven years since leaving school, I had played for five professional football clubs. Now I was unemployed again and wondering whether my football career had come to an end.

Billy Meadows came to my rescue. He contacted Dexter Adams at Barnet and convinced him that his talented squad would benefit from the addition of two much travelled forwards who lived in the area. Dexter made enquiries and agreed to give us a trial.

So it was that in late July of 1968 I finally came home to settle at the much loved little stadium with the sloping pitch almost under the railway line at the bottom of Barnet hill. However, before that took place I had one very important engagement to fulfil.

Chapter Ten
One Rumpel

Throughout the turmoil of going from one club to another, one thing in my life had remained constant for over six years.

Patricia was always philosophical about my football career. It may have been because deep down she did not really regard it as a 'proper job'. In a way, she was waiting for me to burn out and get down to making a serious living.

There was nothing unkind about her attitude. She came from a background where football had never been an issue. I should imagine that until she met me, the subject was never discussed at home in Totteridge. When I first met her parents shortly after Valentine's Day, 1962, I remember very well I was wearing my Spurs blazer. When her dad asked me what I did for a living, I was amazed that he didn't know, assuming that because football had been such an important part of my life it was the same for everyone else.

As I drifted from one free transfer to another, our relationship never altered or faltered. Our times together in those first six years are a wonderful memory. Holidays, weekends spent together in hotels, motels, caravans and my digs in Oxford, and one or two scrapes we got into like naughty children strengthened a bond that had never seemed likely to form.

We were from different backgrounds with perhaps different perceptions on life as a result of our upbringing. Today those perceptions remain issues in our lives as we continue to differ greatly on certain matters. But when I met her I knew she was something special.

Being a basic sort of animal I was attracted to Patricia Pointon when she was in First Alpha at East Barnet Grammar School. There were four levels in the first year. I started off two above her and ended up one below her.

I was informed by Michael Reeves shortly after we had all started our new school that the girl who sat at the back of his class by the window was very well formed. He was right. However, as a twelve-year-old she was very reserved and gave the impression of being aloof and totally uninterested in boys, particularly me. When she did finally agree to go out with me in the third year, I really think it was because she was beginning to come out of her shell and probably thought that would be a thing to do.

From that Valentine's Day dance we grew to know and understand each other. After a while I guess she discovered that there was possibly more to me than popular myth had decreed. For my part I discovered a forthright, intelligent and extremely funny lady.

Some of Pat's sayings and actions are legendary amongst those who know us well. Here are some examples:

1968 - 'You can talk to me until I'm blue in the face.'
1972 - 'Oh dear, how embarrassing, I think he's done something famous.'
1972 - 'It's somebody called Bobby Moore on the phone.'
1988 - 'I'm not buying any more taramasalata, everybody eats it.'
1992 - 'I've told Adam he can have a television in his room on the express condition that he doesn't watch it.'
1998 - 'I don't think our lottery numbers are any good.' (after three years of the nat.lott.)
1998 - 'Honey, can we get this blinking horse race over and get home?'
1974-ish (after nearly 200 games for Barnet, at Underhill) 'What slope?'

There are dozens more, too many for this story.

We married on July 6th 1968 at St Andrews Church, Totteridge. It was a stunning day. The sky was brilliant blue and the sun shone on a happy and memorable occasion. My best man was my brother Michael. As we took our places at the front of the church he turned round to look at the congregation and whispered to me, 'Doesn't Mum look beautiful?'

The only cloud on the horizon for me was the absence of

my grandfather, Albert George. He had passed away some eight months before, peacefully in the tiny front room at 28, Old Barrack Yard, my favourite place in the whole world. For nearly all his working life he had worked for the aristocracy. To me, he was the perfect gentleman.

After the reception at Pinks Hotel in Shenley we left in Ken Nicholas' Jaguar to drive south, eventually to Rome.

I had arranged for us to stay in a motel near Folkestone. A bottle of champagne was in an ice bucket in the room and I opened it immediately upon entering.

I had been planning this moment for nearly eight years.

As the cork popped and I poured the fizzy stuff into two glasses I turned round to face my bride of half a day.

She was fast asleep on the bed, fully clothed, looking like a little girl tired out after a long day.

I gently undressed her and put her to bed.

After all, we were married.

The journey to Rome took us through Belgium and we were driving along the autoroute just south of Brussels discussing this and that. It was then that she told me how much money she had saved up over the years we had been going out together. It wasn't a fortune but if it was £500 it was £510 more than I had.

I'd had no idea she'd been saving. We had not discussed money at all, which was typical of me. Now I had been taken into her confidence well and truly. It was like winning the pools as far as I was concerned and in my genuine delight I told her I thought she must have been spinning straw into gold. It was there and then that I nicknamed her Rumpelstiltskin after the fairytale character who came to save the lonely princess.

I may not have looked like a lonely princess but my Rumpel had come up trumps – not for the first time, nor for the last.

Chapter Eleven
Underhill

I had to make it at Barnet otherwise I was finished. It was as simple as that. Now I was a married man I had to start to make 'a proper living'.

I got a job as a representative for R Whites, the soft drinks manufacturer. The job came with a basic salary, expenses and a motor car. My task was to call on pubs and off-licenses to solicit orders.

When we returned from honeymoon, I was probably a stone overweight. In Rome we had been taken out and entertained regally by Count Tullio. For six glorious days he left us alone in his apartment on the tiny Island of Giglio, having left instructions with the only restaurant on the island that they were to provide us with all we required. Incredible but true.

A suntanned and fat right-winger set foot on Underhill for the first time a day after our return.

We were playing Hendon in a pre-season friendly. It was a hot late July day and behind the top goal stood what seemed to me like several hundred of my old school friends. Did I take some stick! I was exhausted going up the famous slope second half and could not have beaten an egg. Every time the full-back took the ball off me, a roar went up from behind the goal. What must I have looked like?

Dexter Adams sat down next to me in the dressing room after the game and spoke kindly. He told me he would give me a month to get fit. If, in the meantime, I decided life was too short and I really did not want to make the effort, I was just to tell him and he would understand.

He gave me a parting comment. 'You can play, you know.'

Five simple words, spoken after a game when I could fully have expected to be told how crap I was. That was not Dexter's way and it had the most amazing effect.

Of course I had been through all this before at Watford and Oxford. The month's trial where I worked hard to get a contract and then screwed it up.

This time I was determined to see it through and restore some self-esteem. Dexter turned out to be an intelligent and perceptive man. I thought Barnet were a great side. I wanted to play with Gerry Ward. I wanted to be a local hero.

I made my calls to publicans and shopkeepers in the mornings and trained at Underhill on my own in the afternoons. How strange this was when a few years before I'd been desperate to sign full professional so that I wouldn't have to work in the afternoons.

Patsy put me on a diet and I lost a stone. I had not been included in any more matches until I felt I was ready. After two and a half weeks I was raring to go.

We played away at Kings Lynn on a Wednesday night in a mid-week league fixture.

On the hour and 1-0 down, Gerry threaded a ball down the middle for me to run on to. I outpaced the Lynn defence and crashed the ball home. The lads congratulated me and Dexter gave a short 'Well done' afterwards.

I didn't get in the side on the Saturday, but the following Tuesday night we played Arsenal in the London Challenge Cup at Underhill. The stadium was packed to see a Gunners side that contained Frank Mclintock, George Graham, George Armstrong and Ray Kennedy. I was substitute.

After twenty minutes Delvin Stevens fell awkwardly and I was sent on.

I imagined I knew every person in the 5000-strong crowd. I was the only player actually from Barnet. I *had* to do well.

Billy Meadows had equalised an early goal by Kennedy. I was told to play wide on the left and attack the Arsenal right back. I can't remember who he was but he must have had an off night. I was allowed to go past him at will and send in a stream of crosses, much to the delight of the crowd on the so-called 'popular side'. From one cross Bill headed home past Geoff Barnett in the Arsenal goal. At half-time, 2-1 up, Dexter pulled me to one side. 'Another few performances like that and you'll be back in league football in no time'.

I felt fantastic, couldn't wait to get back out on the pitch.

We beat Arsenal 4-1. Meadows got a hat-trick and I scored from close in to cap a truly memorable night.

I was back!

I stayed in the team for the rest of the season and on Good Friday, 1969, heard the sweetest words any manager had ever spoken to me:

'You're retained for next season.'

Dexter Adams had become my greatest hero, my role model, there was no way I would let him down.

Ask any player who played for Barnet in the last thirty years what they thought of the club and I will bet any money that ninety percent would say it was a happy experience.

This view was summed up perfectly by the late Jack Mclelland.

Jack had spent his career at the top. A goalkeeper for Arsenal and Northern Ireland and then for Fulham, he came to Underhill in the close season of 1969. By then Dexter had put a team together that, with two exceptions, Barry King and Les Eason, had all come from professional clubs.

Jack found a friendly, welcoming atmosphere that just did not exist at the bigger clubs. After a very few weeks he told me that he was at his happiest, hoping to end his career with Barnet.

Of course, Dexter was a great influence on everyone but it was more than that. At all clubs, large and small, there are lots of people doing things. On match days in particular the same faces would turn up to do a hundred different jobs for nothing, for the love of the club. At away matches they would be there supporting the team. It creates an environment that makes you want to be part of it all.

At Barnet there was an indefinable aura that made it special. It may have been the ghosts of the great amateurs who had graced the Underhill slopes in years gone by, the spirit of men like Lester Finch and Doctor Dennis Kelleher, famous English and Irish Internationals respectively.

Whatever it was, it created the most tremendous team spirit.

This was a completely new experience for me. At all the other clubs I had played for there were one or two guys I got on with but, being in and out of the first team, I was never really part of anything. Also, it seemed to me that when it is a full-time occupation, it's more intense. At times you are competing with so-called team-mates to maintain your living.

I am speaking personally now, not generally, but the Barnet

squad of 1969-70 were all similar to me with their soccer backgrounds. Apart from Jack, Jimmy Lye had been in the Spurs youth team with me. Jim had come from Cambridge City with Gerry Ward. Peter Jenkins had been a left back at Charlton Athletic. Ben Embery was also an ex-Spur from our Youth Team. Ben had gone to Exeter City before coming to Barnet. Gordon Ferry played in an Arsenal youth side that contained Peter Simpson, Peter Storey, John Radford and John Sammels. He arrived from Dallas Tornadoes in Texas, having spent some time at Orient.

Barry King and Les Eason had cut their teeth on amateur football and had both played for England at that level. They were very good players, particularly Les, who had great ability. He was a small, diminutive guy with a 'Greaves-like' sense for goals. Les Eason was to form a devastating partnership for two years with Billy Meadows. In season 1969-70 they scored an incredible ninety-two goals between them.

I played wide on the left in this great team. On the right wing was a guy who should have played for England, and I mean the *full* England team.

Colin 'Paddy' Powell was signed from Stevenage Town, as they were then, at the same time as Bill and myself signed from Hastings. Tall and wiry, Paddy was a winger to thrill any crowd of spectators. It was clear to everyone as soon as he arrived at Underhill that this boy was something special. His demolition of opposing full-backs created goal after goal for Meadows and Eason and if the ball by-passed them, I occasionally came in at the far post to profit from his skill.

It remains a mystery to everyone who played with Colin Powell that he stayed at Barnet for so long. He was nearly twenty-nine when Charlton Athletic took the plunge and paid £5000 for him. He went on to become a legend at the Valley and features proudly in the Charlton hall of fame. The famous South London Stadium now owes the superb condition of its playing surface to one, Colin (Paddy) Powell, groundsman.

As I said, our team spirit was second to none. There wasn't a player in the side that didn't get on and this fact was reflected in our performances.

That second season at Barnet, 1969-70, rates alongside the 1971-72 campaign at Hereford as the most memorable of my career.

We didn't win the Southern League but we turned in some

displays that delighted all those who witnessed them. A 10-0 thrashing of Burton Albion at Underhill when the Meadows-Eason partnership shared eight goals. A 6-0 demolition of Hillingdon Borough when Paddy Powell twisted the blood of Jim Langley, the old Fulham left-back, down the slope. Romford away produced another 5-0 win, a result that created a classic anecdote from the Romford dressing room.

Harry Clarke, centre half for Tottenham in the 50s, was manager of Romford.

Our 5-0 win was played on a Wednesday night at the old Brookfields Stadium. To say we murdered them would be an understatement; it could have been ten. Romford were a good side, up there in the top six with us, boasting a team of experienced professionals. Curiously, the following Saturday we were due to play them at Underhill.

Harry called the players in for training on the Thursday night. But they didn't train. Instead, he brought in a Subbuteo table and decided to spend the evening discussing the way they were going to deal with the Barnet goal-scoring machine on Saturday.

He placed the two teams of players at opposite ends of the table as the players sat quietly.

'Now,' Harry began, 'if we're kicking up the slope first half . . .' He lifted the table up to indicate the famous Underhill slope. The meeting never got any further. As the table was lifted all the players rolled off and onto the floor, followed by the Romford players, who collapsed in hysterics.

The meeting was abandoned. When the Romford team arrived two days later, this story was told to us by Terry Tapping, their left-back and another former Arsenal player. Told in our dressing room, it produced the same degree of mirth; it was very funny particularly if you knew Harry who was a big, genial cockney.

We lost 5-0.

Season 1969-70 was special for another reason. The Football Association had decided to introduce a cup competition for non-league teams, culminating in a Wembley final. This competition was called the FA Trophy, the object itself a huge and ornate cup which had lain unused in the cabinet at Lancaster Gate for decades.

We had expected to do well in the early rounds of the FA Cup. A draw at Wycombe Wanderers was followed by a brilliant 3-0 win in the replay. We then beat a strong Walton and Hersham side 1-0 away from home before being drawn at home to Sutton United in the second round proper. On a most disappointing afternoon we let the fans down by losing 2-0.

It made everyone even more determined to do well in the new competition.

We were drawn away to Bath City in the first round. Bath were in the same league as us and had been the first visitors at the start of the season. On that day we won a good match by three goals to two. I took note of the guy who scored their two goals, a centre-forward by the name of Brian Owen.

We were confident taking the pitch at Twerton Park. The surface was good and spacious, it suited our passing game. But no-one could possibly have been prepared for what Dexter Adams would later describe as 'the best I have seen in twenty-five years'.

At half-time we were 3-0 down, Owen had scored two. As we walked off Jimmy Lye said to me in his own inimitable way, 'This is good night campers, son.'

Never before has what a manager said at half-time had as great an influence on his team as the words Dexter spoke that day. He sat us down and talked in his usual, composed and serious manner. He convinced us that the score was false, recalling the comments of the Bath supporters in the stand. He had overheard two of them discussing the fact that the game was far from over. Above all, he urged us just to keep passing the ball, that if we did that we would continue to open up their defence. We went out with our heads up.

I will never forget that second half.

If ever I took part in a better performance I do not remember it. Gerry Ward took control of the midfield and sprayed passes to all corners of the park. We seemed to have the ball all the time; from the kick-off it seemed as if they knew what was coming. Paddy Powell got an early goal and we were on our way. Eason made it 2-3 and we knew there was no way we would lose. As our supporters roared us on, Paddy scored twice more to seal a wonderful 4-3 victory.

After that result the Barnet Press headlined Dexter's 'twenty-five year' quote. It was quite something for a man of his background. Dexter Adams had played for Hendon and the England Amateur side. He had played in front of 100 000 people at Wembley in the Amateur Cup Final and managed some great Barnet sides before this one.

We all now believed we could win the FA Trophy

There were four rounds to be played to reach the semi-final. We did it in style: Rushden away by five goals to nil, Hereford United at home 2-0, Bromsgrove Rovers 2-1 also at home and then an 8-2 thrashing of Northern league side Mossley at Underhill saw us race into the semis.

Our opponents were Macclesfield Town. The venue, as decided by the FA, was Stoke City's Victoria ground, just eleven miles from Macclesfield.

Dexter, as thorough as ever, travelled up to Stoke midweek to inspect the pitch, the length and width, the playing surface, the dressing rooms. In short, he wanted to see if this famous league football stadium where Stanley Matthews had begun and ended his career was good enough for his team.

We had one major injury worry. A week earlier Les Eason had received a terrible kick on the back of his left leg from Dennis Sorrell at Romford. We had no 'hard men' in the team but I think all eleven would have taken Sorrell on after that tackle. Les' leg was black and blue, however the decision was taken to play him. Tragically, he was little more than a passenger for most of the game.

That in itself could not be given as the reason for our 1-0 defeat.

Eleven thousand watched the game and witnessed us 'freeze' against a physical and determined Macclesfield side. It was the biggest disappointment of all our careers, including Dexter.

Those two famous imposters, triumph and disaster, had combined to convince our great manager that it was time to call it a day.

Dexter Adams privately believed that his team of 1969-70 was the best he had put together in his eight years as manager of Barnet. The fact that we had entertained all season did not compensate for us winning nothing. He felt he could go no further.

His resignation was a bitter blow to all of us. As far as I was concerned, he had saved my career and given me back my self-belief. I owed so much to him. Many years later I told him that coming to Barnet in 1968 was my salvation and he told me a little story. We were playing Tottenham reserves in a pre-season friendly at Underhill and he sat next to Bill Nicholson. During the game Bill said, 'I see you've taught Ben Embery to head a ball at last.'

Dexter was amazed. 'I thought to myself: "You had him five days a week for four years. Why didn't you teach him?"'

I never heard him shout or swear or lose his temper. He was a serious man and got his point across in no uncertain manner. His knowledge of the game was apparent to all who played for him and had I ever become a manager I would have tried to be like Dexter Adams.

Chapter Twelve
What Odds Brazil?

In the summer of 1970 we went on holiday to Minorca. Patsy and I drove through France and Spain down to Barcelona with Martin and Jan Webb. We caught the overnight ferry to the island of Mahon, where Lord Nelson and Lady Hamilton were lovers, allegedly, 170 years earlier. We travelled third-class in the bowels of the vessel, the experience bringing a whole new meaning to the word dehydration.

In the middle of the night I staggered up on deck in search of water. Desperately, I tried to open the doors that separated us from the second- and first-class passengers. The terrified face of a Spanish sailor appeared at the glass doors. 'Que Passe?' he yelled at me, thinking the boat was on fire or something.

'De Nada,' I said, which actually means 'Think nothing of it, you're welcome'. No wonder he looked at me as if I was stupid as well as crazed.

The sight of the beautiful island soon compensated for our interesting voyage and we met up with Ken Nicholas and his girlfriend Jill, who had flown in that day.

After a few days the humour tended to wane a bit, particularly in the mornings after long and late boozy nights. One morning we had gathered in the Pons Bar for breakfast. We all ordered our croissants and coffee, except Ken, who had decided to have two lightly boiled eggs. That particular dish does not translate easily into Spanish and he got very irritated with the poor waiter, who was doing his best but did not understand at all what he had been asked for.

At the height of Ken's display of bad temper, the waiter suddenly burst out laughing. No-one could fathom what had amused him and with Ken's face getting darker and darker, the little waiter started pointing at his tongue. We all looked in Ken's direction to discover that his tongue had turned black.

This was obviously the gallons of cheap red wine we had consumed the night before. We were still laughing as a miserable and very hungover full-back trudged unhappily back to his room, minus two lightly boiled eggs.

Meanwhile, the World Cup was in full swing in Mexico. On the night of England's quarter-final against West Germany we were all in the Pons Bar drinking San Miguels. There was joy unconfined when Alan Mullery's powerful strike put England 2-0 up. We were dancing and singing and there was a great atmosphere; even the German holidaymakers were enjoying themselves. They must have known something because all of a sudden the lights went out, literally.

A power cut plunged all of Mahon into darkness and brought a premature end to our celebrations. The cut lasted well into the night and by the time we went to bed the game in Leon was long finished. We were sure England had triumphed, however, and when I heard the strains of 'Deutschland Uber Alles' in the middle of the night, I was convinced I was dreaming. Sadly, I was not and goals from Beckenbauer, Seeler and Muller had put the world champions out of the Cup. It was quite unbelievable. Up to the power cut we had been in total control, marching towards a semi-final against Italy and then surely a final against the glorious Brazilians.

We tried hard not to let the result spoil our holiday. It didn't.

On the night of the World Cup Final, Ken and I positioned ourselves at the bar of the hostelry calling itself the Dutch Bar and proceeded to open a book on the result. We were offering 4/6 against Brazil and 3/1 Italy. There were no takers so twenty minutes before kick-off we pushed Italy out to 5/1. Now there were a few bets laid, 100 pesetas here, 200 there.

We grew a little bolder and with a few hundred pesetas in the bag, eased Brazil to even money. An English guy steamed in with an even tenner and we immediately cut the odds back to 6/4 on, but not before taking two more bets, both at an even 200 pesetas.

A quick reconciliation showed us to be holding the equivalent of £5 against a payout of £25 should Italy win, and approximately £12 against a victory for Brazil which would lose us an even twelve. Even a couple of cowboys like us could work out that if it stayed like this, we would lose either way. The fundamental principle of running a book is to ensure that it balances. At that time in my life I wasn't capable of balancing my backside, metaphorically speaking.

We decided to go for broke, not for the first time or the last. We knocked Italy out to 7/1, in the unshakeable belief that Brazil could not lose. There were less than five minutes to kick-off and the bar was packed. As word spread, we found a little line had formed behind our bar stools. By the time the game kicked off we were holding over £30 against an Italian victory. Such a result would have meant a payout of £200, more money than any of us possessed, certainly on holiday in Minorca.

Even though Brazil were favourites, they were by no means the sort of odds on shot we had made them. Italy were a great side and their 4-3 semi-final win over West Germany was one of the most memorable of any World Cup. The Italians were also twice winners of the Jules Rimet trophy, as were Brazil. No country had won it three times.

On reflection, we were completely mad, but when the world's greatest ever footballer, Pele, headed Brazil into the lead after twenty minutes, Honest Ken the bookie yelled out 'Ten to one Italy!' That little exhibition produced a few laughs but no more bets.

Riva equalised and amidst the roar that went up from the punters you could see Ken and me exchanging glances with each other prior to surreptitiously glancing around for easy exits. We were actually alone that night as far as our holiday companions were concerned. Patsy, Jill and the others were bar-hopping in Villa Carlos while we tried to supplement our spending money.

Our heroes did not let us down and goals from Jairzhino, Gerson and a wonderful strike from captain Carlos Alberto had us calling odds of 50/1 against the Italians well before the final whistle.

I believe that Brazilian team were the best eleven players I ever saw gathered together on a football pitch. I also believe the England team of that World Cup were the best side ever to represent this country.

I have great memories of that holiday in Minorca: the quarter-final against West Germany, England's 1-0 defeat by Brazil, encapsulated for all time by the photograph of Bobby Moore and Pele exchanging shirts, and the heady night in the Dutch Bar when we gambled and won.

When we returned home we found a postcard from one of our friends, Ian Main, who had stayed on in Minorca.

It read simply: 'Two lightly boiled eggs and a black tongue, please.'

Chapter Thirteen
'Happiness Is Not Having What You Want, It's Wanting What You Have'

The above is a quotation that Patricia gave me for this book. It summed up how I was feeling about life in the summer of 1970.

I was happy playing at Barnet. In spite of the disappointment of Dexter Adams' retirement, I was settled at my home town club *and* retained for another season. Tommy Coleman had been assistant manager and was now in charge.

But there was another blow awaiting me on our return from holiday.

Billy Meadows had asked for a pay rise to reward his amazing total of seventy-eight goals in two seasons. The club refused his exorbitant demand for an extra £5 a week and he was sold to Southern League rivals, Hereford United. Inevitably, he scored against us when they came to Underhill on the opening day of the 1970-71 season, inflicting a 2-3 defeat.

I remember some of the crowd chanting 'traitor' at Bill. He had only scored seventy-eight goals. We were earning £15 a week; I suppose a thirty percent pay rise was too much to ask. But, as Ruud Gullit would say twenty-eight years later, 'Why not negotiate?'

During November Bill called me several times. 'They [Hereford] want you down there.' I was flattered but had no intention of leaving Barnet. In that same month I scored a hat-trick in a 6-1 defeat of fourth division Newport County in the first round of the FA Cup. In the Newport side was a midfield player called Ronnie Radford.

I couldn't have been happier.

Then, on a cold January night, I collided with what felt like a brick wall during a home game against Poole Town. I was sure I had broken my ankle. In fact, the doctor told me it would have been better if I had. Badly torn ligaments put me out of the game for about six weeks, the first major injury I had ever suffered.

When I returned to action I learned that Barnet were prepared to sell me to Hereford United.

Maybe they knew something I didn't, though I doubt it. But I never fully recovered from that impact. Twenty-six years later I had a total hip replacement. The X-rays showed an old fracture in my groin never detected previously that ultimately caused osteo-arthritis. The fracture was due to the tackle against Poole.

I suppose the fact that Hereford were prepared to pay money for me, no matter how little, was a key to why Barnet were not opposing this transfer. Even though I did not want to leave Underhill, everyone knew how ambitious the border town club were and at that time they were playing to home attendances of 5000 plus. It was a small step back up the ladder – or was it?

There was another, very exciting aspect of playing for Hereford United at that time. The player-manager was a true legend of world football: John Charles, once described as the best centre-forward and centre-half in the world, at the same time.

The tall, impassive Welshman had left Leeds United for Juventus in 1957. His performances for the Turin Giants won him almost divine status in Italy. After a brief return to Leeds in 1961, Charles had a spell with Roma before returning to Britain for good in 1966. Cardiff City was next stop but not for long and in 1967 'Il Gigante Buono' (The gentle giant) became player-manager of Southern League Hereford United.

I had played against him a few times while at Barnet. On one occasion, in my first season, 1968-69, we were away in a Southern League Premier fixture. Dexter Adams, in an attempt to counter the threat of the great man, detailed Roger Thompson to man mark him. In the first half, Charles scored three headers. We changed the system in the second half. He was impossible to mark, particularly at set pieces. There were stories from his time in Italy that opponents would be literally hanging on to him with arms round his waist as corners came over. 'Charlo' would just shrug them off and plant the header wherever he felt it should go.

I went to a match at Edgar Street with Bill Meadows to meet Charles and the chairman, Mr Frank Miles.

John Charles was an impressive looking man. Over six foot, he had the physique of an ancient Greek athlete. His face matched his body: square chin and straight nose, like a statue. He had a permanent suntan. Whenever I had seen him before, unless he was playing, he had been wearing a beige camel-hair overcoat, the belt tied loosely at the waist. If you looked like that and could boast the glorious career that had made Charles so famous, you would not need to say a lot.

I think it would be fair to say that big John was a man of few words.

I stood in the tiny treatment room at Edgar Street with him and the chairman, who, in contrast, was a good speaker. Frank Miles was a businessman, a man used to speaking and getting what he wanted.

In little more than three minutes I was promised what amounted to a small fortune. Ninety percent of it was based on results. 'If we win the league, you'll get £500 [Hereford were in second place], if we win the FA Trophy you'll get £250 [Hereford were in the semi-finals], if we get into the Football League . . .'

He had said enough. Of course there would be a signing-on fee and a two-year contract. The wages were forty percent higher than I was earning at Barnet – £25 a week part-time was good in 1971, but did I really want to leave Barnet?

Charlo waited for the chairman to leave. He took one last drag of his cigarette and doused it under the cold water tap.

'You don't want to believe a fucking word he says, boy, get it in writing.'

I was speechless and just nodded stupidly. The big guy grinned at me. 'Do you want to come here?'

'Er, yes,' I said quickly.

'Well, make sure you do then.' He grinned again and walked out.

And so I became a Hereford United player. I wasn't sure why, but it was exciting.

My debut was at home to Bath City. The ground was packed and the crowd roared every time I touched the ball. But I was ineffective and did little of note. We drew a disappointing game 1-1.

On the following Wednesday night we played away at Wimbledon. Another average performance. This time, my ankle swelled up after the game and I knew I wasn't 100 percent fit.

There were less than two weeks to the FA Trophy semi-final. For Bill Meadows and me it was the second time in two years.

We were due to play Hillingdon Borough at Filbert Street, Leicester City's ground. No more than a six weeks before, Hereford had beaten Hillingdon 6-3 in a League match.

I had extensive treatment on my ankle – in London. Bill and I never trained at Hereford, that was part of the deal. We trained at Barnet with our old team-mates.

We lost the semi-final by two goals to one. At 1-2, with fifteen minutes to go, I missed an easy chance from no more than six yards. I felt very miserable. There were no recriminations from the manager. Instead, he told me how he'd seen Omar Enrico Sivori miss easier chances. I didn't believe him. Sivori, an Argentinian, was one of the greatest players who ever lived. He and Charlo had played together at Juventus and were room-mates on away trips.

Big John told us about the time they'd been at an Italian Cup away match in Palermo, Sicily. He and Sivori were resting in their hotel room on the afternoon of the game.

'I was dozing,' he said in that quiet Welsh lilt. 'There was a knock at the door so I got up and opened it. There were three blokes standing there in dark suits and sunglasses. They said they wanted to speak to Sivori. I woke him up and he went to the door. A minute later, he rushed back in the room and started packing his things. I said, "What are you doing?" He said, "If I play, they're going to shoot me, I'm leaving."

'So I telephoned down to the coach, Herrera. He came running up to the room. When he heard the story, he told Sivori, "Things like that always happen down here. If you leave you'll never play in Italy again."

'Well, he played but he ran away from the ball every time it went near him. It was nil-nil and the ball came to him in the penalty area. He deliberately shot wide but it hit a defender and went in. Sivori immediately flung himself to the ground, covering his head.

'Two minutes later the other team equalised from what looked like yards offside. With five minutes to go the ref gave them a penalty for nothing and they went 2-1 up. Sivori was trying to leave the pitch but Herrera wouldn't let him. Just then I got the ball, beat two men and scored from twenty-five yards. The referee disallowed it. I went crazy and demanded an explanation. "Shut up," he said, "they're going to shoot me if they don't win." '

We didn't win the league either.

But it was an experience playing with John Charles and you could see, even though he was now thirty-nine years of age, why he had been such a great player. There cannot have been a better header of a football in the history of the game. It wasn't his height, although that was an advantage. His timing was faultless, immaculate. He could hang in the air, it seemed, for as long as he wished.

When he was playing for Hereford he wasn't as mobile as in his youth, of course, but possessed the most delicate touch when required. If you add all that to great strength with either foot, you have a superb specimen.

I will never forget an end of season game at Gloucester City. Big John had made himself substitute. It was nil-nil with about fifteen minutes to go. We got a free kick and during the break in play, Charlo brought himself on. He literally walked into the penalty area, saying to the referee, 'Hang on'. When he was ready at the far post the free kick was taken. Big John met it perfectly and powered it back into the far corner of the net. He just walked back to the centre spot, saying, 'There you go then, boys, 1-0 to us'.

Chapter Fourteen
Hereford United

Had I made a mistake leaving Barnet? It was too late now, although it crossed my mind several times after the Trophy semi-final.

At the end of that season Hereford went on a close season tour to Brest on the west coast of France. The journey from Southampton to Cherbourg was horrendous, the coach trip from Cherbourg to Brest just as bad. I think the whole team were sick at some point.

Halfway between Cherbourg and Brest, a trip of about seven hours in total, we stopped in a remote village to obtain relief and some refreshment. As we staggered into a tiny cafe on the main road, the two old guys sitting quietly in the corner looked up in utter amazement. They had immediately recognised the imposing figure of John Charles. This was some years after his retirement, in a foreign country, not the one he made his name in and long before the era of satellite television. He really was a superstar, and very uncomplicated.

He approached the counter and addressed the owner (moustached and wearing a striped apron, what else?) in perfect Italian. 'Quindici cafe per favore, grazie.' The owner looked completely mystified.

'Quinze cafés, Monsieur, s'il vous plaît, merci,' I assisted, standing alongside Big John.

The big man turned to me, a huge grin on his face. 'You didn't tell me you were French, boyo! Hey lads, Ricky speaks French! Have you got any French money?' I pulled out several hundred francs. I had assumed that, going to France, I would need some local currency. Charlo didn't have a penny on him. I paid for the coffees.

He was so excited to find that one, I spoke a little French and two, I had French money, and it suddenly dawned on me that, of course, all his life he had been looked after. When he travelled with Juventus to a foreign land, he didn't need money, he was just a player, everything was paid for by someone else. Now he was in charge. There were no club gofers in dark glasses ready to cough up whenever one of the stars needed a few quid, or even the price of a cup of coffee.

I found it all very amusing. Suddenly, I had status in this group of guys, all because I had thought to change some money.

When we finally arrived at our destination we found our hosts absolutely charming. There was an English player, formerly at Hereford, by the name of Nigel Page-Jones. He had married a French girl and was now playing for Stade Brestois, in the French third division.

John introduced me to everyone as being French-speaking, which I was not. I spoke a little after four years of learning the language at school. Nevertheless, I was regarded as something of a curiosity. It seemed every time I looked at Charlo he was grinning at me.

By all accounts, the trip was to be paid for by the host club, out of the gate receipts which were to be split fifty-fifty. After the game, in which I scored the only goal, John was given a bulging envelope in full view of his players.

We followed him around the whole evening. He was like the pied piper; every time he turned around he saw fourteen guys behind him.

'What's the matter, don't you trust me?'

'*No!*' we chorused loudly.

Sitting in his hotel bedroom much later, he doled out the francs – 'One for you, two for me'– it was hilarious, we never stopped laughing. 'Il Gigante Buono' never carried a penny on him.

That short and funny trip helped me settle at Hereford. I got on really well with the other players, particularly Dudley Tyler and Brian Owen whom I had encountered in Barnet versus Bath City matches. Dudley told me about a close season trip to Germany the previous year. John Charles was feted wherever he went and at a banquet given in honour of the visitors and their famous manager, he was asked in front of several hundred people if the trip had been enjoyable. 'Oh yes,' said John, 'we flew Luftwaffe, very comfortable'.

Billy and I did our pre-season training with Barnet before the 1971-72 campaign and we didn't see our team-mates until the first friendly, away at Shrewsbury.

There were three new faces. Ken Mallender, a left-back signed from Norwich City, had previously played for Sheffield United. What a character! He had the most infectious laugh I have ever come across and was the greatest audience to a couple of cockney impersonators. Billy and I used to do Blakey from 'On the Buses' and Alf Garnett from 'Till Death Do Us Part'. We only had to say a couple of words and Mallender was in fits. His laugh started everyone else off. Ken was a classy player, but he could kick you over the stand if he wished, still laughing.

Tony Gough came from Bath City. Vastly experienced and with two terrific feet, Goughie became a midfield general and skipper. Quiet and thoughtful, I can still hear him calling me to 'get back, Ricky, you lazy git!'

The third signing was a guy who played for Newport County when Barnet beat them 6-1 in the FA Cup the previous year, a midfield player with talent, commitment and a warm and generous nature. Everybody loved Ronnie Radford.

We sat in the dressing room before playing Shrewsbury. Charlo's team talks were legendary. Sometimes there weren't any.

'Out you go then, boys,' he said this time.

Raddy asked a question, 'Where do you want me to play, John?'

Charlo looked at him in disbelief. 'You're a midfield player, aren't you?'

'Yes.'

'Well, play midfield then!'

After three games we were second in the league. We were due to play Yeovil at home on a Wednesday night and Dover, the league leaders, on the Saturday.

Billy and I arrived at the ground for the match. Charlo was standing in the doorway to the players entrance, grinning at us.

'Hey you, Douglas Fairbanks!' he shouted at me. I never knew why he called me that but I knew who he meant. 'Come into my office.' I went in and he told me to sit down. It was brand new, built in the close season. I could have sworn he'd never been in it.

'I think you're feeling your ankle, boy, I'm going to leave you out tonight'

I was stunned. 'But John, it feels fine, I really want to play,

I've been looking forward to this all day.' I looked at him pleadingly.

He thought for a moment. 'All right, you play then, I'll drop someone else.'

We thrashed Yeovil 3-0. I realised he'd wanted to drop me but, faced with my pleas, he couldn't. I played my heart out.

I won't say I admired John Charles in the same way I admired Dexter Adams but I thought the world of him. To be so famous and yet so completely unassuming was his greatest asset. As a communicator he was just like a kid, still loving every minute of what really is a simple game.

However, Frank Miles was a chairman going places and John was just too laid back for his liking. He was fired at the beginning of October 1971. Yet John Charles did a great deal for Hereford United. He will always be regarded highly by those who worked with him and fondly remembered by his players.

When the manager was sacked Hereford United were in second place in the Southern League premier division – not exactly the end of the world, but I suspect there were reasons other than the playing side. There had to be, the club was very ambitious and it was no secret that Football League status was the target for that particular season. For some time, the chairman had wanted a full-time manager, one who would live in Hereford. Big John still lived in Cardiff and did not attend Edgar Street every day.

Another famous ex-player stepped in as caretaker manager while the club advertised the position. Joe Wade had been a stylish full-back for Arsenal in the 50s. He played in the same side as Joe Mercer and had the unfortunate distinction of being the man who finished Mercer's career. A collision during a first division match at Highbury resulted in a broken leg for the veteran wing-half. Witnesses in the 50 000 crowd say you could hear the crack all over the stadium. As Mercer was carried off, he waved just once, knowing it was the end.

Joe Wade was and still is an absolute gentleman. He ended his own career at Hereford, became manager for a spell and then retired to run a sports shop in the town.

Colin Addison was appointed a couple of weeks later. He came straight out of the old first division from Sheffield United. A midfield player of some repute, Colin had played for Arsenal and Notts Forest at the highest level. Jack Mclelland told us that when he was at Highbury, Addison was the best five-a-side player in the club. He could work marvels on the training pitch but never quite fulfilled his undoubted ability on a Saturday.

A player of his class – he was still in his early thirties – was a huge bonus to a team like Hereford. Colin Addison took over John Charles' good team and made it great.

I will never forget his first game in charge. It was away at Poole Town in a Southern League Premier fixture. The usual dressing room banter was taking place. Billy and I were trying to make Mallender laugh, which wasn't hard. Dudley Tyler and Brian Owen were trying to make Goughie laugh, which wasn't easy.

Suddenly, the new manager clapped his hands for silence. 'OK, lads, concentrazione!'

There was silence for two seconds and Brian Owen said in a broad Somerset accent, 'Blimey, I thought we'd got rid of the Welsh Git!' This was a reference to Charlo's oft used Italian phrases.

I don't think the roar of laughter that followed Brian's quip was quite what Colin had in mind but to his credit he saw the funny side of what he had said. I never heard him quote Charlo again.

I scored after five minutes with a far post header. This was about as rare as getting a pass off Billy Meadows anywhere within twenty-five yards of goal. There was no dream start for Addo though, and we lost 2-1.

At just thirty-one years of age, Colin Addison had made a wise move into management. He was very ambitious and impatient for success. What a brilliant appointment by Frank Miles; Addison was just the man he'd been looking for.

The following week I was dropped.

I have often wondered over the years how I would go about dropping a player had I become a manager. At the league clubs I had played for, apart from Arthur Cuncliffe's 'It's not the end of the road, son' at Bournemouth, nothing had been said. The team sheets went up on a Friday and you read where you were playing.

Dexter Adams at Barnet would tell the player first, explaining clearly why he was doing it. I've told you about John Charles; he tried to drop me and I wouldn't let him.

Colin was unique. He took me into the treatment room at Edgar Street and sat me down.

'Good header last week, Ricky son, took it well. I felt you faded badly second half, in fact you faded first half. I'm not looking for scapegoats, but I need to get things going quickly and I'm not saying you were our worst player but you did go very quiet and it was a bad result, Ricky, a bad result, specially as we were in front and it was a good header, Ricky, I've said that. I told the other lads everyone's fighting for their places now, we're going all out for league football which means we have to win this league and all I'm saying, Ricky, is that you'll be treated like everyone else, but in a nutshell, Ricky son, basically and I'm not singling you out, it was a bad result, Ricky, a bad result, anyway, you're dropped.'

I knew what was coming as soon as he invited me into the treatment room, but bless him, it took 150 words when twenty would have sufficed.

So I became more or less the permanent substitute.

We climbed to first place in the league. I came on in most matches and scored one or two goals to assist the efforts of the other lads. Playing for twenty minutes at a time suited me as the ankle continued to give me trouble. I spent more time getting treatment than I did training, but things weren't too bad.

'OUR GLORY LIES NOT IN NEVER HAVING FALLEN, BUT IN RISING WHEN WE FALL.' This is the Hereford United FC motto. I guess you could apply the same quotation to a racehorse.

We entered the FA Cup at the fourth qualifying round, drawn at home to Cheltenham, nearly a local derby. On 6th November 1971, in front of 6441 fans, we embarked on our historic journey. Cheltenham were dispatched 3-0 with two goals from Gough and an own goal.

In the first round proper we were drawn away to Kings Lynn. The night before, in a telephone call to my parents from our hotel, I had received the sad news of my grandmother Francis George's death. She had been ill for some time and died in St George's Hospital, Hyde Park Corner. She was eighty-six years old. So the last link with my grandparents was gone and I was left with many precious memories of a lovely lady.

The game, played in thick snow on November 20th, ended

in a nil-nil draw. The replay, four days later, was attended by 7758 people. Goughie scored again, the only goal, to put us into the second round.

Northampton Town, of the fourth division, were the visitors to Edgar Street on Saturday 11th December 1971. Now the excitement began in earnest as 9510 spectators witnessed a hard fought nil-nil draw. I came on for the last twenty minutes and, as I took the field, I heard their manager, the late Dave Bowen, call to the right full-back, Lew Chatterly, to keep an eye on me. Chatterly looked up, grinned and tapped the back of his shorts with his right hand, indicating that he had me in his pocket. Not today, I thought. The atmosphere was electric and as I went past Chatterly for the third time in as many minutes, I reminded him that he should get his pockets sewn up. As we walked off at ninety minutes, he gestured to me, 'See you Tuesday, we'll see how quick you are then'.

In the event, I sat out the replay, which was drawn 2-2 in front of 9099 people at the County ground. On that night, all my relatives from the Peterborough area sat in the stand along with my mum, dad and brother. It was tremendous game, enough to compensate for my non-appearance.

The second replay was scheduled to be played six days later at the Hawthorns, home of West Bromwich Albion.

As our cup run began, I started a brand new job with Umbro International Ltd, UK distributors for Adidas, the famous German sports shoe company. My area as a sales representative was North London and the Home Counties. However, the training included spending a week in the North West with a guy called John Cooper, who was a famous athlete. In the 1964 Tokyo Olympics he had won two silver medals, for the 400-metre hurdles and the four by 400-metre relay. Coop was a big, ebullient guy and his success as an athlete owed a great deal to his amazing courage. He was the type to push himself even harder when his lungs were ready to burst. He was a Loughborough man, a great friend of Bob Wilson, the Arsenal 'keeper and TV presenter. Jeffrey Archer, now Lord Archer, was another contemporary.

Cooper's greatest friend, though, was Robbie Brightwell, captain of the Great Britain Olympic team and himself a 400-metre finalist in Tokyo. Brightwell had become general manager of Adidas and it was he who had appointed myself and John Cooper to join the first all-Adidas sales team in the United Kingdom.

Coop was good company. He came to the first Northampton replay and joined with the lads in a good drink afterwards. Later, he became sales manager for Adidas and was responsible for the England Rugby Union squad in a public relations capacity. In 1974, he attended the France versus England Five Nations game in Paris. Anxious to get home, as always, he caught an earlier than planned London-bound flight from Charles de Gaulle Airport. It was a Turkish Airlines DC10, en route from Istanbul.

Thirteen minutes after take-off, a cargo door burst open and depressurised the aircraft. The plane crashed into a heavily wooded area, killing all on board.

In the short time that I knew Coop, I discovered a man of almost disarming honesty; a man with great courage and character, someone you wanted in your team.

John Cooper was a true Corinthian.

The second replay, at the Hawthorns, came right in the middle of the first Adidas UK sales conference, at Wilmslow in Cheshire. I was given permission to leave early for the match.

By now, of course, we knew who our opponents would be in the third round, should we succeed against 'the Cobblers'. The added incentive to beat this fourth division side was a trip to St James' Park, Newcastle to play one of the most famous clubs in the country.

Our third meeting in the space of nine days turned out be an amazing football match. At least 6000 Hereford fans journeyed up the M5 to make up the bulk of the 8331 spectators.

Again I started substitute, except this time I played a much larger part. Tyler and Owen had scored for us in the 2-2 draw, Hawkins and Large replying for Northampton. It was Large, a much travelled centre-forward, who put the Cobblers in front in the first half. At half-time, 1-0 down, Colin told me to get warmed up as soon as the second half started. After about fifteen minutes I was sent on in place of Tony Gough. We attacked for practically all of the remaining half hour. I had two shots cleared off the line as our supporters frantically screamed for us to equalise. The minutes ticked by and the ninety were up when the ball came out to Ken Mallender on the edge of the penalty area. He drove it back in, first time, along the ground and it whistled into the back of the net. The laughing policeman had scored and did he celebrate? He sprinted fifty yards back to the halfway line with the whole team in pursuit. They kicked off and the referee blew his whistle for full-time.

Our wonderful supporters had urged us back into the tie. We owed them a victory now and a goal from the brilliant Tyler in the second period of extra time finally settled the marathon and ensured our trip to Tyneside.

We celebrated in time honoured fashion in Birmingham after the game. As I was leaving for the drive up the M6 to Cheshire, Billy Meadows stuck a huge cigar in my mouth. When I pulled into the hotel car park an hour and a half later, it was still in my mouth, unlit. I was still at the Hawthorns, in a complete daze of joy.

Meanwhile, the Adidas sales conference opened with a word of congratulations to the North London sales rep from Mr John Humphries, the managing director of Umbro International Limited. I must confess to feeling great pride about that too.

It was to be a month before we would play in the third round of the FA Cup. I had to pinch myself several times. The greatest domestic competition in the world had succeeded yet again in firing up the imagination of the nation.

I remembered the first final I ever saw on television: 1953, Blackpool versus Bolton Wanderers. Stanley Matthews was thirty-eight years old. He had already been on the losing side in two finals; this had to be his last chance.

What a game it turned out to be, with Blackpool, 1-3 down with ten minutes to go, grabbing a dramatic victory in the dying seconds as Matthews crossed from the by-line for the South African Bill Perry to crack home the winner.

I remembered the Spurs cup wins of 1961 and 62, and my own experiences. Losing to Reading in the first round in my brief spell at Watford. Losing to non-league Bedford Town while playing for Oxford United. Then the hat-trick against Newport County for Barnet in 1970, only to lose in the third round to Colchester United, who then went on to a famous fifth round win over Leeds United, the league leaders and cup favourites.

94

Everybody loves the FA Cup. We couldn't wait to get up to St. James' Park.

History showed Newcastle to be great cup fighters. They reached the cup final five times in seven seasons in the early part of the century, winning the trophy just once, after a replay against Barnsley. By all accounts this side was a formidable one and the theory was that the turf at Crystal Palace (the venue before Wembley) was thicker than that at St James' and did not suit their slick passing game. In 1924, the second Wembley final, Newcastle conquered the heavy pitch to defeat Aston Villa 2-0. The scorer of their second goal, Stan Seymour, went on to be manager, director, chairman and vice-president of the club. In 1932 the Geordies beat Arsenal 2-1 with the help of the infamous 'over-the-line' goal. This was nearly as controversial as Geoff Hurst's goal in the 1966 World Cup final. But while that dispute remains unresolved, old film of the 1932 Cup Final shows that when Newcastle's Jimmy Richardson reached the ball at the by-line, it was clearly over the line before he hooked it back for Allen to score.

In 1951 and '52 Newcastle United became the first club in the 20th century to win the cup two years running. In 1955 they won it again, this time creating another record when folk hero Jackie Milburn scored the fastest ever Cup Final goal in forty-five seconds. 'You have to be a Geordie to understand what the cup means in these parts,' he is quoted as saying. 'It means, glory, glamour, excitement and, above all, it is instant.' I cannot think of a better way of describing the great competition.

The legendary Milburn was to play a significant role in my own Cup memories.

Six weeks after Newcastle's 2-0 victory over Aston Villa in 1924, two local Herefordshire teams, St Martins and RAOC, announced an amalgamation. They made an application to enter the Birmingham Combination under the name of Hereford United FC. The new club was to share the use of the Edgar Street ground with Hereford City. Football had been played on the same ground since the latter part of the 19th century, including many historic matches between Hereford Thistle and the old Hereford club, better known locally as the 'Old Reds'.

The first ever competitive match Hereford United played was a Birmingham Combination game against Atherstone

Town at Edgar Street on 30th August 1924. The following week they lost 7-2 to Kidderminster Harriers in an extra preliminary round FA Cup tie. The early and somewhat inauspicious introduction to the competition gave no hint of the reputation the club would gain as formidable non-league opposition in the years to come.

In season 1932-33 Hereford United reached the first round proper for the first time, away to one of the Football League's founder members, Accrington Stanley. In a hard fought game, United went down by two goals to one. Having reached the second round proper in 1948-49 and 49-50, the club recorded their first ever win over Football League opposition the following season when Scunthorpe United were beaten by a single goal at Edgar Street, in front of 10 527 people. The nearest league club, Newport County, were the visitors in the next round, when a 15 526 crowd saw the Welsh side triumph by three goals to nil. In season 1957-58, with Joe Wade as player-manager, Queens Park Rangers were the visitors to Edgar Street in the second round.

This was to be United's finest hour as an incredible 6-1 victory sent them into the third round for the first time. Sheffield Wednesday were the visitors in what was the club's first ever competitive match against a first division side, when 18 114 people witnessed a 3-0 defeat. But Hereford United's name was now on the football map.

In 1965-66, they reached the third round again but after beating Millwall at home, the club had the misfortune of being drawn away to Bedford Town, only to go out by two goals to one.

By the time Billy Meadows joined John Charles and company in 1970-71, Hereford United had reached the first round proper in every season since 1954, a great achievement for a non-league club. In 1970, Northampton Town became the first league side to be beaten by Hereford away from home in the FA Cup when goals from Meadows and Brian Owen sealed a 2-1 replay win. Brighton and Hove Albion then cancelled out a Charles goal to win 2-1 at Edgar Street in front of 12 769 spectators.

The Cobblers had now been brushed aside for the second year running and there were great compliments paid after the victory. Dave Bowen, himself a former Welsh International and distinguished Arsenal wing-half, said that Hereford were the best side he had seen all season and contended: 'It really takes some believing that Hereford are a non-league side, it was a terrific tie.'

Newcastle United's boss, Joe Harvey, having spied on the future opponents, stated: 'I was surprised by Hereford's performance, considering they are a non-league side. I thought the standard of football was very high. We should get 37 000 at St James' Park. Our fans are mad about cup football, and Hereford as newcomers should be attractive newcomers. We're not taking anything for granted.'

In the event, 39 301 spectators witnessed the attractive newcomers.

The FA Cup third round ties were scheduled to be played on Saturday, January 21st, 1972.

The club, under the guidance of chairman Frank Miles, was prepared to do things in style. We were to travel on the Friday before the game and stay at the Gosforth Park Hotel, at that time the premier hotel in the north-east.

The entire squad and their wives, together with the chairman, directors and other officials of the club, gathered together in the dining room of the Gosforth Park on the eve of the game. There was one wife missing however – mine. Patricia, as was her wont, was travelling up on the Saturday morning with her own personal entourage, her sister Teresa, brother-in-law Peter and half a dozen other of our closest friends.

It had been raining all day in the north-east. As we began our meal, an announcement was made that the game had been postponed due to a waterlogged pitch. There was complete silence for three seconds as this news was digested. The first to speak was Bill Meadows. 'I'll have a large gin and tonic then.'

The disappointment was immense but like the good troopers we all were, we consoled ourselves at the Dolce Vita night club in the centre of the city.

As Patricia wasn't there, I shared a room with one of the few single players, David Icke. David was a goalkeeper, at that time understudy to the great Fred Potter. He was a quiet, thoughtful guy and I got on very well with him. To my shame, I got in very late that night and kept him awake as I described the delights of the Dolce Vita. After I left Hereford I never saw him again until three days after the 1998 Grand National. We immediately recognised each other and I was pleased to see and hear that he is doing very well with his own book publishing company.

The game was rescheduled for Tuesday 24th, kick-off 7.30pm.

Again we were to report the night before, this time at the Swallow Hotel in the heart of Newcastle. I was operating Adidas stockrooms in London, at the Regent Palace Hotel. It was a very important time of year for the business. The retailers were invited to view the new season's range and place orders six months in advance. I had to keep asking for permission to leave early and take the following two days off. To his great credit, Robbie Brightwell, as a sportsman himself, had no problem with this and made sure my customers were looked after.

'Get it played, kid, and enjoy it,' he said. He was a great guy.

We trained on the Tuesday morning at Newcastle's facilities. They were training as well and I could see Malcolm 'Supermac' Macdonald going through his paces a couple of pitches away.

Supermac was just one of five internationals in the Newcastle squad. The others were the goalkeeper Willie McFaul, full-back David Craig, centre-back Bobby Moncur and inside-forward Tony Green. It was a formidable task but what, to use a very well worn phrase, did we have to lose?

When we arrived at the foot of the steps that lead up to the main entrance of St James', a familiar face was there to greet us. John Motson, a young BBC football reporter, was covering the match for Radio Two. John and I knew each other well. He had been a junior reporter on the Barnet Press in the early 60s and I met him first in 1964 when the paper covered my move from Tottenham to Watford. An old schoolfriend, Roger Jones, later to become sports editor of the local rag, introduced Motty to a lot of people in the Barnet area, many of those from our old school, East Barnet Grammar. One of them, my old buddy from Barnet boys' days, Bob Sims, held a pyjama party at his parents' house, a wonderful Edwardian structure in Lyonsdown Road, New Barnet in 1968.

On a warm, summer's evening more than hundred people, dressed in a variety of bedwear, had been raving it up when Motty arrived. He was very smartly dressed in a dark suit, white shirt and tie, all of which, I recall, stayed intact for the evening. He hasn't changed much, although I have seen the tie removed occasionally.

Anyway, back to St James'. The first thing we did, having had a quick look in the dressing-room, was to go out and look at the pitch. This was Colin Addison's first instruction. 'You've earned the right to be here, get out and have a walk on the park. Get your heads up, look confident, you have a chance to show the world what you can do.'

That last phrase is a key to why teams from lower divisions so often give at least one stunning performance when confronted with top-class opposition. We all start out the same, wanting to be professional footballers. Most of us, if good enough, will go through one of three stages: being signed by a big club as a junior, then, as in my case, being released to smaller clubs until a level is found; or making the grade and being kept on, as in the case of say, Bobby Charlton. Some, like Malcolm Macdonald, will start at a much lower level and improve to reach international status. In the final analysis, we are all in the same profession, operating at different grades. Without exception, every player wants to play in front of 30 000- or 40 000-strong crowds every week. For those who are fortunate enough to get even one chance to experience it, that chance lets them prove to themselves how good they really are.

There were no twenty-minute warm-ups in those days, so when we next emerged from the tunnel it was into the cauldron that is a full house of passionate and knowledgeable Newcastle United supporters. It was weird; the terrace opposite the tunnel was closed for refurbishment so although you could hear the crowd, until you were actually on the pitch taking in the whole stadium, you had no idea of the hordes of people waiting to watch this match. There were, in fact 39 301 packed into three sides of historic St James' Park, anticipating a slaughter. Were they in for a surprise?

We kicked off amidst a deafening roar. The ball went back to Alan Jones who struck a long pass downfield. It skimmed off the head of Newcastle's Pat Howard and into the path of the running Brian Owen. Without halting his stride, Brian cracked the ball with his right foot.

Straight into the top right hand corner of the Newcastle goal.

We were one nil up – in precisely seventeen seconds.

As 5000 Hereford supporters celebrated, so the Geordies

recovered from the shock to produce a noise so loud it made the hairs on the back of your neck stand up. The thundering chant of 'SUPERMAC, SUPERMAC!' rolled off the terraces. We hadn't been playing a minute.

For the next twenty it was like the proverbial charge of the Light Brigade. John Tudor equalised and when Macdonald smashed home a penalty five minutes later, I thought the roof of the stand would collapse with the noise.

But just when the world was expecting a flood of goals, Newcastle relaxed. They left the door open a fraction, and we crept back in. Almost imperceptibly, we took control. Minutes before half-time, Colin Addison took a pass from Ken Mallender and moved forward in space, looking about him for a colleague to give the ball to.

No Newcastle player approached Colin; those who were defending backed off, marking the Hereford runners. The tactic proved fatal.

Sensing his chance, the player-manager struck, right-footed, from twenty-five yards. The ball never rose above knee height and before McFaul moved, the net behind him was dancing.

We had delivered the psychological blow, and although they didn't know it at the time, Newcastle United were on the way out of the FA Cup.

It was all in the mind, that second half. We grew in confidence, theirs drained away.

I had sat on the bench knowing that I had more chance to take part if we were losing. I desperately wanted to get on and experience this living dream, if only for the memory. With under twenty minutes to go and the match finely balanced at 2-2, I came on. As excited as I was, I was surprised. The team had been outstanding and, if anything, we were on top. It could have been that Colin sensed an incredible victory because I found myself with a constant supply of passes delivered with shouts of encouragement, urging me to attack David Craig. In the dying seconds, Billy Meadows' diving header was turned around the post by McFaul. Newcastle United, sixth in the top division, six times winners of the FA Cup, had survived the newcomers.

The sporting Geordie fans applauded us from the pitch.

As we sat, savouring the moment, in the big, circular bath in the visitors' dressing room, we were visited by the West

Ham United manager, Ron Greenwood. He congratulated us on a fine result and then turned to Billy Meadows, whom he had known from their days at Arsenal.

'If you had just glanced that header, Bill, it would have gone in, you know.'

Thank goodness he didn't.

After a long and mellow night in the Swallow Hotel, where we were joined by Supermac and Motty, Bill and I travelled back to Kings Cross the following morning. The very enthusiastic young BBC reporter accompanied us, unaware of the effect the result would have on his life and career.

I realised why Ron Greenwood had been at the game. The winners were drawn to play West Ham at home. Bobby Moore, Geoff Hurst, Trevor Brooking.

'Hold on a minute,' I said to myself, 'we could be playing them.'

Chapter Fifteen
The Goal

The replay was postponed so many times because of the appalling weather in the Hereford area that the game was finally played on the day of the fourth round ties.

I carried on with the Adidas stockrooms. The final one, ironically, was at the Oxford Motel on the A40, en route to Hereford. I spent Thursday and Friday there and trained at the Manor ground on the Thursday night.

On the Friday afternoon, Billy and Pat Meadows arrived at the motel with John Motson. Motty was on trial at BBC television, and they had given him our game to commentate on for 'Match Of The Day'. During the journey he began his now legendary research. We went through every Hereford player in detail, where they had come from, how old they were, what position they played in, what their wives looked like.

For some reason, I stayed in a separate hotel from Bill that night and John and I dined together in the Green Dragon Hotel. Over dinner we went through the team again and I told him the most probable line-up. It wasn't hard; the twelve players had remained unchanged for several weeks, through each one of the seven cup ties we had participated in.

The twelve were: Fred Potter, Roger Griffiths, Ken Mallender, Alan Jones, Mike Mclaughlin, Colin Addison, Tony Gough, Dudley Tyler, Billy Meadows, Brian Owen, Ronnie Radford and me.

Fred had once been an inside forward for Aston Villa. He was a superb goalkeeper, deservedly winning 'player of the season' in the historic '71-'72 campaign. Unflappable, phlegmatic, a real Brummie.

Roger Griffiths was the one local boy in the team. He had been player of the year in season 1967-68, before transferring to local rivals Worcester City. In 1970 he returned to feature prominently in three great years, completing 250 games for the club. Roger was very much like Fred Potter in character, a real pro.

Ken Mallender, who is written about in the previous chapter, is one of those guys you will never forget. His bright, infectious personality was a highlight of the team and I thought the world of him. I still do.

Alan Jones was by a long way the longest serving player in the '71-'72 team; indeed the 335 appearances he made for the club places him fourth in the all-time list. One of the two 'Welsh Lions' who were the central defenders, Alan had been signed from Swansea in 1967. Along with Mike Mclaughlin, signed from Newport County in 1970, Jones formed a barrier of steel in front of Fred that was to concede fewer goals in a season, thirty, than ever before achieved by a Southern League Premier team.

In a four-three-three formation, Colin Addison was the inspiring player-manager running the mid-field. His class was there for all to see and having him in the side was like Stevenage's 1998 side obtaining the services of Roberto di Matteo. Alongside Colin was the skipper Tony Gough, the best passer of a ball with either foot over thirty yards I had seen since Johnny Haynes. And Ronnie Radford. A Yorkshireman, like Mallender, Raddy was always smiling. He was quiet – most of the time – unassuming and remarkably modest. He was to become part of football folklore, a fitting testament to a wonderful guy.

Brian Owen and Billy Meadows were hewn from the same rock that all great centre-forwards are made from. Brian, from Bath like Goughie, was the most affable person you could meet. On the pitch he was fearsome, not nasty or dirty, just very, very hard. I think it was Ben Embery at Barnet who said trying to tackle Brian Owen was like tackling an iron bar. He scored over fifty goals in his time at Hereford and I suspect he would be number one on most team sheets.

Dudley Tyler had arrived at Edgar Street in 1969 from amateur club Pinehurst in the Hellenic league. He became a sensation immediately, scoring twenty-one goals in his first season and voted 'player of the year' by the fans. He continued to be a sensation, starring in the cup run to such an extent that West Ham United paid £25 000 for his services at the end of the 1971-72 season. Having Dudley on your side, playing down either wing, was like having Tom Finney in the team. Bill Shankly, the legendary former manager of Liverpool, used to say that when the Preston defence got tired they would give the ball to Finney 'so that he could run their defence around for five minutes'.

So Motty got his research and then, late that Friday night, he returned the favour in memorable fashion.

It must have been well after midnight and we were strolling through the hotel when we stumbled upon some journalists, gathered for the big game. Immediately recognisable was a football and FA Cup legend: Newcastle's favourite son, the great Jackie Milburn. He was now a football writer for the *News Of The World*.

John introduced us. I was awestruck, Milburn was appalled.

'You should be in your bed,' he said to me, looking at his watch.

'I'm only sub,' I ventured lamely.

'You know, it's lads like you that made me give up management. Only sub? You might come on and score the winning goal!'

My irresponsible and undedicated past flooded back, right there, in the snug bar of the Green Dragon Hotel. Here was a man, a real hero of the game, telling me what Bill Nicholson, Ken Furphy, Reg Flewin, Freddie Cox and Arthur Turner had all thought about Ricky George.

I mumbled something about being pleased to have met him, went to bed and never slept a wink.

February 5th, 1972, dawned chilly and bright. It was a February day, a football day.

The pitch, rolled flat, was very muddy underneath. After all the postponements, it was just about playable. The Newcastle squad had been in a hotel nearby in Worcester for ten days, waiting to get this over with.

We had our usual pre-match meal at the Spread Eagle Hotel, and walked to the ground. The official attendance was 14 313, but there must have been more than 20 000 spectators if you added those who were up trees and floodlight pylons, and on roof-tops.

There wasn't a great deal to be said before the game. A national newspaper printed a photograph of Malcolm Macdonald holding up two hands, predicting a score of ten goals against us. Colin pinned it up on the dressing room wall. Enough said.

The Hereford pitch slopes left to right as you look from the main stand. The slope is nowhere near as pronounced as Barnet's Underhill or other famous sloping pitches, like the old Yeovil surface, the Huish.

Newcastle, playing in red shirts, attacked right from kick-off, down the slope. They created several goal-scoring chances early on and only a mixture of poor finishing, bad luck and some great goalkeeping from Fred Potter kept us in the game. Gradually, our boys edged their way into the match and after the early onslaught the tie evened out into one of fascinating proportions. What the enthralled spectators were witnessing was a football match between two teams separated by nearly ninety places and four divisions, slugging it out toe-to-toe like a couple of old-fashioned prize fighters. There were no bad tackles, no bookings, and no petulance, just twenty-two professionals doing what they had been born to do, play football.

On the bench, I sat anxiously watching my mates play themselves into immortality. I was praying for a chance to get on, just like the first game. At nil-nil anything could happen. If it stayed like that there would be extra time. Surely then I would play.

At half-time the players walked off to thunderous applause. They had been magnificent, every one of them. Who would come off for me? I couldn't have told you. Roger Griffiths was feeling his left leg but reassured Colin that it was okay. As usual, before we left the dressing room, Colin told me to keep warm.

The second half went the same way as the first with Ken Mallender hitting the post for us and big Alan Jones, who had gone forward, missing a great chance from close in.

As eighty minutes approached, Tony Green dragged the ball away from Goughie in mid-field, before slipping a pass out to Viv Busby on Newcastle's right. Busby was on his last day of a month's trial from Luton Town. At the right corner flag he crossed, high and long to the far post. Macdonald climbed, hung in the air for a split second and thundered the ball into the back of the net with his forehead.

'That's it! Newcastle have scored!' cried Motty to future zillions of people.

Before Fred had retrieved the ball from the net, Colin looked across and motioned for me to come on straight away. Griff limped off, shouting encouragement to me in that wonderful Herefordian accent. It later transpired that he had played seventy-six minutes with a broken leg. That summed the team up in many ways. You would not want to shirk a tackle in front of that lot. Mind you, if couldn't run through the proverbial brick wall during an FA Cup tie against Newcastle United, then you surely should not be playing the game.

I ran across the mud to take my place on the left wing, just below the BBC gantry. I had about nine minutes to do something, anything. For myself, for my team, for the cameras, whatever. I chased every ball, desperate now not to waste this once-in-a-lifetime opportunity.

On eighty-seven minutes, I won the ball, chasing back on our left flank. To great cheers I slipped the ball inside to Ken Mallender, who knocked it first time into mid-field. Ronnie Radford challenged for the ball with John Tudor and won it at the second attempt. Composing himself, he stroked the ball forward ten yards to the feet of Brian Owen and kept running. Brian laid it back into the path of the oncoming number eleven.

Ron Radford was at least thirty yards from goal. In the split second that it had taken for the ball to roll back towards him he had decided to shoot. The urgency of the situation, his awareness of precisely where he was in relation to the Newcastle goal and the knowledge that he did possess the ability to strike the ball correctly if he were to aim for goal, computed itself in time for him to perform the act that would make history.

The connection was perfect. The ball whistled off his right boot towards the top right-hand corner of McFaul's goal. For the third time against Hereford, the Northern Ireland International goalkeeper got nowhere near making a save. It was struck with such force that had the goal not been there, the ball would have disappeared into orbit, somewhere down the Leominster Road.

The pitch was invaded by a thousand little boys in parkas and Motty went into memorable overdrive. Amongst the thousands of delirious supporters another television man was savouring the moment. John Shrewsbury, BBC's producer of Match of the Day, had caught the flight of Raddy's goal every inch of the way. Having secured it on camera for all time, Shrewsbury became a part of the Hereford story. Twenty-six years on, he, Motty and I share a regular lunch date to enshrine the special moment. John Shrewsbury, like John Motson, was on the first rung of success that day.

Ronnie Radford, the most laid-back of us all, had laid the foundations for the greatest FA Cup upset of all time, and for the title of this book. Not only had he scored what became the 'goal of the season', not only had he pulled us level at the eleventh hour but, bless his huge heart, he had given me another thirty minutes on the stage.

In the first period of extra time, we kicked down the slope again. On 103 minutes of the tie, the same R Radford, from a similar position thirty yards from goal, decided to push a short ball just six yards to Dudley Tyler. No great urgency now, his brain said, no panic, we've got the ball, do the simple thing, keep it.

Dudley dragged the ball from his right to his left and cut inside to gain space. I was standing on the edge of the Newcastle penalty area facing Dudley. He drove the ball, left-footed, straight at me. I tried to cushion it but it popped up in the air to my left. I followed it, turning all the time towards goal. The ball fell under my foot and I got a second touch. I was lucky to get the chance but this time the leather sphere behaved itself, moving obediently in the right direction under my control. My brain said 'Shoot', and I struck the ball right-footed across the outstretched leg of the Newcastle captain, Bob Moncur. I looked up to see, once more, McFaul nowhere near it. Behind its flight, my heart leapt as I saw it hit the back of the net.

The elation is immediate. Your reaction is spontaneous. To run, to jump, to hug, to kiss, to laugh, to cry and do all those things at the same time. I *knew* I had done something very, very special. I still feel the emotion today, seeing that ball hit the net. It still brings tears to my eyes. After all the disappointments and the failures. The unwavering support of my family who were always faithful. My great friends who cried themselves when the goal went in. For a moment, this was *my* moment.

But the glory for all time would be the team's. The magnificent men who had fought tooth and nail to keep the Hereford United dream alive became instant legends. How lucky I was to have played just a small part. It was a great team, a truly great team.

I was engulfed by a sea of little boys and men in mud-spattered white shirts. Billy Meadows came hobbling across the muddy pitch. He was completely knackered, covered in mud with his front teeth missing. The nose looked even more crooked than ever. He finally threaded his way through the mass and planted a great big kiss on my mouth. Who says footballers shouldn't kiss? I wouldn't have missed that for the world.

We were never remotely in danger of relinquishing our hold on the game. The Newcastle lads were shell-shocked, you could see it on their faces.

The second period of extra time was played out in a carnival atmosphere. We should have scored more, such was our dominance of that final fifteen minutes. My confidence had reached an all-time high in a football match. Never again would I experience this feeling. I had entered the tunnel of exclusion, where all around you is out of focus in comparison to the clear, sharp outline of what you have to do. The ball seemed bigger than ever before, my opponents smaller. I could run fast with no effort and the white shirts of my team mates were luminous compared to the dull red of the defeated.

This brief transcendence to a higher plane was because I had scored a goal, a goal to win an historic football match, a goal to reward my courageous colleagues, a goal to reward the wonderful Hereford supporters, a goal to show my children and their children, *the* goal.

At the final whistle, the pitch was invaded for the third time and it was some minutes before we got back to the dressing room. Ron Radford was sitting in the bath, shampoo all over his head, grinning from ear to ear. He had been the nearest to the tunnel at the end and he had quietly slipped off before the rest of us.

The photographers piled in and the champagne was opened. Raddy rinsed his hair, climbed out of the bath, put his shirt back on and posed with the rest of us. Ten minutes later, along with his two children, he joined Colin Addison and myself on a very muddy pitch to be interviewed by a very excited Motty.

The adrenaline was still pumping away in my body and when John made reference to the previous night's encounter with Jackie Milburn, I reminded him, in front of the world, that he had been there as well. Behind his microphone, out of camera, he gave a little grin. What a day for the young would-be commentator! It was his first FA Cup Match of the Day.

' "The goal was somewhere near so I just tried my luck," was George's high-tech description of that historic moment.' So wrote Bryon Butler in his excellent book, *The Official Illustrated History of the FA Cup*, which Adam bought me for Christmas 1996.

The significance of my appearance in any publication about the great competition game is not lost on me.

People often ask rhetorically, 'I bet you had a few drinks that night?' Actually, Patricia, her sister Teresa, brother-in-law Peter Main, along with his best friend, Dick Crook, Motty and myself went back to Bill Meadows' house in Edgware to watch Match of The Day while eating fish and chips and sipping a few celebratory lagers.

The following day, *The Daily Mirror* sent round a photographer to snap me sitting up in bed getting breakfast from Patsy. We had been married four years and that was one thing I had not yet experienced.

'Whatever next?' as those who knew us well would say.

Chapter Sixteen
The Aftermath

Our victory over Newcastle United was reported in the *Bangkok Times* where we shared the headlines with the royal family's tour of Thailand. The achievement was hailed in Europe, Africa, Australia (where a millionaire made a serious bid to buy the club lock, stock and barrel), New Zealand, Canada and Malaya. Hereford United became a household name and we were labelled 'the Giantkillers of the century'.

Trevor Bond from *The Sunday Telegraph* wrote: 'Hereford, kept waiting like an impatient bride for their three-times-postponed third round replay tie, swept first division Newcastle out of the FA Cup – they then invited West Ham to a delayed fourth round reception in the same parish. Best man at yesterday's affair was substitute Ricky George '.

Jackie Milburn wrote in *The News Of The World*: 'What a fantastic FA Cup third round victory by the Hereford miracle workers. There was no fluke about the tanning of the mighty Geordies. The Hereford Tigers, 5000-1 outsiders, kept their cool when Malcolm Macdonald and company threatened to pull them apart.'

Next was West Ham United, just five days later.

The late, great Bobby Moore led his team out at Edgar Street on the 9th February, 1972. Alongside England's World Cup captain that night were Bobby Ferguson in goal, John McDowell, Frank Lampard, Billy Bonds, Tommy Taylor, Harry Redknapp, 'Pop' Robson, Geoff Hurst, Trevor Brooking and Clyde Best.

Forgive me if I take a temporary back seat and defer to the true professionals of journalism to relive that match.

The legendary Desmond Hackett in *The Daily Express* recorded: 'Had this been a boxing match instead of a splendidly-contested soccer duel, Hereford would have won

110

on points. When the wild excitement had finally died down, it was West Ham who went off gasping, exhausted...and relieved to find themselves still in the Cup.'

The Sun's Peter Batt: 'In one unbelievable spell towards the end Hereford were going so berserk that I would not have bet against them reaching Wembley.'

Jeff Powell in the *Daily Mail*: 'Hereford blew a rich, ripe agricultural raspberry at West Ham and all the football aristocracy they represent. Colin Addison's part-timers reduced West Ham to a rabble, scrambling to prevent Hereford's historic FA Cup run escalating into the sensation of our time.'

Fourteen thousand eight hundred and nineteen people witnessed the nil-nil draw.

I was on for the full ninety minutes; even the brave Roger Griffiths could not recover from a broken leg in five days. Billy Tucker, a tall young central defender, was now the substitute.

It was an amazing match, because on this occasion, incredibly, we weren't the underdogs. I lined up opposite Harry Redknapp on West Ham's right wing and remember shaking hands with him as we wished each other luck. This made me very proud. Harry and I are the same age, we had played against each other in Spurs-West Ham youth matches. In the intervening years, I had played for six clubs; Harry was still at Upton Park, in the first team. Yet, on this special night, we were equals. The Hammers came to Edgar Street that night nurturing a healthy respect for us. The world had announced that the win over Newcastle was no fluke, and so it proved because West Ham were forced to defend for their lives, just as if they'd been playing away at Leeds United or Liverpool.

Ron Greenwood, as gracious as ever, came to our dressing room again and congratulated us, admitting that they were lucky to be still in the competition.

This wasn't just another draw, another famous result. There was more to come just five days later, a replay on a Monday afternoon in London's East End, about half a mile from where my mother was born.

Trying to compare my feelings about the Newcastle and West Ham United matches reminds me of the time I received a fax from a business associate in the United States sometime in the mid-eighties. It was headed 'TRIVIA' and went on to say that the sender had read in a soccer magazine somewhere about my goal against Newcastle. Of course, it is part of Trivial Pursuit, but I answered swiftly, in positive fashion: 'It may be trivial to you, but apart from my marriage and the birth of my kids, it was the greatest day of my life.'

There is no disputing that, but I have to say the anticipation of playing at Upton Park in the fourth round replay was the most exciting. I don't know how much excitement the body and the brain can cope with; what I do know is that we had now played nine FA Cup matches since the 6th November, three of them against first division opposition on centre stage, and I was so high I didn't recognise myself.

The Evening Standard wanted a picture of me in action, so I donned a tracksuit and went down to the astroturf at York Way, Islington to meet the photographer. When I got there the first person I saw was Bryn Jones, brother of Cliff and an ex-playing colleague from my Watford days. Bryn was teaching at Holloway school, coaching the kids. He stopped the session, called the kids together and told them to take a good look at an FA Cup hero.

I stood there self-consciously as this group of ten and eleven year-olds stared at me as they might at some inanimate object on a trip to a museum. I could understand it; I wasn't a famous player who they would have heard of, like *Charlie* George (now he *was* a good player). I was a curious species: a Giantkiller.

Anyway, when the time came, the club did it again – in style. On the Sunday night before the game we met up in the Britannia Hotel in London's Grosvenor Square, where the huge eagle atop the American Embassy surveys the statue of Dwight D Eisenhower, thirty-fourth president of the United States.

The Britannia's east wall, on the south side of the square, is actually in Carlos Place, where thirty-eight years earlier my parents had first laid eyes on each other. When I was a little boy, I would walk on summer Sunday evenings with my parents and grandparents from Knightsbridge to South Audley Street, passing the Grosvenor Chapel in South Street, listening to the chapel bells. As I arrived that Sunday night in February 1972 to rendezvous with my team, I heard those same bells.

The fantasy continued.

Photographers arrived in the morning, again from the

Standard, and snapped Fred Potter, Ken Mallender, Bill Meadows and me in the gardens of Grosvenor Square. The paper produced a souvenir edition which paired me with Bobby Moore on the front page – something more to cherish from this golden period in my life.

Kick-off was scheduled for 2.15, Monday February 14th. The nation had been hit by a power strike, so like the old days before floodlights, an FA Cup replay was being played on a weekday afternoon.

Nothing captures the imagination of the nation like a Giant-killing. We were heroes all over the country, coming from a football backwater where prize bulls are reared and cider produced. Now we were coming to town, having given West Ham the fright of their lives five days before. Everybody wanted to get a look at this curious collection of journeymen footballers.

We left Grosvenor Square at 12.30, not early enough. As we edged our way through the London traffic towards the East End, I sat quietly taking in familiar landmarks: the Lord Nelson pub in Old Street, where my great friend Richard Bernard had lived in the 60s; Petticoat Lane, where Martin Webb and I used to scoff doughnuts on a Sunday morning; Blooms Restaurant in Whitechapel, once the most famous kosher eating place in London. I could almost smell the chicken soup as we drove by, and down Commercial Road.

I looked out at all the people coming and going in that incredibly busy part of the great City, thinking: 'I'm going to play football this afternoon, while you are going about your business, I am going to be running out in front of a huge crowd to play against the England Captain.'

And then, suddenly, I thought, 'I wish my grandad was here to watch me', and my eyes filled up.

The traffic was so bad that we had to abandon the coach somewhere near East Ham station and pile into a police van to ensure we actually got to the game. We realised, as if it wasn't obvious before, that the reason for the roads being jammed in and around Upton Park was that the world and his brother were trying to see this match.

Having seen Dave Underwood as we arrived, I was anxiously looking around near the players' entrance for any of my friends and loved ones to make sure they were OK. There were literally thousands milling about and I couldn't pick anyone out at all. We were already late and I was about to go and get changed when suddenly I saw this small, middle-aged lady with a familiar face. Her name was Nancy Hunt and she was the mother of a school friend of mine, Peter. I had played in the school team with Peter Hunt and his mum and dad were always at the games. After I left school, I heard that Mrs Hunt had followed my progress, particularly when I came back to Barnet in 1968. Nancy was a big Barnet fan and I never missed seeing her, home and away.

Amongst all these people, there she was. I called to her to see if she had a ticket. Her reply was incredibly moving, even more so in my emotional state: 'I just came to wish you good luck,' she said with a shy smile on her lovely face.

'Wait right there!' I shouted and rushed into the dressing room, where the lads were nervously getting into their kit. 'Anyone got a spare ticket?' I yelled. Colin Addison, bless him, had one left. I will never forget the look on Nancy Hunt's face when I handed her that ticket. I will never forget her.

The dressing rooms in big stadia like Upton Park are always well heated. It is warm and soothing, like being back in the womb. You can't hear the crowd but the expectancy is so great, you can cut the atmosphere with a knife. My hands shook as I tied my bootlaces. I rubbed oils into my legs and then smeared my eyebrows with vaseline. Looking in the mirror to do this, I noticed how flushed I was. If anyone was speaking, I didn't hear them. Dave Underwood was standing in our dressing room, just standing quietly by the door, bless his great big heart.

The bell went and amidst a few nervous voices of encouragement we filed out into the corridor, studs clattering on the concrete. As we approached the pitch all I could see was bright daylight and a massive stand packed solid with people. We were greeted with a thunderous roar and prolonged applause.

I was indeed in paradise.

Even now, twenty-eight years later, the memory sends shivers down my spine. As Giantkillers and conquerors of Newcastle United, we were as fascinating to the 42 219 people crammed into Upton Park that afternoon as Brazil would have been had they turned up. Ten thousand more were locked outside.

The generous reception we received was a combination of thirty-odd thousand East Enders and nearly 10 000 wonderful Hereford supporters. Special trains were put on and a film crew recorded forever happy fans in black and white singing a song especially written by Russ Lowe, a local disc jockey. The film, 'Cup Glory', was released later that year to celebrate 100 years of the FA Cup.

After less than ten minutes, I had a chance easier than any goal Hereford had so far scored against first division opposition. Dudley Tyler crossed from the right and Tommy Taylor mis-kicked on the slippery pitch. The ball spun up into the air and dropped on the volley onto my right foot. I was inside the penalty area and stabbed at the ball instead of striking it with confidence. It beat Ferguson but whistled inches past the post.

Just before half-time, Geoff Hurst put the Hammers one up.

We gave another good account of ourselves, losing Ken Mallender with an injury in the second half when Hurst scored twice more to end our glorious run. Fittingly, our great goal-scorer, Billy Meadows, was the player to score the last goal ever for the Giantkillers.

We were defeated 1-3 but left the field to magnificent and prolonged applause.

I was still only twenty-six years old but my glory had come and gone. My fifteen minutes of fame were up. As a footballer, my achievements had peaked for all time and were consigned to history.

Could it be possible that, twenty-six years later, in 1998, the events of 1972 would be recalled in such dramatic fashion?

Chapter Seventeen
Rodney Marsh's Jersey

After Hereford's cup exit at West Ham, I was able to concentrate more on trying to build a new career outside football.

My job at Adidas was twofold. I was a salesman in London and the South-East. I was also involved in what they called 'Soccer PR'. This was by far the most interesting and exciting aspect.

As a salesman I was answerable to Robbie Brightwell. As a PR man I worked for and alongside a man by the name of James C Terris, Sales Director for Umbro/Adidas who had been instrumental in securing the famous German brand for Umbro back in the very early 60s. It was his work with the top clubs that had raised the profile of Adidas in the UK.

For some time Jim had been looking for an assistant, someone to accompany him on the never-ending search for greater exposure for Adidas. Someone to share the work load, someone to put him to bed at night.

James Terris was a Scot. Born in Rothesay on the Isle of Bute, he was in his early 50s when I went to work for Umbro/Adidas in late 1971. The Hereford cup run obviously improved my chances of becoming Jim's right-hand man and we got on very well. I think it would be fair to say that Jim had three loves apart from his charming wife Chris: bottles of Bells, football and Umbro/Adidas. I would not wish to place any of the three in front of the others. My experience of the man was that he did a fantastic job for his employers while having the remarkable capacity to pour his first whisky at one minute past eleven every morning. Football and football people were his favourites and he generally gave short shrift to those outside that magic circle, of which, I have to say, he was very much a part.

Football people are pretty much an insular group,

suspicious and wary of so-called 'outsiders'. Therefore it was always a difficult task for one of those 'outsiders' to infiltrate. In the days before money was the key to gaining access to anyone at all, you really had to be accepted into the magic circle. It was generally OK if you had been a player; anyone else was regarded as a nosey busybody.

Jim Terris had gained the confidence of most in the game. Even though he was promoting a product and at times bore gifts, his approach was subtle and well thought out. There are several golden rules. The first and most important is: Do not discuss the game, any game, it doesn't matter. Do not discuss players. Do not proffer an opinion unless specifically asked to do so. In short, if you are accepted inside, find the right moment to get your business done and the rest of the time just shut up and listen. There is nothing a manager likes better than an audience, particularly one that doesn't disagree with him.

Jim was intelligent enough to have worked all this out early on. Even when he may have been on the Scotch all day, he maintained an incredible awareness that never let him down.

He also had a great ally, in the shape of a man named Ronald Goodman. Ron had been born to the business of dealing with professional football clubs. His father Barney had been a supplier of essentials, such as pumps to blow up footballs or replacement bladders or laces, to Tottenham Hotspur shortly after the war. Barney's cycle shop in Palmers Green was developed by Ronald into the largest supplier of all football kit, including boots, to major clubs in the country during the very early 60s. This booming business was the result of Ron's ability to gain the confidence of the clubs by making himself reliable, helpful and never, never a bloody nuisance. He came, did his business and left. If he arrived at Cardiff City, for example, on a Monday morning to deliver some shin pads and the team had been beaten 6-0 the previous Saturday, it was absolutely not mentioned unless the manager requested an opinion.

Jim, in his capacity as Sales Director of Umbro, took on Goodman Sports in Southgate, North London, as his personal customer. And how wise he was. The two became firm friends and Ron's advice and assistance became invaluable to a man promoting a product at the sharpest end of the public relations scale.

Consequently, the office at the back of the shop in Chase Side Southgate became a meeting point for Jim on his frequent trips to London. Since I was living in Barnet, just two miles away, it was extremely convenient for me and I slotted in neatly as Jim's number two, or 'gofer'.

We met up there just before the European Nations match against West Germany at Wembley in 1973. The England team were staying at the Hendon Hall Hotel, as they had done during the Ramsey era and the World Cup of 1966. Jim and I drove to the hotel on the afternoon of the game. He was on first name terms with the England manager and introduced me. Alf said hello politely, but was clearly uninterested and I should not think my presence even registered with him. That is not surprising in view of the fact that England were playing their most important match since the 1970 World Cup.

My job was to collect all the players' boots and paint in luminous white the three Adidas stripes that were the trademark of the famous German company. An easy task on paper, except that I had to approach very famous players on the day of a game and mess around with the essential tool of their trade. I don't think Alf ever fully appreciated how and why this sort of thing happened.

The marketing policy was brilliant. In 1966, the entire World Cup squad were paid £50 a man to wear Adidas boots throughout the tournament. If one were to try and estimate the advertising value obtained by the television exposure it would run into millions. But football was naive then; not so now, I hear you cry.

In that same never-to-be-forgotten World Cup, Adidas' main rivals, Puma, owned by Rudi Dassler, brother of Adi, had sponsored Brazil, Portugal and Argentina amongst those countries likely to be in contention. Everything went against Puma. Brazil and Pele were kicked out of the tournament by a brutal Portuguese side and Argentina won no friends with their infamous 'animals' display against England at Wembley, Alf Ramsey being the one to apply the label to Señor Rattin and company. In the semi-final, Bobby Charlton's double finished off Portugal and the wonderful Eusebio to leave the final as a 100 percent Adidas jamboree.

West Germany were tied to Adidas for all time so Puma made a dramatic last minute move to save face. At the eleventh hour, literally, they approached one England player to play in their boots in the Final. The player in question was offered £2000, just forty times the amount he had signed a contract with Jim Terris for. Not surprisingly – and who is anybody to judge? – he went for it. I will not name him here, but any photograph of the Final will disclose all. It was a *coup de grâce* in many ways because it certainly ruined the game for the Adidas contingent sitting in the stands who were more concerned with the identity of the boot than the ability or identity of the player. So while millions watched and enjoyed and England celebrated, the Adidas hierarchy demanded retribution from the contract breaker.

Here was the moment when Jim Terris was presented with the opportunity of making a friend of Alfred Ramsey for all time. At a suitable time not long after the match, Jim met with Alf to tell him of the displeasure felt by those who had, in good faith, entered into a contract with all his players, had abided by the terms of that contract and had it breached at the most critical and damaging moment. There was so much anger in the Adidas camp that they had already instigated legal proceedings for damages against the player who had so blatantly cheated them.

Alf's response was remarkable. Looking completely bewildered, he said, 'Are these players getting paid?' Even Jim was taken aback. Naive, perhaps, but putting it into perspective, Alf came from a football generation that did not look outside its own self-created environment. Money was secondary to the honour and glory of playing the game and if you were selected to play for England your travelling expenses were all you expected. The power of advertising played as little a part in your thinking as did the rate of the dollar against the pound or the theory of spontaneous combustion.

Once Jim had delicately explained to the England manager how it all worked, Alf thought long and hard. He wasn't a stupid man, far from it, and he reasoned that it would not be good PR for any sports company to be seen to be suing a World Cup hero on his own doorstep. Jim took this on board and promised to relay the thoughts of the man they called 'the General' when he was a player to his principals. Alf promised great co-operation should the matter be quietly put to bed.

So it was, and the man was true to his word. Jim Terris was afforded the run of the England team hotel and the assistance of the back room staff, Harold Sheperdson and

Les Cocker. The officials from the Football Association never questioned our presence and I was able to do my job.

In spite of all this help, I still had to get hold of the boots and I carefully approached the players one by one. I did know Bobby Moore from our two games against West Ham and he was typically helpful. If any of the players hesitated, a quiet word from Bob did the trick. England, by 1973, were not 100 percent Adidas any more and the deals were on a match-to-match basis. For a game like this European Nations tie, we were paying £75 a game.

Eight players were wearing Adidas, two Puma and one Hummel. The Puma players were on the same sort of deal as ours. Hummel, a Danish company, had recently signed up several notable British players to wear their football boots. Adidas, as mentioned, were distinctive by the three white stripes. Puma had a white caricature of the fleet-footed animal reproduced on their boots. Hummel's boots were white all over.

Jim and I discussed the white boots over a cup of tea with the player in question. I offered to clean the shoes for a small fee. It's not often that you pay someone for the privilege of cleaning their boots but as JCT said in his broad Shankly-type accent, 'There'll be no fucking white boots at Wembley tonight, Ricky boy, make fucking sure of it.' I put a tin of black boot polish on, that's all.

Jim was happy.

I had a great time working with the man. He was always pissed; I don't know what he was like sober, even though I saw him early in the morning and last thing at night. He was only ever about five hours away from the next one. He and Ron Goodman were like blood brothers but they were very good to me and I learnt an awful lot from them.

Of the many phrases of Jim's that stay in my memory, one springs to mind regularly. We were at a sales conference in Wilmslow, Cheshire, where the Umbro Head Office was. There was a lot of hype going on, with various sales managers and accountants prattling on about figures and bottom lines and production schedules. Jim, who said very little on these occasions, suddenly put his hand up for quiet. Everybody waited as he composed himself.

'Nothing happens, you know,' he said very deliberately, 'until somebody fucking sells something!' The last word came out so loudly that everyone jumped. Jim winked at me and took another mouthful.

I have reminded myself of that simple sentence many times.

England lost 1-3 to West Germany that Wembley night and the game heralded Geoff Hurst's last appearance there in an England shirt. The return match some weeks later was to be my first trip abroad for the company.

My phone rang at 11.30 one night. 'Berlin for you in the morning, my son,' came the familiar voice, and he told me to check in at the Karwendelhof Hotel, where the team were staying.

We sat in the Olympic stadium in Berlin – me, Jim, Ron Goodman and John Humphries, managing director of Umbro. We got completely soaked. Hitler's stadium, built for the 1936 Olympics, had no cover anywhere, except the podium where the Führer had stood aghast as a black American called Jesse Owens captured three gold medals.

In the England side, the two Puma players we had tried so hard to poach for this game on Adidas' home territory were performing well. Roy McFarland at the back alongside Bobby Moore was keeping Gerd Muller, 'der Bomber', very quiet. Up front the Puma player was Martin Chivers, the Spurs centre-forward, whom I had approached several times to wear our boots.

Jim wasn't happy with Chivers. He couldn't understand why the man appeared so aloof. It wasn't true actually, the big fellow is a really nice guy, he just gave the impression of aloofness.

Our little group, three middle-aged men and a part-time professional footballer, had an Umbro shoulder bag containing a bottle of Bells, four glasses and a bottle of water. Sitting alongside us were about 200 German police in green leather coats, watching the match intently.

Jim, soaking wet and with scotch in hand, was singing periodically, 'Chivers is a jelly, Chivers is a jelly' and then laughing his head off. The nearest German policeman sitting next to me kept looking across at us. 'What's he fuckin' lookin' at?' Jim asked me. I tried to ignore the question but Jim was on a roll. 'Hey, you, d'ywant a drink, yr miserable 'kin German bastard?' He was holding up the bottle as he spoke; I was praying the man didn't understand English. He just shook his head and I breathed a sigh of relief. Jim went back to his baiting of the England centre-forward and the match ended nil-nil.

True to form, we got into the official after match reception and I was introduced for the first time to Adi Dassler, now in his eighties, and the German team manager, Helmut Schoen. Jim was now on his best behaviour even though he had been scotching it for the best part of ten hours. Later on in the bar, he thrust a hundred Deutschemark note into my hand and sent me over to buy champagne for Bobby and Tina Moore and Mr and Mrs Franz Beckenbauer. I was embarrassed doing this but the two players and their wives thanked me graciously.

During the evening, I handed out envelopes discreetly to any England player that I bumped into, still doing the PR bit.

At around three in the morning, Jim and I grabbed a taxi to go back to his hotel. We had one more task to complete before leaving Berlin. As we were about to move off, the door to the taxi was thrust open and in jumped Gerd Muller himself. Here I was sitting with a true legend of German football. He had had a few and Jim and I agreed to drop him off. As the taxi sped through West Berlin, Jim was singing 'Chivers is a jelly, Chivers is a jelly' and Muller was studying him with a look of curious amusement on his face. Jim spotted this and started laughing. The great goal-scorer started to laugh too and suddenly we were all bent double in the back of this taxi, crying with laughter. 'Aye,' said Jim, just like Shankly, 'der Bomber, you little bastard.' At this, Muller began to laugh even more. When we dropped him off he was still laughing. He didn't have a clue who we were.

Back at Jim's hotel we went to his room and reconciled the amounts of money I had doled out that night. I left him at ten minutes before five, with his eyes disappearing into his head. My flight was due to leave at 7.30. I got back to the hotel at just after five to see an amazing sight. Alf was sitting in the lobby surrounded by journalists, travel agents and Ron Goodman. The players were wandering about in groups, everyone was still having a good drink. What I realised was that this was the tradition. No-one sleeps after a big match, at least almost no-one. I had been told once that on the night of England's 1966 triumph, Martin Peters had had an early night. However, that was just a rumour.

After a European Cup match against Borussia Monchengladbach one night at Anfield, Jim took me down to the famous Liverpool boot room. This event was the clearest evidence of the confidence that Jim enjoyed amongst the top names in the game. A knock on the door and we were welcomed by Bob Paisley, Joe Fagin and Ronnie Moran. I can't remember who else was in there that night but I will never forget the moment the door opened and in walked Jock Stein. The great Celtic boss sighed, sat on a bench next to me and said, 'I can't stand those bloody boardrooms, son, can you?'

There was no sign of the other great man, Bill Shankly. I was hoping, nervously that he might walk in any minute, but apparently he always stayed in his room alone after a game. We had been sitting there for about half an hour or so, listening to these icons of the game when suddenly Paisley held up his hand for quiet. 'Listen,' he whispered and sure enough, echoing down the corridor of that famous stadium were the strains of 'Amazing grace', being whistled by the great Shankly himself. 'He's ready to go home,' Paisley explained. 'He won't come and ask me, he just stands out in the corridor whistling.'

I did get to meet Shankly, finally, at Hampden Park after the England-Scotland game there in May 1973. As always, Jim made the introductions. We were in the main boardroom at Hampden, another bloody boardroom. 'This is Ricky George, Bill,' said Jim.

'Ricky George, aye, that's a good name. Tell me, Ricky, do you make Rodney Marsh's jersey?'

'Well, the company does,' I said, completely taken aback.

'I suggest you make the sleeves on his jersey a few inches longer so he can keep his hands warm while he's standing aboot doing nothing.'

He winked, slapped me on the back and moved on.

Just two seasons after their inglorious FA Cup exit at Edgar Street, Newcastle United reached the Final itself, where their opponents were Shankly's mighty Liverpool.

In my capacity as Adidas Soccer Public Relations person it was my task to meet up with the Newcastle squad at their hotel on the eve of the match. As I strode into the lobby of the Selsdon Park in Croydon, United's manager, the late Joe Harvey, was standing with his assistant, the future Tottenham Hotspur boss, Keith Burkenshaw.

The look on their faces when they saw me would have been worth filming. Poor Joe Harvey looked stricken, as if he had seen all his worst nightmares reappear just when he was getting over them.

Once they realised there was a valid reason for me being there and that this was not some sick joke, they were friendly and welcoming. After all, it was practically the same team to a man as the one we had beaten two years before. That in itself was compensation for their disastrous day, and made our achievement all the more remarkable.

My job was to paint three white stripes on the team's Adidas boots. To accomplish this, Malcolm Macdonald allowed me to use his room for as long as it took and all the squad's footwear was placed at my disposal.

While I painted, Supermac sat on his bed and we chatted about how football throws up so many strange coincidences. I discovered that Malcolm, before his football career took off at Fulham, had a trial at Barnet and was rejected by Dexter Adams. Also that as youngsters we had both idolised Johnny Haynes, the Fulham legend of the 50s and 60s. When Macdonald finally broke into the Fulham first team, Haynes was player-manager at Craven Cottage. I told him how, through Dave Underwood, I had finally got to play alongside Haynes for 'Gerry's' showbiz team.

'Did he moan at you?' Malcolm asked.

I nodded, smiling.

'He absolutely slaughtered me, left me with no confidence at all,' he went on. I remarked that as he was now England's centre-forward his confidence had certainly been restored.

'That was entirely due to one man, Harry Haslam.' Haslam had been manager at Tonbridge and latterly at Luton Town where Macdonald had played before his £180 000 transfer to Newcastle.

Interesting, again, how one person can influence an entire career.

After a while, Supermac left the room to join his team-mates for a training session. When he came back I was fast asleep, from inhaling the white paint.

The following day, a very smart Newcastle United team was destroyed by a small, dark-haired young winger by the name of Kevin Keegan, who scored two goals in a 3-0 victory.

When Kevin Keegan made his International Debut against

Wales at Ninian Park in November 1974, Jim Terris and I were there.

My job, once more, was to paint the three stripes on the Adidas boots worn by the England players. At a certain point during the afternoon, I made my way from one bedroom to another with the small bottle of white, strong-smelling luminous paint, displaying all the artistic skills I had learned at school.

When I got to Emlyn Hughes' room I was not surprised to find his young Liverpool team-mate resting in the other bed. I sat down quietly to do my job, watched by a fascinated Keegan, who was also looking questioningly at Hughes.

At this time, the young superstar was wearing Stylo Football boots. Stylo were an English Company trying desperately to compete with Adidas and Puma. They had gone for one high profile player at a time to wear their product. George Best had been the first.

The problem was, the players didn't like wearing Stylo, as they were not as comfortable as the German-made products.

Keegan's curiosity finally got the better of him. 'What's happening?' His question was directed at Emlyn.

'Ricky works for Adidas, he's painting the stripes on the boots so that they show up on television and in photographs. Are you getting anything from Stylo for tonight?' he asked the future England coach.

After a negative response, Emlyn then went on to explain that Adidas were paying £75 per man to wear the boots in this particular game. He was surprised that Stylo had not seen fit to mark Kevin Keegan's International debut by highlighting which footwear he used. From Stylo's point of view, he was wearing their boots and maybe they were not as thorough as their German competitors.

I knew what was coming.

It would be a major coup for Adidas and a serious blow to Stylo should Keegan be seen to be wearing three stripes in his first appearance for England. To close this unexpected deal, I needed the assistance of my boss, who at this moment was sitting happily alongside Ron Goodman in the hotel bar cuddling a large Bells.

It took a matter of minutes to conclude the deal and Jim returned to his soul-mates. Meanwhile, I was given the problem of finding a pair of Adidas football boots for Kevin Keegan.

125

I didn't have to look far. As the young striker handed me his 'Stylo' boots, I noticed some familiar characteristics.

'I couldn't wear that Stylo crap,' said Keegan, 'so they put their flash on my Adidas 2000s.'

'Some people have no ethics,' I said to Jim as I re-joined him in the bar.

I have so much to thank Jim Terris for. Regrettably, when England failed to qualify for the 1974 World Cup finals, I resigned from Adidas. I had put in an inordinate amount of time on both England and Scotland but the decision was taken not to send me to Munich. This was not Jim's decision but nevertheless I felt aggrieved. I never forgot the times we had together and was greatly saddened by news of his premature death in the mid-eighties. He was sixty-one.

Chapter Eighteen
Tom Or Mick?

Having resigned from Adidas I was now struggling to earn a living. Part-time wages at Barnet in 1974 were £20 per week, not enough to support a family.

Patricia and I had been married six years, we wanted children, and in September we discovered the wonderful news that Patricia was pregnant with Daniel.

For a couple of years our home had been a two-bedroomed flat in Warwick Road, New Barnet. One of our neighbours was a man about ten years older than me. He was married but I had never seen his wife. One winter's day in late '74 I was trying to make some sense out of our small garden when my neighbour introduced himself.

'Call me Mick but my real name's Tom,' he said.

'Call me Ricky,' I said.

'OK, Tricky,' he replied.

Mick had taken a week's holiday from his job as an MTO (material take-off) engineer, and volunteered to give me a hand in the garden. His wife, he told me, worked for Joe Lyons in South London.

Appreciative of his help, I offered to buy him a beer at lunchtime. We went to the Hadley Hotel in New Barnet and got completely pissed. About 3.30 we caught the tube at High Barnet and I found myself in Leicester Square having more drinks with this relative stranger, during which both our life stories poured out. He had been married for about fifteen years. They had no children – by choice – and both, by all accounts, held down well-paid, secure jobs. The marriage was one of programmed and unchanging routine: roast beef on Sunday, liver & bacon on Mondays, lamb chops on Tuesdays and so on, all prepared, cooked and served by Tom or Mick's wife, whom he affectionately called 'Shitface'.

We staggered home very late. He was on holiday, and I

discovered that weekends (Friday night to Sunday afternoon) and holidays were spent seeking oblivion through as many pints of light & bitter as possible.

I saw plenty of Tom or Mick that week, managing to stay sober for most of the time as we had a game coming up.

As we were kicking in before the game at Underhill on the Saturday I heard a voice calling to me from the terraces. 'Oi, Tricky, Tricky!' Tom or Mick was standing, or rather swaying, at the foot of the steps of the terraces on the Barnet Lane side. He managed to stay there for the ninety minutes, periodically shouting at me, 'Tricky, go on my son!'

I don't think he ever saw much of the game but in the bar afterwards he told me that he had got me a job as an MTO engineer starting the following Monday morning. I was on the same hourly rate as him and I would be working from an office in Baker Street on the design of oil rigs in the Arabian Gulf. I was absolutely speechless. I didn't take it seriously, he was so pissed he couldn't stand, but when I finally poured him out of my car and into the Queen's Arms pub around 7.30 that evening, he left me with the words, 'Seven o'clock Monday morning, Tricky, don't be fucking late' and disappeared singing 'Oh Tricky, Tricky.'

On the Sunday evening he was beginning to sober up and knocked on my door about six. 'Wear a suit, seven o'clock, don't be late.'

The following day, now stone cold sober, he briefed me as to what to say and what to do as we travelled up on the Northern line to Baker Street via Kings Cross. I was very apprehensive. Going into a job I knew nothing about, far less was qualified to do, I wondered what lay in store. I needed the money and £6 an hour in 1974 was a huge salary. I couldn't believe this was happening.

I needn't have worried. The firm I was to work for had been sub-contracted by BP to design these rigs, and the man in charge shook hands, handed me a contract, told me where to fill in my bank details and clocked me in at just before 8.30am. I never saw or spoke to him again. I was given a desk in Tom or Mick's office and given the simplest of tasks to perform while Tom or Mick gave me a crash course in material take-off engineering.

During that first week I saw a different Mick or Tom. Monday through to 4.30 on Friday afternoon, he never touched a drop. He was serious, morose even, most of the time and we hardly spoke during the morning and evening journeys. On Friday evening he went home, bathed, changed into a white shirt and best suit and disappeared through the public bar door of the Queen's Arms, surfacing only to eat, have a bet or, when Barnet were playing at home, to come and shout at me from the terraces.

I kept this strange existence up for about six months, when both my conscience and my bank balance had returned to near normality. I was dreading telling Tom or Mick of my decision to leave the job, thinking that he would consider me ungrateful. In the event, I told him one Friday morning that I was giving a week's notice. He didn't bat an eyelid, just sat reading his newspaper and murmured, 'What're you going to do then?' I told him I was thinking of starting my own business. He grunted and without taking his eyes off the paper said, 'Fucking good luck.'

In spite of the dubious terms of my employment, I did actually learn the basics of material take-off, which is calculating the weight and lengths of the legs which hold the oil platforms in the shallow waters of the Arabian Gulf. I didn't make any dire mistakes as Tom or Mick saw to that, and in a perverse way I did earn my corn.

On the Friday I left the job we parted at our respective front doors and he just said, 'See you' as he walked into his weekend world.

Sure enough, as we took to the field at Underhill the following day, there he was swaying in his usual place, shouting 'Oh, Tricky, Trickeeee!'

Chapter Nineteen
Skateboard

The only real contact I had with any of the great Spurs of the 60s was Jimmy Greaves. Jimmy opened a sports shop in Chingford in the early 70s, shortly after joining West Ham, and in my capacity as Adidas rep for the area, I would call frequently at the premises in Hall Lane. He wasn't often there so I would see his partner Ron Penn and the youngster who worked for them, Glenn Chalkley. However, the establishment that was 'Greaves and Penn' ran a soccer team that would play friendlies against local schools or clubs. Most of these games were played on a Wednesday afternoon at the Mann Crossman sports ground at Walthamstow. I was invited to play for the team.

It was tremendous fun. Apart from Jimmy himself, Trevor Brooking, Frank Lampard and Alan Sealey, amongst other famous Hammers, would turn out occasionally. Roger Morgan from Spurs was another and it was a great pleasure for me to play alongside these guys.

Greaves' stay at Upton Park was short and the world of soccer was saddened when he decided to hang up his boots prematurely at the age of thirty-one. But after a year or so, whatever demons had tormented his soul since his absence from the team that won the World Cup in 1966, compelled him to make a comeback in the game. He signed for Chelmsford City in the Southern League.

By now I was back playing for Barnet again under manager Billy Meadows and chairman Dave Underwood, and I was still seeing Greaves on a fairly regular basis. I approached him on behalf of the club and during the 1977-78 season he became a Barnet player.

Since 1975 I had also been running a small company in the sports business. During 1977 a guy called Peter Davies joined me as a director. He was a passionate supporter of the Underhill Club. We were banking at Barclays in Guernsey in the Channel Islands and the bank manager was an enthusiastic member of the Guernsey Round Table. He was also a big football fan.

As a gesture of thanks for the help the manager had given us, Peter Davies and I offered to take some famous football personalities to the island. There were to be two events, a football forum for members of the round table and a football match against the waiters of the Old Government House Hotel, where we booked rooms for about twenty people. The match was for the California Rainbow Trophy. Barnet were playing Peterborough United in the FA Cup on a Saturday in November of 1977. The team flew out on the Saturday evening for a football match to be played the following afternoon. The forum was booked for Sunday evening at 8pm.

Meanwhile, we had jumped in and gambled on the skateboard phenomenon which hit the UK in the latter part of 1977, ordering 3000 boards at the equivalent of £10 each from a company based in San Diego, Southern California. This company sold skateboards, colourfully designed under the attractive name of California Rainbow. We borrowed £30 000 from Barclays in Guernsey to join the bandwagon.

We had hoped to receive the goods in the UK for the Christmas sales. With the facility from Barclays, we opened a letter of credit to California Rainbow Inc. We took a stand at a sports exhibition in Birmingham and played in Guernsey for the California Rainbow Trophy.

The team consisted of Bob Wilson, John Motson, Alan Parry (soccer commentator), Jim Rosenthal (sports commentator), Jim Combes (ex-Worcestershire cricketer and goalkeeper for WBA), Billy Meadows, me and James P Greaves.

The game was well contested and entertaining for a small audience, with the trophy going to the captain of the all-star team, me. Far more entertaining, though, was the evening forum, hosted by John Motson.

The panel consisted of the five famous names referred to earlier, and by far the funniest and interesting was Greaves. The first question was directed at him. 'What is the main difference between international and non-league football?'

Jim thought long and hard. So long, in fact, that for a while it seemed as though he was not going to speak. After what seemed an age, during which you could hear a pin drop, he spoke.

'Basically,' he drawled in his unique Cockney manner, 'not very much.' A further long silence, then, 'Take yesterday, for example, we played Peterborough in the FA Cup, pissed all over 'em for ninety minutes, got beat 2-1.'

A split second while everyone took it in and then the place erupted. For the rest of the evening, the other speakers were regularly interrupted and made fun of, including the chairman. It was hilarious and turned what could have been a very low-key affair into one memorable event. I for one had never realised what a funny man Jimmy Greaves was, a fact recognised by ITV for many years immediately following his performances on the World Cup panel of 1982.

Greaves' problems have been well publicised and I would not presume to pass comment. That unforgettable night, however, he sat with Patricia and me at dinner and poured his heart out to us. He probably won't remember but we recall every word and it was incredibly moving. Pat was five months pregnant with our second son Adam and at the end of our conversation Jim looked at her and said, 'The only really important thing, Pat, is that little baby in there.' How right he was.

Footnote: We had hoped to get the skateboards in time for Christmas. They arrived in the first week of 1978 and overnight the demand died completely. At the end of January 1978 we had 3000 California Rainbows in stock and no orders or interest. It was another turning point in my life. We waited about six weeks before, on March 17th 1978, two weeks after the birth of Adam, I put a dozen samples in the boot of the car and went travelling. I went all over France trying to sell the stock that now owed Barclays Guernsey £30 000. After a week of fruitless search, I ended up in Brussels and a meeting that would ultimately have an enormous effect on our lives.

Chapter Twenty
Man of the Woods

I nearly didn't go to Brussels. I spent a week in France visiting wholesalers in Grenoble, St Etienne and Lyon, without success. On the Thursday morning I arrived in the centre of Paris for my appointment with Marcosport, a big distributor in toys and sports. I was offered £18 000 for my stock of skateboards for which Barclays Guernsey were owed £30 000. 'First loss is the best loss,' is the phrase used in the trade. Reluctantly, I accepted.

Driving away from Paris that lunchtime my depression was accentuated by my indecision as to whether to keep the final appointment in the famous suburb of Brussels, Waterloo, where Napoleon finally met his match in the shape of the 'Iron Duke'. At the last minute I took the Lille Bruxelles exit off the autoroute. Why was I going? I'd sold the stock, what was there to discuss? I have never been able to answer that question.

Pierre Boizard, a giant Frenchman, ran a company called GIGC from his tiny house off the Chaussée de Waterloo. When I saw the premises I almost drove away. Another lesson in life: don't pre-judge.

Pierre was extremely intelligent, spoke excellent English and explained that GIGC was only six months old. He had formed the company specifically to sell skateboards, and was so convinced of the future of that particular business, I didn't have the heart to tell him how vehemently I disagreed.

Having established that my skateboards were, to all intents and purposes, now sold, he was interested in acquiring further stocks at low prices, *and* skateboard accessories: helmets, gloves, elbow- and knee-pads. Here I sensed a chance to retrieve some losses. I knew, of course, that I was not the only company in the UK to have caught a cold. Although he didn't appear to have a great deal of money, Pierre kept mentioning the names of retailers and cash & carry wholesalers in Belgium whom he intended to supply. One such company was Makro, with a head office in Antwerp. Boizard had an appointment to see the buyer the following morning; he insisted that I go with him.

The buyer's name, Van den Bossche, translated from Flemish means 'man of the woods'. His first name was Marc, and when I was introduced to him he grinned. 'I know you, you were an Arsenal player some years ago.' I was taken aback, first by his apparent knowledge of English football, second by his apparent lack of knowledge.

'Actually, it was Tottenham Hotspur,' I contradicted him.

'Oh yes, Tottenham, sorry.'

He spoke so quickly and positively, I was reluctant to question him any further on how or indeed *whether* he really did know who I was. I've always suspected he was referring to Charlie George, who scored in the FA Cup final for Arsenal against Liverpool in 1971, the year the Gunners won the double. But, keen to make an impression, I kept quiet for fear of disillusioning him.

We covered the matter of skateboards and accessories in a matter of minutes. When Marc heard I had sold 3000 Taiwan-made fibreglass boards with cheap wheels to France for £6 each, he complimented me. 'I would have offered you half that price, if I were you I'd hurry up and send them to Paris before they change their minds.'

I smiled, but inside I began to panic. Accessories were of interest, but they would have to be very cheap, less than £1 per item. I didn't imagine I would find any that cheap, but I promised to try.

Up to this point, Boizard had been sitting quietly, digesting the market knowledge the stocky little Fleming was imparting. As we rose to leave, Van den Bossche said to me, 'If you ever find any Adidas goods, I'm interested' and a lightbulb went on inside my head. Since 1975, I had been buying small quantities of Adidas from Peter Black Leisurewear in Ilkley, Yorkshire. They had been appointed to sell the famous brand to outlets other than the traditional sports trade, wholesalers, mail order and department stores. I bought T-shirts and bags from them. They had footwear but carried remote, unknown models. Up to now that particular business had not been successful.

'I'll make a call now,' I said, and Van den Bossche dialled an outside line and handed me the phone.

My contact at Peter Black informed me of a stock of three models of footwear totalling just over 6000 pairs. He gave me details of sizes and the price they were hoping to get. I put the phone down and informed a speechless 'man of the woods' what was available. What I didn't realise was that for years, Makro had been trying to buy this world-famous brand and for years Adidas in Benelux had refused. A giant cash & carry wholesaler who sends out thousands of sales flyers when they have a promotion was not the type of outlet big brands like Adidas wanted to be associated with. My man at Peter Black had not asked where I would be selling; they were keen to get rid of the shoes, it was obvious.

I put on £2 per pair and told Van den Bossche the price. There was no discussion. The irony of the situation was beginning to dawn on me. Profit on the 6000 pairs would make up the loss on the skateboards. I might even be able to negotiate a lower price with Peter Blacks: things were looking up.

As we took the lift to the ground floor, I gazed in disbelief at the purchase order for £72 000. Then a giant French hand landed on my shoulder. 'And what about me, bastard?' said Boizard.

I had almost forgotten his existence. Of course, he was entitled to commission. Shit, I thought, but then without him I would never have come to Makro. He wanted half the profit, but I told him he could have 4% of the total deal. We agreed at 5%. I decided to barter with Blacks to cover the commission.

I drove to Ostend and caught the ferry. My mind was racing and the four-and-a-half-hour crossing zoomed by.

On Monday morning Brian Kirk at Peter Black called me. They had another 2500 pairs of yet another strange model. I called Van den Bossche: deal done.

'I need a discount to take the lot,' I said to Kirk.

'I'll give you 3¾%, seven days payment,' he said.

'Make it 5%, thirty days,' I countered.

And so it was agreed. Blacks sold their strange, unwanted Adidas shoes, Boizard got his commission, I salvaged our losses and got Barclays out of the way, and the 'man of the woods' got his Adidas. Overnight, he became a hero at Makro and I became his greatest friend. For the best part of the next twenty years, I sold Makro Belgium millions of pounds' worth of sports and leisurewear.

One night in 1985, I got a call at home.

'How are you, Bastard? I saw Van den Bossche today, you owe me 5% of everything you have sold him since March 1978.'

'Fuck off,' I said.

'If you don't pay me, I'm going to tell him you're not Charlie George,' he said seriously.

'Fuck off,' I said again.

'You know something, Bastard, in the short time I knew you, you taught me to swear like an Englishman, fuck off yourself.'

We both laughed, wished each other well, and Boizard hung up.

The 'man of the woods' still doesn't know whether I'm Charlie George or not. He knows all about Earth Summit, though, as BBC is his favourite TV channel.

In any case, he is well named. My meeting with him in the spring of 1978 well and truly got me out of the woods.

Spurs youth at Highbury 1962.
I'm firth from the left, out of line, as usual.

Photo: local Photography

Back row (left to right): Peter Isaac (trainer/physio), Colin Addison (player/manager), Ken Mallender, David Icke, Ron Radford, Fred Potter, Billy Tucker, Mick McLaughlin, Roger Griffiths.

Front row (left to right): Alan Jones, Ricky George, Brian Owen, Dudly Tyler, Tony Gough (capt), Calvin Palmer, Ivan Hollett, Billy Meadows.

Raddy's goal of the century.

Ronnie Radford.
He'd actually been in the bath already. God I love him.

Celebrating in style!

"We won!"
Delighted Hereford United fans pour onto the pitch to congratulate
their heroes after their 2-1 momentous victory over Newcastle United.

Estartit 1966.
Jan, Dennis, me, Patsy & The Count.
(I never noticed how close he was before).

Thirty odd years later, *she* still looks good.

Rebecca, Adam, Daniel & Patricia
Santa Monica 1996.

Earth Summit two weeks before the 1998 Grand National.
God, I love him.

Chapter Twenty-One
A MacDonalds In LA

In June 1984 I received an order for 2000 Prince tennis rackets. My customer was based in Dusseldorf, West Germany. His name was Wilhelm Bungert and he was a famous tennis player. In 1968, he was the losing finalist in the men's singles championships at Wimbledon. John Newcombe, the brilliant Australian, beat him in straight sets.

Wilhelm was a terrific guy: friendly, approachable and he spoke excellent English.

My supplier for the Prince rackets was based in West Hollywood, Los Angeles. Two guys ran the business, Barry Smith and Warren Levy. I didn't know them very well at that time, though I had met Barry when he came to London a couple of years before. Their business was the same as mine. We were parallel traders dealing in major brands of sporting goods: Prince, Dunlop, Adidas, Puma, Wilson, and so on.

Prince was a hot number. A very astute man by the name of Howard Head had discovered that the rules governing tennis-playing equipment allowed for a considerable tolerance in the size of the head of a tennis racket. Mr Head had already made a fortune, having founded the Head Sporting Goods Company and then later selling it to the giant AMF Inc.

He went to Taiwan and had a prototype racket made with a large head. It became a sensation, perfectly legal and within the laws of the game. Overnight the large head made the game easier for kids and old people alike. Prince rackets were Howard Head's second fortune.

Wilhem Bungert's customer was Metro, a giant cash & carry superstore. The Prince distributor in West Germany would not supply Metro, who would discount the prices, thereby affecting the sales of the sports shops. It was common for groups like Metro to source such brands through the parallel market. This was a business I knew very well, as I had been sourcing and supplying this sort of merchandise for nearly ten years.

This transaction was typical, but there was a problem that needed to be overcome before anything moved. Tennis rackets, traditionally were wooden and had been manufactured for donkey's years in Europe. Dunlop and Slazenger, for example, were made in England. When Howard Head moved production to Taiwan he gained the advantage of cheap labour but opened up the trade to the counterfeiters. Hand-crafted wooden frames were replaced by lightweight aluminium and graphite produced with modern technology in factories all over the Far East. It was easy to copy a Prince Pro with its large head and thousands of copies began to flood the western markets.

Metro had fallen foul of the counterfeit Princes. By purchasing through a middle man like me they ran that risk. A German supplier had delivered several thousand copies and they were all seized by German trading standard officers. Prince Deutschland sued for damages and court cases were imminent.

Business must go on, however, and the search continued for the genuine product. Bungert was a highly respected person in his native country but Metro were ultra cautious.

Wilhelm called me one night at home. He explained that before he could actually buy the ordered rackets, Metro would have to be completely satisfied of their originality. Other than a letter from Smith and Levy warranting the fact, there was nothing I could supply. Even then, by providing such a letter I would be breaking the golden rule in business by divulging the name of my supplier. In this case, if the deal were ever to go through, I had little or no choice.

Bungert suggested that he and I and Dr Harkotter, Metro's in-house lawyer, would travel together to LA, inspect the stock to the good Doctor's satisfaction, eat a Macdonalds and fly home. It was quite funny, every time we spoke about this he said the same thing. 'We fly, inspect, eat a Macdonalds and fly home.' I guess Wilhelm at that time regarded the hamburger phenomenon in the same way as the rest of the world. He had travelled round the world several times and had a condominium in Fort Lauderdale, Florida, but I guess in 1986, a Big Mac was still something of a novelty to Europeans. Actually it was psychological: fast trip, quick look, fast food, get back. He wouldn't have said 'We fly, inspect, have cocktails in the Polo lounge of the Beverly Hills, dine at Spagos and watch the sunset over the Pacific then fly home', would he?

I reasoned that the profit I hoped to earn was worth risking supplier and customer cutting me out in the future. If I didn't set it up there was no deal anyway. I could have arranged it and let Bungert and the Doctor fly 6000 miles for one night. Then I would have to rely on either the Americans or the Germans to pay me my $12 000 commission. As nice a bloke as Wilhelm was, that was too much of a risk, particularly when they all discovered my whack wasn't exactly peanuts. I had been in this position so many times and the standard phrase is, 'I don't care if you're earning a hundred grand, it's none of my business.' The truth is they *do* care, everyone cares what the others are earning, it's human nature.

I set it up. Barry Smith and Warren Levy assured me there would be no discussion on price. If the Doctor wished to inspect that was fine, the goods were already in the warehouse in West Hollywood.

Before I arranged the flights, Bungert explained to me that he and I would share the cost of the Doctor's flight. The other thing was, he liked to fly in business class. I watched my profit begin to drain away.

We flew out on British Airways flight number BA283 on June 18th, Wilhelm and I in economy, the Doctor twenty-odd rows further forward in club.

The Los Angeles Olympics were two weeks away.

About two hours out of London I recall very well I was beginning to relax. I started to doze. The captain came on over the tannoy. He spoke calmly, very matter-of-factly. 'Ladies and Gentlemen, for security reasons we are required to land at Keflavik airport in Iceland. As we are shortly to begin our descent I would ask you all to please fasten your seat belts immediately'.

The 747 banked steeply to the right, straightened out and descended – rather rapidly, I thought at the time, more so than usual. Yet I had absolutely no feeling of fear or trepidation. The quick descent did not alarm me, it just registered, that was all. I did not doubt that there was a very good reason for the unscheduled stop but I had no thoughts of anything other than an inconvenient time delay to a trip that was already excruciating, timewise.

We touched down perfectly and the giant aircraft taxied to a halt. The captain spoke again, still calm. 'Ladies and Gentlemen, we do have some problems this morning so I have instructed the cabin staff to make an emergency evacuation of the aircraft.' As he finished speaking, the exit doors were thrown open by the crew; I hadn't even noticed them taking their places as the captain was speaking. They literally hurled people down the chutes. Anyone hesitating was thrown, for their own good.

I grabbed my briefcase and when it came to my turn the stewardess yelled, 'Jump and sprint for a quarter of a mile!' I jumped, landed halfway down the big yellow chute and slid the rest of the way, clattering into the guy who had just jumped and was struggling to get to his feet. I was hit by the guy behind me and we all apologised to each other as we gathered ourselves for the sprint across the tarmac. Wilhelm was a few yards behind me but I didn't look back. Then I glanced to my left and saw the Doctor. He obviously hadn't run for a while but was doing OK. His running style was so funny that I found myself laughing; it must have been some sort of nervous reaction.

When I arrived at what most had judged to be the safe distance, we were miles from the airport terminal. I looked back at the strange sight of people running towards me. Behind them was the eerie vision of the Boeing, looking like a modern Noah's ark that had been abandoned.

By the time the crew reached us the plane had been stationary for fifteen minutes. That is how long it took to evacuate the entire aircraft. We were told the reason by members of the crew as we stood shivering in the Icelandic breeze. Shortly before the captain made his first announcement, a first-class passenger had visited the toilet. As this person took a paper towel from the pile he or she had noticed a message written on the next towel. It read 'Bomb on board, land ASAP - Libya'. The message was given immediately to the flight crew and the decision was made.

Several buses came and deposited us at the terminal. Ambulances arrived to take care of the injured, mostly elderly people who had been hurt as they tumbled out of the plane.

We were herded into the small area where Departures and Arrivals remain air side. The local police sealed off all passengers and crew and we were held for the next seven hours in this confined space. Mercifully, there was a toilet, a telephone and a bar. We had left London at midday, UK time. It was now sometime after three in the UK, sometime after seven in the morning in LA. After an age I got through to Barry Smith. 'I hope the Doc's OK,' he said, facetiously. More importantly, I got through to Patricia before she heard anything on the news.

Wilhelm and I decided to kill the time by sampling the local schnapps, an evil concoction suitably named Black Death. The doctor sat quietly and tried to do some reading while the other 300 or so passengers kicked their heels.

We sat on the floor drinking the schnapps while Wilhelm took me through his tennis career. It was fascinating listening to a guy that had actually played in a Final at Wimbledon and had played against the likes of Laver, Rosewall, Hoad, England's Roger Taylor and any big name you could think of during that era. Bungert had been an amateur, even so at one time he had been in the top ten players in the world and was remarkably modest about his achievements. I could think of worse companions to share a dirty floor with for seven hours in Keflavik Airport.

At around ten o'clock the Icelandic police finally released us and the entire plane-load was bussed to the Lofleider Hotel where sleeping bags were doled out to all. We chose the bar to sleep in, probably because it was closest to home, metaphorically. I wanted my Mum that night.

After the worst night imaginable, we were taken back to the airport to await a replacement 747 flying out from London. Our abandoned ark had been thoroughly searched and if they ever did find anything, we were never told. The incident was reported on the news and in the papers at home just to add to the drama.

We resumed our journey to Los Angeles, finally arriving at around 4.30pm local time. To say that we were tired and a little stressed would be an understatement. However, LA immigration were sympathetic and there had obviously been instructions to speed our passage. As we approached the barrier, a customs guy yelled out, 'Auf Wiedersehen, you're British.' This greatly amused my two German companions and the Doctor smiled for the first time in thirty-six hours.

A smiling and urbane Barry Smith was waiting as we emerged into the bustle of the arrivals terminal. Barry was a cool individual with a very dry American sense of humour. At times this could be very appealing; it could also be incredibly irritating. As we piled awkwardly into his four-wheel drive Toyota he drawled, 'I hope you don't mind but we sold the Prince rackets this morning when you didn't show up.' The Doctor looked stricken and his mouth dropped open. I quickly reassured him, but even Bungert was taken aback by this stab at black humour that Smith was so good at. He apologised and then tried to ingratiate himself by telling us how truly grateful he and Warren Levy were to us for making this effort.

He looked at us over his Raybans. 'Now, d'you guys wanna go freshen up or go eat some rackets?' Every time Barry spoke the Doctor looked terrified and although he spoke excellent English, I don't think he had ever heard it spoken quite like this.

After a thirty-minute drive through the LA rush hour we arrived at the warehouse and offices of American Sales Inc. Inside, with his glasses round his neck and a pen behind his ear, was a busy-looking Mr Levy. He obviously did not originate from Southern California and the accent was pure Noo Joisey. Levy was small and dark, Smith tall, slim and dressed in highly polished penny loafers, beige Chinos and an immaculate Polo cotton oxford. His Raybans were now on top of his head.

We went straight into the warehouse. The cartons containing the 2000 frames were conveniently arranged to enable the inspection to take place.

The Doctor, although shattered, went about his task professionally and Bungert assisted while they picked their way through the stock. He obviously knew what he was looking for there were secret codes in secret places, something the consumer would know nothing about. The Doctor was careful not deface the goods and he was very thorough. I was confident that now we were here, the deal would go through. This thought sustained me as I fought to stay awake while the Herr Doctor carried out his painstaking task.

It must have been around 7pm (3am UK time) when the two Germans emerged. It was positive. The Doc was satisfied the goods were original. I was beginning to relax. My mind wandered to a king-size bed somewhere, anywhere.

'There's just one final check I need to make,' said Harkotter.

'I need to see the original invoices from your supplier. Only to look, I do not need to take them away or even make a copy. I must have sight of at least one invoice which states the supplier is an authorised Prince distributor.'

One look at Smith's face and a pang of anxiety raced through my stomach. He shook his head, solemnly. 'No can do, no way. Sorry, but we weren't asked to provide this.'

The Doctor looked shocked and directed a questioning stare at Bungert. It was terribly embarrassing. He looked aghast as he admitted that he had not covered this point with me. I felt badly for him but my feelings were rapidly changing to despair. We could not fail on this, surely. I took Smith and Levy into another office. I pleaded with them to reconsider. They were unbelievably adamant. It would be a betrayal of trust. They had given their word to their supplier, who was an authorised Prince distributor in another country, that they would never, under any circumstances, reveal his name. By allowing Doctor Harkotter to look at the invoice they would be breaking the agreement.

I fought hard. 'No-one will ever mention the name. The Doctor just has to have sight of a genuine invoice; in the event Metro should ever be in court he can swear under oath to have seen an original Prince invoice.'

They would not budge. I would not give up and for the first time, I became a little angry. I thought that things were being taken too far by these people, that they weren't attempting to understand what was actually required here.

They agreed to put the question and the circumstances to their supplier. I prudently left the office while they made their call. Three unhappy Europeans awaited the outcome.

It was not to be and incredibly, after all we had been through, neither side would budge. The Doctor, as dismayed by events as all of us, could not confirm to his employers something that was not true. He was, after all, a lawyer.

In the excruciatingly awkward interlude that followed the telephone call, I tried to come to terms with what had transpired. It seemed there was nothing to be done, certainly no more today and, I told myself, it could have been worse. We might never have even got there!

Warren Levy, obviously feeling very bad about it all, went home to eat with his wife. Barry Smith, at least, had the good grace to take us to a hotel in the Santa Monica area. We had a quick shower and decided to eat, but not before I had sunk several Dewars on the rocks. Four huge steaks and a bottle of California red wine later, we were ready for bed. There was one final irony to complete my day. Barry Smith ate with us but made no attempt to pay the bill. So I paid it - well, Bungert was my customer!

We agreed to meet the following day. After all, our flight home would not leave until 5.30 in the evening and Smith promised to try to find a solution.

Refreshed and with batteries recharged, we hounded them all day long. They came up with pathetic alternatives, the worst being an offer from Warren Levy to sell us Wilson rackets in place of the Prince. That suggestion was the last straw and two hours earlier than necessary, we asked Smith to take us to the airport. We drove in silence along the Santa Monica freeway to LAX, and even Barry Smith refrained from making his usual facetious comments.

He didn't come in, just left us at the kerbside. As we shook hands, he looked at me and, in the absence of any kind of appropriate words, said simply, 'Sorry.'

I tried to think of who was actually to blame here, as if it made any difference. Technically, it was Wilhelm himself. Smith and Levy stated categorically that had they been asked to supply documents they would never have had us fly out. On the other hand, if the Doctor gave his word as a lawyer that he need never mention the name on the documents, only that he had seen a genuine invoice, why wouldn't they do it? Likewise, I thought, why couldn't the Doctor be satisfied with the actual stock? He had confirmed it was all correct, surely that was enough? I decided that the only person blame-free was me. A fat lot of good that revelation was.

We checked in at the TWA desk. Our flights, of course, had been altered and this timing suited us as it meant we arrived in Heathrow around 11.30 on Saturday morning. My companions had booked a flight to Dusseldorf at 1pm. There were no seats free in economy so we had all three reserved in business, which on this particular 747 was on the upper deck. Here, Wilhelm and I got back a tiny piece of luck. When we checked in we expected to pay the difference in the fare. We were told that there was no need; I didn't wait around to ask why.

I had the greatest flight back I've ever experienced from

the West coast. I sat next to a very friendly American guy and we chatted as one Dewars after another disappeared. Flying up the coast with the Pacific gleaming in the evening sun, I went into philosophical mode, occasionally glancing behind to toast Wilhelm and the Doctor.

'What the hell,' I thought, ' I'll write about this one day.'

Chapter Twenty-Two
A Kentucky In Tokyo

A year after my trip to LA with Wilhelm and the Doctor, I travelled with another business colleague, this time a Dutchman, to Japan via Singapore.

Bill Kuiper was younger than me. He was a big, ebullient man who could also be a bit of a bully. His perfect command of English enabled me, once more, to form a close relationship with a foreign customer.

I had known him a couple of years and supplied him with Dunlop tennis rackets, Reebok shoes and Nike shoes when he suggested I accompany him on a selling trip to the Far East. It was February 1985, the time of year when the Japanese importers place orders for delivery the coming winter.

We flew out on Singapore Airlines to rendezvous with a Singaporean Chinese guy named Ron Goh. This gentleman was a supplier to Bill Kuiper. Before we arrived Bill was at pains to ensure that Ron Goh and I did not exchange business cards. This was the rule and I had no problem with it. However, this paranoia on the part of the Dutchman led to an evening of complete farce.

We were taken to eat to an open air restaurant near Boogie Street. It was very hot and the atmosphere was steamy. As the three of us took our seats, Ron Goh looked in my direction, went to open his mouth to speak only to find a huge Dutch hand instantly clamped over it.

Kuiper made no attempt at explanation, settling back in his seat to study the menu as a completely bewildered Chinaman exchanged a nervous smile with me. During the entire meal, every time Ron Goh looked as though he might utter a word in my direction, Bill just said, 'Shut up' And the poor man obeyed.

So we sat and talked in snatches. I was allowed to address

them both on a general subject but the unhappy Ron Goh was only permitted to speak directly to Kuiper. There was a Guinness promotion on and a tiny waitress was constantly refilling our glasses from a huge jug. The atmosphere, the long flight and the Guinness combined to put me in a very funny mood. I asked Ron Goh how long he had lived in Singapore and he answered to the Dutchman without ever looking at me. I asked him if he was married and he told Bill, who already knew he was married – he'd met Ron's wife three times!

Suddenly, as I started to ask Ron if he had any children, I could take it no more. I had taken a mouthful of the black stuff and as my control deserted me, I am ashamed to say I spat out the whole lot over the table, the majority going all over poor Ron Goh.

Bill Kuiper now went into hysterics, so much so that he nearly choked and had to be excused. As he left the table, Ron Goh peered after him until he was out of sight and handed me his business card.

We flew on to Tokyo that very night, leaving Singapore at midnight and arriving at six o'clock the following morning. We checked in at the Imperial Hotel where we had a meeting scheduled for 10am. After showering and changing we met in the lobby at the appointed hour. Mr Takuishi, a charming English-speaking Japanese, acted as agent and interpreter for Bill Kuiper. One minute before ten a solemn group of five business men arrived to be introduced. We bowed to each other in the traditional fashion and settled down to talk business.

I was totally unprepared for the way the next two and a half hours were to be spent. A question from Bill or myself asked through the interpreter was met by a stony-faced silence that could last up to five minutes. When this first happened I felt myself start to giggle. Kuiper sensed this and dug me sharply in the ribs. After that I controlled myself with difficulty, but then another problem arose. The Guinness, the six-hour flight and little or no sleep in two days had combined to make me feel very weary. It was cold in Tokyo and the heating in the Imperial Hotel was full on. During the silences I started to drop off. The first couple of times I got the Dutch dig and quickly opened my eyes.

However, after an hour or so I went off completely during a sombre pause in proceedings. I have had a habit all my life of jerking spasmodically in the first stages of sleep. I could only have been asleep for a second or two when my body suddenly kick-started itself. My right foot shot out at the same time as I leapt up emitting a huge shout. The whole group jumped out of their skins and the man opposite me received a crack on his shins into the bargain. I apologised, sheepishly, managing to stay awake until finally, mercifully, we broke for lunch.

The whole trip Kuiper had been on about Kentucky fried chicken. It was definitely in the UK at that time but possibly not in Holland. Anyway, our hosts took us to a local restaurant where naturally we took off our shoes and ate traditional Japanese fare. However, that night he tried to drag me into a KFC restaurant on Ginza Street. I steadfastly refused to eat American fast food, having travelled 6000 miles to the mystic east, so we went into a bar with some Dutch friends of Bill's. A waitress took our order and we stayed for an hour or so getting steadily drunk on Scotch and Japanese beer.

No money was asked for until we were ready to leave. When the bill arrived it took us some time to work out exactly how much we were being charged. We sobered up quickly; the bill came to the equivalent of £400! Bill, being an obstreperous individual at times, slammed his fist down on the table and shouted, 'I don't pay this!'

The waitress explained in English the details of the bill. Cover charge, service charge etc, etc. We were in no ordinary bar, it was a classic clip joint. Three dumb Dutchmen and one equally dumb Englishman had just strolled into one of Ginza Street's famous dives where presumably in the good old days you would have paid for a Geisha girl to join you. These days the Geisha's are elderly ladies, but had we required company it was available. As I looked about me I could see beautiful young Japanese girls suddenly appear from nowhere.

Bill was having none of it. 'We don't pay this bill, do we?' he shouted at the top of his voice. I was about to answer when I saw two guys appear from a side door and make for us. Bill's two friends and I got the message and began rapidly throwing thousand yen notes on the table. He was still ranting and raving as the two arrived at our table. One of them, who was at least six inches shorter than Bill, gently drew him aside and whispered in his ear. One second later Bill's yen notes joined ours. The waitress quickly counted out the correct sum and with a very pleasant smile and a bow, wished us goodnight.

Outside we asked him to tell us what the guy had said but he was in shock.

Coffee was needed and so we sat down in the nearest western-looking establishment, which just happened to be the KFC restaurant Bill had craved so much earlier. He was still in a state and I wondered just what the gentleman could have said to him that had frightened him so much. He never told us but whatever it was, the experience changed his entire demeanour for the rest of the trip, something I was grateful for, as his bullying manner was becoming a little tiresome.

We stayed another night in Tokyo which was pretty uneventful apart from a heading exhibition I gave in the bar of our friend's hotel. Bill had introduced me to a crowd of Dutch and Japanese as an ex-footballer. One of the party took a tennis ball out of his pocket and attempted to head it in my direction. His technique was pretty poor so I threw the ball up and headed it back as per *The FA Coaching Manual* (1952 edition). The group were so impressed that I was asked time and time again to repeat the act. At one stage, there were people standing in line to have a go, it was the biggest attraction since karaoke. I wonder what they would have thought if they knew my heading record as a player. Rubbish, would be the answer. I don't think I scored more than six times with my head in eighteen years.

For some time I had been chasing a French Company famous for manufacturing ski jackets. The company was Moncler and the boss was a Madame Charlon. I wanted to become their UK distributor but so far I had not even been able to speak to her, let alone get an appointment. The brand was very famous in France, Belgium and Italy in particular. I had faxed for the umpteenth time before leaving for the Far East, not expecting a response.

However, the day after the heading session we left for Osaka on the bullet train, which travels at 250 miles per hour, past Mount Fuji in all its glory. Checking in at the Osaka Palace for three nights was to be the most important part of our trip, for in this city I was to meet three of the biggest importers of shoes and clothing in Japan. Bill had invited me on the trip to introduce me as his partner to discuss possible future orders for sport shoes, Reebok and Adidas in particular.

At the reception I was handed a fax from my office. It read 'Madame Chalon will meet you at twelve o'clock, midday at the SISEL Exhibition in Paris on Monday. This is the only time she has as she would be travelling herself for the next month.'

It was Sunday.

I either had to make plans to leave that very day or ignore the elusive French lady. Waiting a month would be too late, this was my only chance. She and she alone was the decision maker at Moncler. I told Bill of my dilemma; he was seriously pissed off but had mellowed a great deal. His experience in Tokyo had had a weird effect on him and when I asked him if he could handle the meetings without me he just shrugged, as if to say, 'Possibly, I don't know.'

I made my decision to leave Japan on the first available flight to Paris. There was one leaving Osaka at six that evening. It stopped in Tokyo then once at Anchorage, Alaska before arriving in Paris at seven on Monday morning. I had to forfeit my return flight on KLM to buy a business-class ticket (one-way) on Japanese Airlines. I didn't mind though because Moncler was a profitable business if I could strike a deal with *La Formidable*, Madame Chalon. I checked out, paying for one night in the Osaka Palace, bade farewell to a subdued Dutchman and settled in my seat for the long flight to Charles de Gaulle Airport.

We arrived on time and I checked into the Holiday Inn to freshen up for my long awaited meeting. On the dot of twelve I was standing at the Moncler booth, announcing myself to the receptionist. A minute later Madame Chalon appeared. An elegant, expensively dressed woman in her mid-50s, she could have been anything. A politician, an industrialist or the madame of a bordello.

She looked businesslike and she was. We shook hands and she gave me one of those smiles that say, 'I am very busy, let's get to the point.'

My preamble was cut short in mid-sentence. 'We are not interested at this time in the British market.'

'Excuse me, Madame,' I said, 'I travelled from Japan to have this meeting.'

'You are English?'

'Yes—' I began.

'Then I am sorry, where you have come from today is no matter, goodbye.'

She walked away to join a group of other expensively dressed Europeans and in a split second I was forgotten, forever.

Trying hard not to feel like the complete prick I certainly was, I wandered around the show for fifteen minutes and left for the airport and home.

There was a fax waiting me when I walked in:

'It was a pleasure meeting you, please find attached following offers on Reebok, Nike and Adidas. Looking forward to your early response,

Best Regards, Ron Goh.'

Chapter Twenty-Three
Cheltenham 1998

On Tuesday 10th February 1998, I was invited along with Bob Sims to the Martell Grand National weights luncheon at the Dorchester Hotel in Park Lane. It was an amazing and memorable day for me.

Earth Summit, with a confirmed entry in the great race, had provided the media with a possible angle with which to write up that year's contest. It turned out to be me: Ricky George, famed only for scoring the goal that knocked mighty Newcastle United out of the FA Cup in 1972.

As surprised as I was, I could understand it. I had had one live television interview with the BBC's Jonathon Powell immediately after the Welsh National. Then amazingly, Stevenage Borough Football Club drew Newcastle in the third round of the FA Cup and Sky TV invited me to the game as the studio guest. But I didn't see myself as a media star and this was endorsed by Andy Gray and Richard Keys when I arrived at Stevenage for the live game on Sunday 25th January.

As I took my seat Gray said to me, 'You're doing two jobs for us today, Ricky.'

'I don't think so,' I said naively, 'just the one as far as I know.'

'Oh no, it's definitely two, the first and the fucking last!' Keys joined in with the last five words. I guess they had practised that with countless 'one-offs' like me, but I took the point. It wasn't in any way offensive and I enjoyed the afternoon very much.

Stevenage gained a memorable draw to fire the public imagination and I had the final say. 'How long did the celebrations last after you beat Newcastle?' Keys asked me.

' Twenty-six years,' I replied, truthfully.

On the morning of the weights lunch I did two live radio interviews, Radio Five followed by Radio four. The questions were similar. How would two famous events in a lifetime compare with each other and what did 'the weights' announcement mean? I was flattered, loving every minute. I was able to answer the weights question without stumbling; as for the former, I modestly described both events as 'my great fortune to be involved with two wonderful teams'. Fingers down throat? Probably.

'The weights' were as expected. Suny Bay with top weight of twelve stone, Earth Summit with a handy ten five. The excitement was beginning.

During the lunch I was again singled out by Cornelius Lycett, Radio Five's racing correspondent, for a filmed interview, followed by a 'quickie' with Clare Balding...on camera! Nigel Payne had of course arranged for Bob Sims and myself to attend and afterwards we shared a drink with Peter and Marilyn Scudamore. It was just over five weeks to the Cheltenham festival, and they kindly invited me to spend the three days with them.

The Scudamores live on Grange Hill Farm Racing Stables in a glorious converted barn in the bottom yard. The Twiston-Davieses live in the top yard where from the Cotswold stone farmhouse they survey the horse boxes on one side and the steep drop away towards Naunton on the other.

Mr and Mrs Michael Scudamore, Peter's parents, live in the wonderfully named Mucky Cottage, just a short walk from the barn and no more than thirty-nine inebriated steps from Earth Summit's box. Nigel Payne and I shared a room there for the duration of the 'Festival'.

Apart from the family's generous hospitality, the three days proved to be memorable in other ways. Michael Scudamore was a National Hunt jockey of considerable repute. Winner of the 1959 Grand National on Oxo, Scu senior was regarded as a fearless pilot and had suffered some horrific injuries during his career. He confided in me that the National fences were not what they had been in his day. 'You had to stand on a bucket to see over the top,' he laughingly told me one night in the Hollow Bottom.

In Mucky Cottage I awoke to the beautiful experience of a Cotswold dawn followed by a slow meander down the stairs where the career of the eight-times champion's Dad was captured in one photograph after another. A brisk walk past the horse boxes to 'the Barn' and awaiting all and sundry was a true Gloucestershire breakfast.

Sharing a room with Nigel Payne was yet another experience. He was always asleep within seconds, and the gentle 'engine-like' sounds emitting from beneath the hairy upper lip were actually quite soporific. On the way back from the course on the first day of the meeting, Peter, Marilyn and I were treated to one of Nigel's 'ten-second slumbers' – every ten minutes!

The main treat for us, though, was being in close proximity to our four-legged hero and every morning after breakfast we would stand with Bob Sims who had made his way from his Broadway Hotel, and watch 'Digger' gallop up the seven furlong all-weather surface which begins down in the valley. Coming up in twos in the bright morning sun, their coats gleaming and their nostrils pumping out the air from their lungs, the horses were a picture of superb fitness and happiness.

'What a life!' we echoed each other's thoughts as we watched, enthralled.

After racing on the second day of the Festival, Wednesday, I sat with Nigel and Scu in the hospitality tent of 'the Bunker Hill Mob', a group of owners headed by former Warwickshire cricketer, Andy Lloyd. Their horse, Frantic Tan, had just finished second in the 'Bumper', and we were sharing a few whiskies.

N Payne, in a mellow, reflective mood, posed a question to his friend and assistant trainer, P Scudamore, one of the greatest N H Jockeys of all time. 'Do you think Earth Summit knows my voice by now?'

Peter, with characteristic directness answered him. 'No, he only knows the voice of the one who feeds him.'

Nigel took a sip of his Scotch and I could swear I saw a tear. Scu and I looked on and stayed silent, not wishing to intrude on this touching display of genuine disappointment.

We spent another riotous night in The Hollow Bottom pub, the hostelry owned jointly by the Twiston-Davieses, the Scudamores, Charlie Egerton the trainer and two of racing's most charming patrons, Mr and Mrs Raymond Mould.

Sometime after midnight, having been deposited by Sims at the entrance to the bottom yard, two very pissed part-owners of Earth Summit stumbled over the uneven surface towards our hero's box. We couldn't see him in the dark as he stood quietly at rest at the back of his stable.

Nigel, with his shirt hanging out the back of his trousers, began cooing sycophantically into the dark. Sure enough, the sound of straw rustling was heard as the gelding made his way towards the noise. Sticking his handsome head out into the moonlight, he was then treated to our slobberings as we stroked and nuzzled him before finally wishing him goodnight, leaving him wondering what the hell we had woken him up for when there wasn't even a polo mint in sight.

As we staggered away towards Mucky Cottage I said to Nigel, 'There, he does know your voice.'

'Do you really think so?' he slurred happily.

'Yes,' I said, 'and so do all the others.'

We turned round and there, in the moonlight were six heads, all gazing expectantly in our direction.

As a footnote to that memorable night: while standing in the marquee that the owners had thoughtfully erected at the back of the pub, both Sims and Payne approached me on separate occasions. Amidst the noise of the revellers dancing to the Irish band, they both confided to me their identical thoughts, albeit in slightly different terms.

'George, as we're both completely pissed you probably won't remember what I'm going to say but if you do, don't say a fucking word to anyone.' I looked at Sims in anticipation. 'I think we're going to win the big one.' Coming from the world's number one pessimist that was a statement no-one would ever forget, no matter how pissed.

Within ten minutes, Nigel Payne, flushed from having his bum pinched by a very lively and attractive Kathy Twiston-Davies, sidled over with a pint in his hand. 'You know something, Ricky, I have this incredible feeling that we're going to win the National.'

'Do you know something, Nigel?' I replied. He looked at me through seriously glazed eyes. 'So do I.'

He grinned, I grinned and turned round to look at Sims, who had finally managed to tear his eyes away from a tiny blonde girl who was dancing. I grinned at him and he grinned back, not having a fucking clue what I was grinning at.

The following day, Gold Cup Day, the Twiston-Davies trained Upgrade won the Triumph hurdle at odds of 14/1. Having supported most of the stable's runners at the Festival, I was on with my case £100, plus £50 on the phone to William Hill.

The sun was shining, I had got back all my losses so far and was sure to end the meeting in profit. Was I lucky, or what?

As we sped away from the glorious Cotswolds in different

cars, Nigel Payne and I mulled over the three brilliant days we had just shared.

'It was a good thing, on reflection,' I mused knowledgeably, 'that we [Earth Summit] didn't run at the Festival.'

'Ricky,' Nigel's rich, full-bodied tones crackled back over the airwaves, 'do you realise that the National is just over two weeks away? Of course we were bloody right not to run. Marcella says he'll be bang on in two weeks! Speak to you soon.'

I felt the butterflies zip around my stomach as I pointed the BM up the Burford hill.

Up to Cheltenham I still had not placed my major bet on our boy. Prior to the Welsh National the previous December, Motty had obtained an incredible 50/1 with Ladbrokes. Star that he is, he offered Russell Townsend, another great friend, and myself part of the bet. We took it. After the gelding's amazing victory at Chepstow, I took 25/1 for Aintree. Still I held back. It wasn't because I had doubts about him getting round the National course; we all knew that would not be the problem. I suppose I just did not want to tempt fate with arrogant over-confidence. We all knew how fragile these animals are and the slightest training upset or cough in the yard would mean withdrawal and no money returned.

Tom Jenks had ridden Earth Summit to victory in the Welsh National and would certainly have piloted him in the big one, but sadly, Tom broke his leg in a fall at Hexham a couple of weeks before Cheltenham. Stable jockey Carl Llewelyn would take the ride as a deputy, which most certainly was not a problem.

The Twiston-Davies stable was still firing on all cylinders and Carl was picking up winners all over the place.

On Thursday, March 26th I returned to Grange Hill stables for a *News Of The World* photo-shoot with Earth Summit. I arrived to find he had been moved up to the top yard as one or two coughs had been heard in the bottom yard. He looked an absolute picture, coat gleaming, bursting with health. On a cold, blustery morning he stood patiently alongside his sixth part-owner and with customary grace permitted dozens of photos to be taken for the newspaper.

Marcella bade me farewell with a thumbs-up and a wink that said 'He's right on the button.'

On Saturday, March 28th, one week before the 1998 Martell Grand National, I took the plunge and placed the biggest bet of my life.

Chapter Twenty-Four
Only For Jo

Even though the gamble I was about to take was by far my largest, I had had some memorable moments on the turf in previous years.

In the summer of 1973, Barry Silkman joined Barnet from Wimbledon. It proved an excellent signing for the club as Silkman was clearly a player with outstanding ability. He was also a racing fanatic, horses and dogs.

As at all football clubs, the gamblers mustered together. Consequently, Barry and I became great friends. Along with Ian Fusedale and Gordon Ferry, we formed an intense and knowledgeable group who, on away trips, would discuss in great detail the chances of a variety of four-legged animals. Invariably Barry took centre stage, for two reasons. One, it was difficult to get a word in edgeways when he was in full flow; secondly, and far more significantly, he was privy to some fantastic information.

The source produced a flow of winners that I have never repeated since. It is impossible to recall them all, but there are one or two that will remain forever in the memory of those who were there.

Legal Tender, at 5/1, finished 7/2 at Lingfield, Hopeful Quaker, 8/1, in a photo at Nottingham; Quizair, at 33/1, started 28/1 in the 1974 Lincoln Handicap, Flash Imp at 5/1, and Only For Jo.

I can't remember exactly when Only For Jo was first mentioned but if anything can be described as a talking horse it was the five-year-old, trained at Epsom by the legendary Ron Smythe. Barry was 'connected' at the stable, so we were told. It was August and the target was the Manchester November Handicap. The Manchester racecourse had long since closed and the race was now run at Doncaster. It is the traditional closing feature of the flat race season run over one-and-a-half miles.

Amongst other bits of information Barry would give us, Only For Jo was constantly brought into the conversation. Even one famous night when he telephoned me in the early hours to tip the six dog in the 7.45 at Wembley the following night and I was desperately trying not to disturb Patricia sleeping next to me, he couldn't finish the call without whispering, 'Only For Jo, Rick baby.'

The ante-post lists for the race appeared during the week before the race and there was great excitement amongst the lads when 'Jo' opened up at 28/1. My £20 each way wager would return £700. To put that into perspective, in 1973 I was earning a total of £46 a week from playing football and working for Adidas. All the players had a bet, even the non-gamblers. The odds were huge.

During this period we had several 'touches' on Silky's tips and this added more excitement to the whole story. One Saturday in October several of us were waiting for the result of the 1.55 at Nottingham standing in Ladbrokes in Greenhill Parade, a couple of hundred yards from Underhill. It seemed to take forever and we were due to kick-off at 3pm. When the announcement was made, 'Photo at Nottingham, between number 15, Hopeful Quaker and—', a huge shout went up from the corner of the shop. Not from us but from the landlord of The Queen's Arms pub. 'Thanks boys,' he said, visibly shaking, 'I had a hundred quid on that.'

In those days, when a photo finish was announced the first named horse was invariably the winner. Hopeful Quaker returned at 8/1, and our pub landlord had picked up £800 – no wonder he was sweating! As we hurried back to the ground we wondered how many £100 losing bets the publican had experienced.

As the big day approached, the excitement grew and although the race was always a competitive handicap with a big field, the word was out and 'Jo' was down to 13/1.

Barry gave us regular bulletins on the horse. He always seemed to be meeting someone at Tattenham corner at night. I had this mental picture of him standing by the rails at the famous landmark on Epsom Racecourse receiving precious information from a shadowy figure who then disappeared into the night across the downs. His meetings were actually held at the train station of the same name.

158

When race day finally arrived, we were away to Grantham in a Southern League Premier fixture. Silky didn't make the trip; he was ill, from nerves!

The race was due off at 3.25. We kicked off against Grantham at three. Ian Fusedale, injured, sat on the bench with a transistor radio. By 3.20 we were losing 0-3.

At just after 3.35 Ian leapt up from the bench punching the air, to the amazement of everyone. The Grantham bench, the supporters sitting in the stands and the linesman who nearly jumped out of his skin must have thought he was completely off his head.

That was nothing compared to the sight of eleven professional footballers jumping and whooping as if they had won the FA Cup.

Only For Jo, ridden by Ian Jenkinson, had won the Manchester November Handicap by three-quarters of a length from Realty.

It was a lot of money to win in those days and such was our gratitude, Ian Fusedale and I bought Silky a gold watch, which he still has, he tells me. I can't remember how much Ian won but he had a new kitchen extension built.

We drew the second half, nil-nil.

The following March I made my first trip to the Cheltenham Festival, with Silky and Ian. We backed the brilliant but erratic Irish novice, Captain Christy at 7/1 to win the Gold Cup.

Favourite to win the Gold Cup was Fred Winter's Pendil, ridden by John Francombe. The horse fell at the second last to an almighty roar from the Irish contingent. Captain Christy, ridden by the late Bobby Beasley, came to the last, needing only to jump it to win. The gelding made a hash of it but stayed on his feet to stride clear up the hill amidst a cacophony of noise, akin to the famous Hampden roar. The atmosphere was electric, I had experienced nothing like it at Ally Pally or Devon and Exeter, or Park Royal dogs, for that matter.

In another race that day, over a distance short of his best, a great Cheltenham favourite was preparing for his third shot at the Grand National. L'Escargot, winner of the Gold Cup in 1970 and '71, was bred in Mullingar, County Westmeath and was owned by the American Ambassador to Ireland, Mr Raymond Guest.

In the great emotion of the day generated by the Irish, I put the twelve-year-old in my mental notebook and decided the handsome chestnut gelding would be the second leg of my attempt at the 'Spring Double', the Lincoln Handicap – the opening feature of the flat season, usually run a couple of weeks before the National – being the first.

Silky had tipped the Ryan Jarvis trained Quizair for the Lincoln so, following the man with the magic touch, on the day of the big Doncaster race, I popped into Ladbrokes in Barnet High Street and placed the following bet: £5 each way Quizair to win the Lincoln at 33/1; £5 each way L'Escargot to win the Grand National at 16/1; £5 each way double the two. *Plus*, for interest, a horse called Legal Tender, trained by Staff Ingham at Epsom, also tipped by Silky and a winner over hurdles on the day 'Jo' won the Manchester Handicap.

So, to complete my investment of £40 I had a £5 *each way treble*: Quizair (33/1), L'Escargot (16/1), Legal Tender (5/1) to win the Yellow Pages hurdle at Lingfield the same day as the Lincoln.

Quizair trotted up, returning 28/1; Legal Tender trotted up, returning 7/2. If the gallant L'Escargot should win the Grand National, my winnings from the treble alone would return nearly £18 000, more than enough to buy a very nice three-bedroomed house in Barnet in 1974. The same house today would fetch close on £300 000

Everything hinged on Dan Moore's brilliant twelve-year-old justifying the support that had reduced his price to shade over half the odds I had obtained ante-post. He started second favourite to the eight year old Scout at 17-2. As a Gold Cup Winner, L'Escargot was unquestionably the class horse of the race. The previous year's winner Red Rum was now set to carry twelve stone, the same weight L'Escargot had carried when finishing third in the same race. There was a big weight pull, Red Rum had carried two stone less in 1973. I was in with a great chance.

On Grand National day, 1974, we were away to Hillingdon Boroughin a Southern League Premier fixture.

I was so nervous that, on this occasion, my team-mates forgave the fact that for the first thirty five minutes I performed as if in a dream. The race was off at 3.30 and I must have glanced at the clock behind our goal a thousand times before, at approximately 3.40 I looked across at our bench.

Billy Meadows, the man I had shared so many glorious memories with at Hereford and Barnet, was sitting, with a transistor radio looking only at me. He held up two fingers in the courteous mode, indicating second place for L'Escargot.

As I trudged off, head down at half-time, I was consoled, not only by my own team but by the Hillingdon players as well, it seemed the whole world knew of my bet.

The amazing Red Rum had defied top weight in phenomenal style, winning by twenty five lengths.

The following year L'Escargot won the Grand National, beating Red Rum into second place, at odds of 13/2.

I had a tenner on.

Chapter Twenty-Five
Barnet Youth

In May 1975 Daniel was born. In April 1975 I started my own business.

I worked hard and after less than one season as a father, businessman and professional footballer, football took a back seat. I still played the odd game and turned out for various sides when asked, but basically it was over. Work took over and when Adam was born in March 1978 I was doing all right in the real world. We had moved from Arkley to Longmore Avenue, New Barnet and in May 1982 when Rebecca was born I knew I had found true and lasting happiness. Football, memories of my childhood, playing for Barnet, scoring goals were all now part of another life.

There wasn't any youth football in Barnet at this time. The Football Club had long since shelved reserves and youth teams for financial reasons. Some enthusiastic and committed parents decided to start a team for under tens in the area. Brian Harrison and Graham Morgan, a lifelong Barnet supporter, started Barnet Beavers in 1983. In 1986, by the time Adam was eight, another team, Barnet Hawks, had been formed by David Jeffrey and Jim Stebbings. I took Adam along to join the Hawks. Two years later the Beavers and the Hawks amalgamated to form Barnet Youth FC.

I attended all the training sessions and matches that Adam was involved in but took no other role. Shortly after the merger of the two teams, I was asked to be the club's first president, a position I accepted with great pride. My involvement with this super group of people gave me enormous pleasure, none greater than watching the development of the hundreds of boys that were to pass through the club from age eight to eighteen. At its peak Barnet Youth boasted twenty-two teams.

In the early eighties, when Daniel and later Adam were old enough I started taking them to Underhill. By the late 80s I was watching regularly again and through a Barnet Youth parent, Malcolm Cussell, I helped begin the Barnet Hospital broadcasts of matches during the 1991-92 season.

When Graham Morgan started Barnet Youth he had a vision of an association with Barnet Football Club. Since the amateur days and the scrapping Youth 'A' and reserve teams, very few local boys had played for the club. Upon reflection, I realised I was one of those locals; I was hard pressed to think of any others apart from Russell Townsend during twenty-five years.

Graham had made some headway with Barry Fry and former chairman Tom Hill. However, when Stan Flashman became chairman in 1983 that came to an abrupt end.

One of my first tasks as President of Barnet Youth was to try to encourage the football club to accept us as a nursery for the development of young local players. Any boys who had shown promise, whether they played for Barnet Youth or not, were being lost to other senior clubs, such as Watford.

I knew Barry Fry, having played against him many times during the Southern League days when he was playing for Bedford Town. I liked Barry, he was a very approachable guy. I also liked Edwin Stein, who had shown great interest in Barnet Youth.

Stan Flashman was also familiar from my days a Spurs. He was not quite so approachable, but always remembered a player, no matter how junior, and I had no problem speaking with him about our ideas for the youth of Barnet.

Barry and Edwin gave us 100 percent support but I was left to put the proposition to Stan. At first, he was pretty negative, saying he didn't like Graham Morgan for some reason. I brushed over that subject and he got rid of me by agreeing to think about it after his holiday in Marbella in July. I tried again at the start of the fatal 1992-93 season but got nowhere. It was terribly frustrating and there was no logic to it. We were self-sufficient with an existing set-up. What we needed was some formal link with the club which would enable them to start schools of excellence with us as a feeder of local talent on the doorstep.

The dramatic exit of Stan and Barry after Barnet's historic entry into the Football League was to change forever the public perception of the Underhill Club. After March 1993 things would never be the same again. This powerful and sometimes

163

farcical duo had achieved every non-league club's dream, in style and amid controversy. Let there be no mistake about it, Stan needed Barry and Barry needed Stan. In spite of the appalling public relations shortcomings of Stanley, without him Barnet would never have become a Football League Club.

Two weeks before the Bees won promotion to the new second division, a new board took over at Underhill. Within days Barry Fry left to become manager of Southend United.

On the day promotion was won at home to Lincoln City, I went to the match with Neil Berry from Barnet Youth and John Motson, a long time supporter of the club. We met the new chairman, Mr Woolfson, and his co-directors, who were very receptive to the Youth scheme. Things looked hopeful, but all three of us left with a less than confident feeling.

During the match I sat next to someone who introduced himself as 'the man who built the clubhouse'. Marc Rowan, one of the club's major creditors, confided to me that he had been treated very badly by Flashman and that he was waiting patiently to see what the new board were going to do for him.

I knew the club was seriously in debt but had no idea to what extent. Mr Rowan, a football man who declared himself a supporter with no desire to see the club suffer, just wanted to be paid. I had no idea at the time what a significant role Marc Sean Rowan would play in my immediate future.

Shortly after the Lincoln game I attended a meeting at Underhill chaired by Mr Woolfson. This was a 'get to know you' affair. There were many interested parties concerned with the future of the club. Barnet Youth was strongly represented and we were introduced as the innovators of the new youth policy to be implemented by the club.

That was the last time I saw or spoke to Mr Woolfson. Within a couple of weeks the new board had resigned, en bloc.

Chapter Twenty-Six
Summer Of '93

The season ended, Barnet were promoted and the newspapers took over. A depressing picture was painted and for several weeks speculation was rife. A few deeply committed and worried people stood firm at Underhill, notably, club secretary Brian Ayres, Supporters Association secretary Liz Ashfield, goalkeeper Gary Phillips, kit man Gordon Ogbourne and ground maintenance man Tony Sharpe. There were many caring supporters constantly coming and going at the ground. A disillusioned Edwin Stein followed Barry Fry to Southend.

The only assets a club like Barnet possesses are its players. This particular group of players had not been paid for ten weeks. When a club fails to pay its players it is in breach of contract and the players are then free to go. In circumstances like these the Professional Footballers Association (PFA) steps in to help, mediate and generally provide what assistance it can. I believe the PFA paid some of the wages to the contracted players. Due to previous disciplinary breaches the club had a transfer embargo imposed on it by the Football League, which meant they were neither able to sell or acquire players.

During May and early June there was further speculation in the press regarding a consortium of businessmen who appeared to be interested in mounting a rescue bid.

On the first of June 1993, the scenario was as follows:

The club had estimated debts of £1 million plus.

All the contracted players owed money from the previous season were technically free.

The squad was conservatively priced at £1 million.

There was a transfer embargo on the club.

There was no Board of Directors.

There was no manager.

There was no money and the staff had not been paid for weeks.

During the next couple of weeks the consortium became active. The press named Stephen Glynne as the head of the ten man group. They were prepared to inject £250 000 into the club with the important proviso that the contracted players would be paid their back wages and therefore remain Barnet players. There was, for the first time in weeks, a ray of hope for the future of Barnet Football Club. There was no mention at this time as to who would ultimately own the club. The Flashman family owned sixty-seven percent of the issued shares, giving them a majority holding. There was no indication as to whether the consortium would buy out the Flashman holding. Within days, however, it all became academic as the Football League, that ancient and revered institution, acted in a most draconian fashion.

They chose to burden their newest member with impossible conditions to retain member status of the League Barnet had fought so hard to join. The League decided that to ensure the club would pay its players in the future, it would have to lodge a guarantee of £250 000 with the League for the duration of the 1993-4 season. On top of this the club would have to provide a further guarantee of £250 000 to ensure its fixtures for the season would be fulfilled.

Unsurprisingly, the consortium withdrew.

If one was looking objectively at the situation you could see the League's reasoning behind these measures. Barnet, during the Flashman tenure, had received appalling publicity. There were constant breaches of discipline off the field and the chairman had not endeared himself to the authorities or anyone else, for that matter. *The Sun* embarked on a campaign to humiliate and shame the man who said on Radio Five, 'The supporters don't matter.' The club suffered as a result and, with the demise of Maidstone United, another promoted club from the Conference, the Football League began to fear a repeat performance. Frankly, I think they wanted Barnet out, after just two seasons. I was right.

On the other hand – and this, in my opinion, shames the Football League Committee – it is precisely those supporters, dismissed by Mr Flashman, who would suffer most if the club was forced out of existence. I don't think the powers that be at the Football League gave any more consideration to those people than had Stanley himself. By imposing the £500 000 of guarantees, they were condemning the club to inevitable closure.

According to recent Football League rules, liquidation automatically means forfeit of membership. Interesting, when you know that football clubs have gone into liquidation in the past yet remain members of the League, that membership having passed into a new Limited Company. New rules drawn up to prevent insolvent clubs escaping their creditors were to be strictly enforced from now on. In a later chapter you will see how one very famous club did precisely that just eleven months earlier. The Football League took no credit for their behaviour during this episode, as you will discover.

When I was a Barnet player in the late 60s and 70s, the treasurer of the club was a man called John Skinner. He was a lifelong supporter and, apart from his occupation as a bank manager, he had three interests in life: his model trains, his mother Grace and Barnet Football Club. John later became a director of the club and remained so until Flashman took charge. He continued to support the club and was one of many anxiously watching events at Underhill during the summer of '93.

After the Glynne consortium withdrew John came to see me on three occasions. We discussed the plight of the club and he gave me more of an insight into the internal problems. The club was still owned by the Flashman family. The balance of the shareholding of thirty-three percent was split between forty or so members. John Skinner and his mother were typical; they owned 200 shares between them. The largest individual holding outside Flashman was 500. Stanley, as his wife Helen insisted on calling him, was completely out of the picture with no money. His creditors had closed in on him and he had vacated his large detached house in Totteridge. John didn't know the full extent of the debt but had knowledge of some of the principal creditors. Marc Rowan's company, GR Construction was owed about £160 000. The police were creditors, the PFA, the staff, including players, and the Inland Revenue. John was sure the amount was insurmountable, but he wasn't sure when he expressed the view that unless something happened quickly, Barnet Football Club would cease to exist.

I made my position perfectly clear, I would help in any way

I could, but as far as finance was concerned there was no way I could afford to bail the club out. I would contribute up to £25 000 if that would support any rescue package. Beyond that and giving time if required, I was unable to do more. I left the door open for John to get back to me.

July 6th 1993 was a beautiful day, our twenty-fifth wedding anniversary. We were just about to leave for Newmarket races with Martin and Janet Webb, our friends for thirty years, when the telephone rang. It was Brian Lowy, a director of Barnet Football Club. He told me the club was doomed.

He had met the previous night with John Skinner, Liz Ashfield and Stephen Glynne. They had pre-empted the worst and formed a new company, hopefully to embrace a new Barnet Football Club. The new club would hope to begin life in the Diadora League Division Three, about five leagues below the Football League. It was hoped that the new club would continue to play at Underhill. The four people who had met the previous night wanted me to be chairman of the new club. The shell company formed for the purpose was called Keybay Limited, and Brian warned me of urgent work to be done if I accepted: meeting the council concerning Underhill, speaking to the Diadora League, speaking to the Capital League about continuing membership, finding a manger – and a team. As far as funding was concerned, that was down to me. He was very frank; none of the others would be putting money in. I was asked to make contact with Stephen Glynne as quickly as possible.

We left for Newmarket with Martin driving. I tried to take it all in and discussed it with Pat and the others on the way. If I agreed I was taking on a huge commitment. They urged me to think carefully but, as Pat said to the others, 'He'll do it irrespective of that if he decides he wants to.' There it was left and everyone returned to the task at hand, finding a winner or two.

We had a wonderful day, meeting up with other old and dear friends. I kept the subject of Keybay and Barnet Council to myself, but I had already made up my mind. I cannot remember whether or not I had any winners.

Two days later I met Stephen Glynne for the first time and together we met with the chief executive of Barnet Council. Mr Max Caller and his colleagues were wary. Here were two people they did not know, neither of whom had any involvement with the running of Barnet Football Club, requesting their assistance in accommodating a brand new club, as yet without a name, at Underhill stadium. In the first place they were adamant that Underhill would always remain a Football Stadium. It was never to be used for any sport other than soccer. They could not guarantee, however, a reassignment of the lease to a new company before the new season and suggested a temporary ground sharing would be an option we would need to consider. In the circumstances, their reaction was reasonable and I felt confident that we could overcome any hurdles with regard to any reassignment of the lease. This subject, though, was of secondary importance to them. The council's primary concern was that the existing club should continue to represent the Borough as a Football League Club. We explained the position carefully and in some detail. Mr Caller hoped that a backer could be found who would take over the club from the present owners and stave off any attempt to put the company into liquidation – in other words, a fairy godmother or father.

Didn't we all.

And so I became a director of Keybay Limited. My co-directors were Stephen Glynne, Brian Lowy and John Skinner. Liz Ashfield was company secretary.

I got on well with Stephen Glynne. I wasn't sure why he was involved, but I didn't question it at the time. The situation required helping hands and he seemed prepared to help. As far as Brian Lowy and John Skinner were concerned, there was no need to question their motives. John had been a supporter for close on forty years, Brian had been around for at least ten to my knowledge.

The night following my meeting with Barnet Council, I went with Brian Lowy to meet with Enfield Football Club to ask if they would consider allowing a New Barnet Football Club to share their ground temporarily. They were extremely helpful and the chairman, Mr Lazarou, agreed a figure with us to share for one season. This would be in the event that Barnet Council would not be able to reassign the lease on Underhill in time for the new football season which, believe it or not, was only a month away.

At this point, a summary of the overall position revealed a bizarre scenario. The club had not been wound up although there were rumours of angry creditors gathering in the wings. There was no appointed director in charge. The club was still effectively owned by the Flashman family who held 67% of the issued shares. A skeleton staff were still going into the Underhill office every day to report to no-one, to receive no wages. The playing pitch had not been touched since the last day of the season. It was like a ship drifting slowly into hostile waters with a worried group of people who, so far, had not been washed overboard.

There was certainly a need to bring that situation into some order. Unless one of the creditors decided to petition for a winding-up, there was no-one in authority to begin a voluntary liquidation. Either way, it would mean losing membership of the Football League. The league rules clearly stated that liquidation meant loss of member status. It was also forbidden to come to any kind of formal arrangement with creditors – remember that, please, as we go through the story.

But the Football League, that ancient and hallowed institution, were hurriedly rushing towards a solution that would speed up the demise of Barnet Football Club Limited.

A Football Association tribunal had already decided that Barnet's contracted players were free to leave the club. Away went Gary Bull, estimated at £½ million pounds, Mick Bodley, £150 000, Derek Payne, £100 000, Gary Poole, £100 000 and so on

Scientists say it is impossible to go back in time, to turn back the clock. Not true.

On 12th December 1993 His Honour Justice Evans-Lombe turned back the hands of time nearly six months to the 24th July. In doing so, he exceeded even his powers as a High Court Judge. Apart from his assumption that he could tamper with the laws of nature, he passed judgement on an issue that was none of his business. He tried the wrong matter.

After Stephen Glynne went on holiday on the 25th July 1993, I was left in charge of Barnet Football Club. We had a little under three weeks to prepare for the opening day of the 1993-94 season. The Football League had failed miserably to expel Barnet at an Extraordinary General Meeting earlier in the month. Glynne and I attended the EGM at Notts Forest's City ground where the great and the good expounded their views upon the suitability of Barnet Football Club to remain a member of their ranks. In the end, the vice-chairman of Wigan Athletic, a solicitor by the name of Bitel, pointed out to the meeting that the essential details of the proposal to expel Barnet was fundamentally flawed. No Football League chairman with any brains could possibly vote in favour of the proposition.

As we drove away from the famous city, Stephen Glynne and I realised what lay ahead if we took it on. We decided to launch a survival fund amongst the supporters, kicking it off with £5000 each.

Our target was £500 000.

Glynne had obtained the majority shareholding in the club, the Flashman holding of 6868 shares, for the nominal sum of £1. His brief was that he would hold these shares in trust until such time as the club could be sold to a new owner. That was our aim. If we could muddle through and be prepared sufficiently to start the new season, the intention was to find a suitable buyer to take over.

In the meantime, at least £140 000 was required if the club were to satisfy the minimum needed to lift the transfer embargo imposed on the club by the Football League.

The supporters responded magnificently, all 300 of them. Incredibly, between that small number of people, enough was raised to satisfy the Professional Footballers Association with regard to the form players' wages and promotion bonuses so that they (the PFA) could inform the Football League that their problem was resolved.

When Stephen Glynne left to go on holiday on July 25th 1993, he left me the following letter, later referred to as 'the Power':

'To whom it may concern

I hereby authorise Richard Stuart George to deal in all or part of my 6868 shares in Barnet Football Club in any way in which he deems to be of benefit to the club.'

Not too complicated. It was effectively a power of attorney giving me the scope and flexibility to deal with any potential purchaser of the club. The letter formed a critical part of the arrangement that Glynne and I had devised to ensure the club survived in the immediate short term. As he had now acquired the majority shareholding he became the new chairman and, effectively, captain of the ship. But he was leaving for three weeks on a family holiday at the most crucial time. The new season was due to kick off in less than two weeks, on August 7th. At a hastily arranged board meeting held at Underhill on 24th July, I was appointed vice-chairman of Barnet Football Club, still members of the Football League Division Two, and handed 'the Power'.

This was not what I'd had in mind when accepting Brian Lowy's invitation eighteen days before. At that time I was to be chairman of Keybay Ltd, trading as Barnet Football Club (1993) Ltd, members of the Diadora League Division Three. Glynne did not wish to be chairman of that particular company, in fact he was on the point of withdrawing his services until the decision was taken to fight on and keep the club in the Football League.

Apart from the commitment I had taken on there was an added complication. We too had a family holiday booked, to depart on 5th August, two days before the big kick-off.

At the crucial survival meeting held amongst 800 or so supporters at Underhill some days before, a man approached Glynne and myself just prior to the start. He introduced himself as an accountant who could raise £½ million for the club by a flotation of shares. We welcomed any help that was offered and he handed Glynne his business card. A couple of days later, I found myself sitting in the crowded front room of a house in Woodside Park, close to Totteridge in North London. Present were Stephen Glynne, John Motson, Liz Ashfield and three or four men I never saw again. The house belonged to the accountant, Mr Alan Kasmir.

A lengthy and complicated discussion took place whereby everything bar the £½ million flotation was mentioned. Kasmir and Glynne discovered that their respective offices were within a few hundred yards of each other in central London. Alan Kasmir joined the board of directors and in doing so, he contributed £1000 to the survival fund. He also offered the services of his practice to deal with the wage bill at the club and the financial state of affairs, a matter that was very unclear in July 1993.

Thus Alan Kasmir and I became unpaid working directors at Underhill.

The race against time began on Monday 26th July. A new manager was appointed in the form of Gary Phillips, the club's popular, long-serving goalkeeper. A potential buyer in the shape of businessman Terry Brady came to Underhill for a meeting. We met by the entrance to the pitch and walked to the centre circle across a terrain that had been untouched for nearly three months. The three of us stood in the circle surveying the scene. Brady's mobile phone rang and he walked away to answer it. Gary and I watched him. 'His suit is worth more than my house,' commented the player-manager.

Brady returned. 'That was the man' he said mysteriously. 'He wants to meet you.'

I met the man later that day at Brady's office in N7.

I hadn't been in Terry Venables' company for nearly thirty years but the greeting was as friendly as it had been then, in George's Cafe in Tottenham High Road, three doors from The Red House. Incredibly, Brady's man was the famous ex-Tottenham manager, currently in bitter dispute with Alan Sugar and, apparently, interested in Barnet.

We had a cordial and workmanlike meeting. Venables' personal assistant Eddie Ashby asked the pertinent questions concerning the club's finances. I was not able to give him the answers he required, only to say that the majority shares were available for a minimum of £250 000, such sum to go straight into the club to deal with the immediate cash crisis. Venables himself was interested in training facilities and the playing staff, naturally.

We agreed to stay in touch through Brady and I left to return to Underhill to interview a groundsman. It took me three minutes to agree terms with Colin Payne, recommended by Gary Phillips as a brilliant groundsman. It was the best signing I ever made.

The Venables connection never got off the ground. Possibly the job he was ultimately offered as England coach was more attractive.

With the survival fund money we restarted the wages, making arrangements with the staff to repay them for the twelve weeks they had stood by the club.

That night I went with Brian Ayres, the club secretary, to meet with the Capital League Committee at the Barclays Bank sports ground at Ealing, West London to ensure we could field a team in the mid-week reserve competition. The committee was made up of old faces, including Barry Fry. There was no problem there.

On the journey to Ealing, Brian gave me my list of priorities in order of urgency. Of the creditors, there were two I had to deal with immediately, Neil Friar and Marc Rowan, 'the man who built the clubhouse'.

Neil is the son of Arsenal Football Club's highly respected managing director, Ken Friar. The club owed him £14 000 and he had a winding-up petition in place, due to be heard in court on September 10th. According to Brian Ayres, Neil was a very angry young man. He needed to be placated, without delay.

Marc Rowan was in his mid-thirties. He was suspicious and aggressive, making no attempt to cover up his feelings, particularly towards a man like Alan Kasmir, who was the epitome of everything Rowan detested. To him, Kasmir was a parasite, a clever accountant looking to pick whatever flesh was on the bones of this ailing company, leaving unsecured creditors like himself to fade away into oblivion. On this occasion, he was spectacularly wrong.

Marc Rowan was owed £160 000. I had met him briefly at the Lincoln City game the previous April. According to Brian Ayres, Mr Rowan need to be dealt with urgently.

Two days later I made my first mistake.

The squad that Gary Phillips inherited consisted of six players. With the transfer embargo still in force, trialists were brought in to play in the first pre-season game away at Lincoln City on my second day in charge. On the morning of the game an old and dear friend, Roger Thompson, called me from his mum's home in Stafford. Roger and I were playing colleagues at Barnet in the late 60s. He had become youth team coach at Arsenal in the 70s before emigrating to the USA after a spell at Fulham as assistant manager. He was home visiting his elderly mother when he heard of Barnet's plight. Roger offered his services to Gary Phillips and we welcomed him with open arms that strange night at Sincil Bank.

After the friendly, I addressed the players for the first time. One of those who had stayed on in spite of the free transfers given to all last year's promotion winning team was centre-back Dave Barnett. Here was a little bit of gold dust left over from the plundered mine that was Barry Fry's team. Gary urged me to provide Dave Barnett with some security. His club car had been repossessed and he needed that sorting immediately. The following day, I leased one for him on my

American Express card. I was now personally responsible for Dave Barnett's transport.

My second mistake came at 7am on the Wednesday morning, when I met with Neil Friar at the West Lodge Park Hotel in Hadley Wood. Neil was indeed an angry man. I placated him by giving him my personal cheque for £5000, in return for which he agreed to hold off, temporarily, on the winding-up order. I was making him a preferential creditor in the event of a liquidation, which was against company law. I also agreed to reinstate him as the club's kit supplier, the job for which, so far, he had not been paid. To complete this second promise I had to go and beg the new supplier, Gilbert Brothers in Barnet, to pull out of the recent deal they had signed with the club. As unhappy as David Gilbert was, he behaved like a true gentleman, taking pity on this grovelling person who was clearly trying to achieve the impossible – keep everyone happy.

Two days later, a creditors' meeting was called at Underhill. Alan Kasmir and I took the chair between us and faced what we expected to be a large group of angry people. In the event, there was only one angry person. The rest were mainly representatives of small creditors, some of whom did not even know they were at a football club.

The one angry person was Marc Sean Rowan, 'the man who built the clubhouse'. What Rowan noticed as soon as the meeting started was Neil Friar's absence. He smelled preference, and in this case he was right. His anger, however, was directed at the wrong person: Kasmir. He approached him immediately after the meeting. 'I can be your best friend or your worst enemy,' he told the accountant. Kasmir took this as a threat and never forgot it. The seeds were sown for the battle. What the sowers did not know was that they were sowing not their own seeds but mine and Stephen Glynne's.

Rowan was owed a reputed sum of £160 000, a great deal of money in anyone's terms, and the absence of this sum had created serious problems for the young builder. Marc was going down fast and the trauma associated with a business failure served only to accentuate his desire for revenge.

But he was venting his feelings on the wrong people. The person responsible for his impending loss was Stan Flashman, who had engaged Rowan to build the new clubhouse, and who had not paid him.. Those who now sought to rescue the club were not thinking in terms of the poor creditors. This was not personal, the survival of the club was.

Therefore, an angry and justifiably aggrieved man like Marc Rowan was regarded as a heartless bastard who cared only about his money, as he had every right to. He had a wife and a family to support; this was personal, to him.

Tragically – and I use that word advisedly – both Kasmir and Rowan attacked the wrong enemy. Alan Kasmir was not at Barnet Football Club to make money. He genuinely wanted to help the situation and his reward would have been some major involvement in the club. He was a pain in the arse at times but he meant well and deserves credit for the assistance he gave during the crucial period between July 25th and August 7th. He saw Rowan as an abusive, aggressive individual, bent on securing control of the club for his own devious reasons, and regarded the man's £160 000 bill with cynical suspicion.

Rowan, for his part, regarded Kasmir as the ultimate vulture, seeking nothing but profit. These two men were to ultimately decide the fate of the football club, no matter how important I thought I was.

A brooding Marc Rowan telephoned me shortly after the creditors' meeting to tell me that he knew Neil Friar had been given preference and that he thought the club was being 'carved up' again. He told me he intended to take over the club on the basis of his position as major creditor. The reason for him telling me this was that he thought I was a genuine participant, as opposed to the Glynnes and the Kamirs of this world. There was nothing I could say that would convince him otherwise. He demanded a meeting.

It took place at the Swallow Hotel, Loughton at 10am on Sunday August 1st 1993. Marc Rowan had his solicitor Michael Kennedy with him. Neil Friar was also present.

For the record, during my six days in charge of a Football League Club, I had arranged cars for Gary Phillips and Dave Barnett; obtained permission from the survival fund contributors to begin spending their money; restarted the wages, allowing a small amount extra per week for those who had gone unpaid for ten weeks; begun negotiations with the Football League and the PFA over the transfer embargo; appointed a superb groundsman to begin work on the pitch; held a preliminary meeting with the FLA (Football Licensing

Authority), Barnet Council and the police. Oh yes, and we bought some toilet rolls! I think I went home once or twice. The survival fund crept up to £80 000.

On the Sunday morning I listened intently to what Rowan and his solicitor had to say. Basically they could not understand why people like Glynne and Kasmir were so interested in the future of Barnet Football Club. They thought they understood what I was doing there, but could only see ulterior motives as far as the others were concerned.

I told them I felt they were wrong. I could not imagine what other motive Stephen Glynne or Alan Kasmir could have other than concern for the club. There was a great deal of scepticism over the fact that Glynne had obtained the Flashman shares for £1, so I explained the background to everyone's involvement. Neither Glynne nor I had heard of Kasmir prior to the survival fund meeting.

Rowan and Kennedy were unconvinced. Even Neil Friar, who had remained very quiet, was deeply suspicious about Stephen Glynne. In their view, Glynne at least was acting as a front for the Flashman family's interests. That was what Mr Woolfson and his colleagues had tried to do: hold on to the club and try to sell it for £750 000. The present scenario was completely different. The shares were available to anyone prepared to put up £250 000, which would be immediately injected into the club. Whoever put up the money would then be in the majority.

After two hours of intense discussion, Rowan agreed to meet Kasmir again. He couldn't meet Glynne, who was in the USA for another two weeks. Even though Marc was fuming over the preference shown to Neil Friar's DMF Company, both he and Kennedy were pro the son of Arsenal's highly respected managing director. Both were season ticket holders at Highbury. At least they had something in common with Stephen Glynne.

The Rowan/Friar/Kennedy plan was to take over the club in lieu of the money they were owed. They felt that Rowan, in particular, had 160 000 more reasons to own Barnet than Glynne. I explained my position with regard to the authority I held and the £250 000 target figure. I explained about the survival fund and about Terry Brady's interest.

We agreed to meet again later in the week, with Kasmir and Brady. I promised to call Glynne in the USA to put him in the picture.

I felt like a tiny piece of meat between two slices of thickly cut bread.

The survival fund crept up to £92 000.

I spoke to Glynne, Kasmir and Brady about the Rowan/ Friar plan. None was enthusiastic about Rowan's suggestion or assumption that as a creditor he was entitled to any shares in lieu of repayment. My view was that he was so hostile at this point that the threat to join DMF's winding-up petition was very real.

I was trying to please everyone. At the back of my mind while this scenario was taking shape was Hull City at home in less than two weeks. There was still a transfer embargo over the club and a stadium as yet unfit to accommodate a football match or one paying customer.

We had some toilet rolls though.

The following evening there was a second pre-season friendly away at Berkhamsted Town. Marc Rowan asked if he could come with me to watch the match. We had a chat on the way up and he was like a different person. Calm and approachable, he apologised to me if I thought he had been rude or offensive. He wanted to be involved, as a director, and was prepared to waive the money owed to him for a significant involvement in the club. He didn't want to be chairman or an autocratic owner like the previous incumbent. He felt he could work with me and was prepared to meet Glynne, reserving judgement in view of what I had said. He was also prepared to meet Brady and listen to his proposal. Marc Rowan was almost unrecognisable from the man I had seen the day before.

I discovered a man with a complex personality. Most of the time, particularly this time of his life, he presented a front full of suspicion and aggression. He had been quite successful as a builder but had fallen upon difficult times and saw the Barnet situation as a diversion from his troubles. Also, he felt the club owed him a great deal, not just the money. It is not pleasant to have your family threatened, but when he tried to collect what he was owed from Mr Flashman that is precisely what happened. I spoke at length to Gary Phillips and Brian Ayres and they described Marc Rowan as a good bloke, someone who had been a generous supporter in and out of the boardroom.

This was not just about money, it was about football and bruised egos. Sadly the latter two go together all too often.

At Berkhamsted we were both to witness a new display of anger and hostility by the chairman of the Supporters Association.

Steve Percy, thirty-something with shoulder-length hair and tattoos, had been a supporter since my playing days. An aggressive and angry individual, he ruled over the supporters with an iron fist. This was ironic because Barnet's supporters have the proud reputation of being extremely well-behaved. Percy would not tolerate any trouble whatsoever and was held in high regard by his members. He was passionate about Barnet FC and had done a great deal of good for the club. However, his personality made him too deeply suspicious of 'the men in suits'.

At the survival meeting he had spoken out in support of the appeal and, as in principle the supporters were his 'province', it was agreed that a representative of those supporters should sit on the board of Keybay Limited. Percy insisted that there should be two representatives on the board so another lifelong devotee, Derek Scott, was added to the growing list of Keybay directors.

At Berkhamsted we were losing 3-0 at half-time. Our team was a mixture of reserves, trialists and ex-players. The score was totally irrelevant; the point of the game from Barnet's point of view was to see if any trialists were good enough, and to try and add some match fitness to players without the benefit of any pre-season training.

Steve Percy was outraged at the team's display. He angrily confronted me and Marc Rowan as the club's only visible officials in the grandstand and demanded to know what the hell was going on. He stood in front of the main stand, shouting as any disgruntled supporter might. However, after I had left my seat and patiently explained that the game and the result were not to be taken so seriously, in spite of everyone's desire to see the team do well, the response was a further demand to know what the hell was going on at the club in general terms. In particular: 'Who are all these people and why have I as director of Keybay not been consulted on what's been happening on a day-to-day basis?'

For the first time, my frustration showed. 'If you want to be treated like a director then behave like one. What do you want me to do, ring you up every time we order toilet rolls?'

There, I had used the phrase again.

Ironically, it was Marc Rowan who calmed things down and advised me to keep cool. Along with Roger Thompson, he helped take the heat out of this angry exchange.

It was an interesting scenario. I was outraged that this person should attack me when I was spending every waking moment desperately trying to get this club back on the road. I was neglecting my business and family because the situation was so damn tight and there was no other way of dealing with it. Meanwhile, Steve Percy went to work every day and just turned up for matches. How could he expect me to consult him on every matter?

In his mind, he spoke for the supporters, the only people who really count at a football club. Those loyal folk continued to pump money into the survival fund and he had been appointed a director of Keybay Limited to control the fund and ensure the money was used responsibly. In Steve Percy's mind it was his club. He viewed directors and the like with grave suspicion; they must be getting something out of it.

'Who are all these people?' he asked me. At least he knew who I was.

For the record, I did agree with him on one thing. The supporters *are* the most important people, and never more so than at Barnet Football Club in the autumn of '93.

Later that week, I drove Alan Kasmir to the Swallow Hotel to meet with Marc Rowan, Michael Kennedy, Neil Friar, Terry Brady and his son. The meeting was brief and to the point. Terry Brady was businesslike and uncompromising. He didn't see any relevance whatsoever in Marc Rowan's assertion that as a major creditor he had more right to own any part of the club than anyone else. As far as Brady was concerned, he was prepared to put £250 000 into the club on the following terms:

The £250k got him the Flashman majority holding. The survival fund was regarded as a charitable donation.

The creditors, no matter who or how large or small, took their chance of being paid or otherwise. Over that he had no control; he simply made the obvious point that a business still in existence has more chance of giving creditors something than one that has been wound up.

He was not prepared to take into consideration any alleged debt to Flashman at all. I noticed Kasmir raise his eyebrows at that. The Flashman family were listed as creditors, how could he disregard that?

But those were the terms, take them or leave them.

Neither Rowan or Friar had spoken a word and there was no comment from them after Brady had finished. Kennedy, the solicitor, now said his piece. 'I think you're being a little unkind, after all Marc in particular is owed a great deal of money.'

Terry Brady pointed out with a smile that he wasn't a successful businessman because of his kindness.

Fair enough, I thought, you'll always know where you stand with this man.

Then all of them asked my opinion.

I said I had discovered that Marc Rowan had some good friends at the club. Brian Ayres, Gary Phillips and the Police Inspector, Dick Hebberd, who had been the director of security at Underhill. All spoke highly of the builder and held the view that he would be good for Barnet should he take up a position on the board.

On the other hand, Mr Brady's offer to buy the club, while generous, made no provision for the survival fund contributors (something that would become a major issue) and no regard for the Flashman debt. I did not see how that would be acceptable to myself or Stephen Glynne.

Brady made a dismissive comment about Marc's popularity and left with a curt 'take it or leave it' farewell. The four remaining accepted my invitation to dinner and we retired to the Swallow Hotel dining room.

If I was to highlight a period during this episode that was to have the most telling and dramatic effect on what lay ahead, it would be those three or so hours that I spent having dinner with the four men, and my drive home with Alan Kasmir afterwards.

There were now nine days to go before kick-off.

The survival fund was hovering around £100 000. My negotiations with the League and PFA on the transfer embargo had reached agreement. We would pay a lump sum of £70 000 to the players, about half of the figure owed. The balance was to be paid in three instalments, beginning September 1st.

The Football Licensing Authority had finally granted the club a licence, setting the ground capacity at 2600, 800 below our break-even figure. The groundsman, Colin Payne, had worked a miracle on the pitch. Gary Phillips and Roger Thompson had put a squad together, signing seven or eight free transfer players.

Apart from the turmoil going on in and around the boardroom, where the directors of both Barnet FC and Keybay Limited were constantly at loggerheads, things were going well.

During dinner at the Swallow, we were unanimous that Terry Brady was not the man for the club. He was too autocratic and too uncompromising and how could we sell the club to a man who so clearly had no regard for the supporters' efforts?

Marc Rowan then made his offer to Alan Kasmir and me. For the foreseeable future he would commit himself totally to the club. If I was to be there every day, then so would he. I was due to take the family away for a week's holiday in two days' time. Rowan pledged himself to carry on with all the things we were putting in place. He would deal with the other creditors and ensure the club was ready for D-Day versus Hull City.

He would await Stephen Glynne's return and keep an open mind concerning how the ownership of the club would be determined. In return, he asked if I, in my capacity as trustee of the Flashman majority, would sign over an authority that would preserve the status quo until everyone had returned from holiday.

His request was fifty percent of the total shareholding in the club, to be held as his security against a sale to a third party by either Stephen Glynne or myself.

The fact that I saw it as reasonable at the time is an indication of two things. Firstly, I needed someone to continue at Underhill while I was away. Someone who could communicate with Brian Ayres in particular. Until you work at a football club full-time you have no idea of how important the club secretary is. He or she literally runs everything. Football clubs only exist to play matches and arrangements for a home match are the province of the secretary. Without him nothing happens.

Secondly, I believed Rowan. The other side of the man that I had now witnessed was a more attractive proposition than the one I had first seen. He had asked me for a chance to be involved and I gave him it.

I told him I agreed in principle but that it was my duty to consult Stephen Glynne in Florida, and that ultimately he had to give his consent for this to work.

Neil Friar's involvement would be to assist on the commercial front, a position he was happy to take up on a voluntary basis, like the rest of us. We shook hands and agreed to meet the following day.

Kasmir and I drove back to Barnet, going over what had been discussed in great detail. We both agreed that if Marc Rowan was prepared to become so involved, then why not?

The most significant part of the conversation, however, was something Kasmir said that I will never forget. 'I've got a practice to run, I can't devote any more time to the club. I'm not travelling to Blackpool and Scunthorpe, are you? If he wants to, then let him.'

I called Stephen Glynne at his apartment in Fort Lauderdale. He wasn't crazy about the plan. 'Why can't we just wait till I get back?'

I explained that Rowan, while in my opinion very insecure, had a genuine desire to assist in the historic victory we were all approaching. With me in Spain, Glynne in Florida and Kasmir in his office, it was vital we had someone in charge at Underhill. Apart from Brian Ayres' tasks, there were still creditors to deal with, police and security to arrange, programmes to be printed, hospitality for visiting directors and other dignitaries...and more toilet rolls to be ordered.

There was a selfish motive here. I wanted a holiday.

Glynne reluctantly agreed to me signing a share transfer of 5000 shares over to Marc Rowan. He wasn't sure it was legal, but we both hoped it would be a convenient stop-gap.

The following morning I met with Rowan in the tiny office under the main stand. John Skinner was present and witnessed the transfer, at the same time witnessing the agreement that this was a temporary arrangement designed simply to preserve the status quo until both Stephen Glynne and I had returned from holiday.

So the deed was done. It was to make me accountable and open to the severest criticism of my life. In some quarters, subsequently, I was condemned as a fool and/or a devious conniving opportunist in collusion with a rogue builder to hijack the football club.

'Rogue builder and second rate footballer,' we were labelled by the opposition.

I went on holiday to Spain on Saturday, August 7th I gave Brian Ayres, Marc Rowan, Alan Kasmir and Stephen Glynne my telephone number.

'Call me if there are any problems,' I said stupidly.

We had been away barely twenty-four hours when I got the first call. It was Alan Kasmir, complaining about Marc Rowan's language to him. I don't remember, much less care what it was about. 'Marc Rowan has told me to fuck off, I will not tolerate that from anyone, I don't need it,' he complained. I agreed with him and promised to speak to Marc.

His side of the story was that Kasmir was poking his nose in and making life difficult. From where I was listening to this nonsense, they sounded like school children. For the entire week of our holiday I received similar calls. I was seriously pissed off, though Patricia had altogether a more graphic view.

Incredibly, in spite of all this, the mammoth task had been completed and against all the odds, Barnet took the field on Saturday August 14th to play Hull City in division two of the Football League. This achievement should never be underestimated and future owners and supporters should be ever reminded of the debt they owe to those 300 or so contributors to Keybay Limited.

We lost 1-2 but by all accounts the team Gary Phillips had put together acquitted themselves well, having drawn level with a header by new central defender Alan Walker, signed on a free transfer from Mansfield Town. The attendance was just short of capacity. The result was practically immaterial. A task deemed nearly impossible three weeks earlier had been completed successfully against huge odds.

Apart from the fund money, individuals played a magnificent part in this exercise and I have no hesitation in naming them here: Liz Ashfield, Alan Kasmir, Brian Ayres, Gary Phillips, Tony Sharpe (maintenance man) Gordon Ogbourne (kit man) Colin Payne (groundsman), Marc Rowan. All of the aforementioned pulled together in difficult circumstances to ensure that Barnet FC fulfilled their opening fixture in the second division of the Football League on August 14th 1993.

The Second League match of the season was the following Saturday, away at Port Vale, one of the pre-season favourites for promotion. This was interesting for me because Vale had been the scene of my league debut with Watford nearly thirty years before. This was to be the scene of the long awaited meeting between Marc Rowan, Neil Friar and Stephen Glynne.

The day was a disaster. Marc and Stephen did not hit it off and the team lost 6-0.

I travelled back to London with Glynne. At this time we

were getting along fine, there seemed to be mutual respect. He wasn't crazy about Marc Rowan's involvement but stopped short of criticising me over this development during his absence.

I can see very clearly now what my enemies would make of this situation in the future. Stephen Glynne obtains the Flashman shareholding for £1. His brief is to find an investor willing to pay a minimum of £250 000 to buy those shares. He entrusts me with the same brief when taking his family on a summer holiday. As soon as he is out of the way, I transfer 5000 of the 6868 shares to a creditor who then joins me in a battle to own the club. I hope most sincerely that I have explained my side of that story already. In any event, you will make up you own minds.

There was still an urgent need to find an investor. Even Rowan, for all his financial problems, recognised the inescapable fact that as well as rescue, this club needed refinancing. He now knew his original plan of taking over the club was unrealistic, and agreed that we should find the right person. The survival fund peaked at £140 000, still a remarkable achievement inside three weeks. About £80 000 had been used up on the past. Last season's players had been paid part of their back wages and promotion bonuses, with a deal in place for the balance. Gate receipts now the season had started would assist the cash flow, but that was all.

There was a list of creditors apart from Rowan, Friar and Flashman. Most of these, I have to say, had been pretty benign. There was no problem whatsoever at the creditors' meeting and we had heard from no-one except police and security people, who were vital if you were to stage a football match. There had been a provision of £½ million put in under the heading 'Inland Revenue'. Kasmir's view was that this figure could be anything as there was an ongoing investigation into the club's affairs under Flashman. If the rumours of cash payments outside of contract to players were true, then there could be a huge PAYE liability, plus a fine. As yet we had not heard from the Revenue.

The stadium needed urgent safety repairs to enable us to have the capacity raised. The estimate for this alone was over £200 000. Anyone wanting to buy Barnet Football Club for £250 000 at this stage would have to be prepared to lose a further £250 000 in the first year, just to survive.

The figures are easily computed. The wage bill was just over £10 000 per week. Revenue comes in two basic forms: ninety percent of gate receipts for home matches are returned by the club, ten percent go to the FA On an average of 2500 people per home match the receipts would be around £18 000, not enough to break even. The Football League donates about £12 000 per month to a club like Barnet.

From other sources you can receive income on advertising, promotion, sale of souvenirs and lottery (club lottery). There are two other areas that every small club prays for: to sell a player for a lot of money, and to draw a big club in a cup competition.

A small slice of luck came the club's way early on. In the first round of the Coca-Cola Cup we had been drawn against Southend United, managed by Barry Fry. A remarkable 2-0 victory away in the first leg, followed by 1-1 draw at home secured a two-legged tie against Queens Park Rangers from the Premier League.

Gate receipts in cup games are shared by the two participants, forty-five percent each with ten percent to the FA. The QPR tie might produce another £50-75K unexpectedly.

So, with Glynne home and back at work, I found myself running affairs at Underhill on a daily basis with Marc Rowan. On one thing we were all agreed: we needed a millionaire quickly.

Apart from Terry Brady, who had been the only serious possibility, there had been numerous other meetings and discussions with other so-called interested parties. All of these, without exception, had so far been a complete waste of time. When I look back at some of those idiots that we gave credence to, I find it very depressing. I wouldn't tarnish these pages by naming them, but there were a couple of guys who drove me mad for months. When I lost control of the club, I never heard from them again.

I was growing sick of the continuing discord between Rowan and Friar and Glynne and Kasmir. I called a meeting prior to two board meetings due to be held that night.

We met at the West Lodge Park Hotel at 7am on Tuesday 24th August. Present were Stephen Glynne, Marc Rowan, Neil Friar and myself. I told them I felt I had completed my task. I acknowledged my mistakes and apologised for them. I did not apologise for the time I had put in nor did I accept any

186

responsibility for the fact that they could not get on with each other.

My stupid ego received an overwhelming boost from these three guys, none of whom I had ever met or even heard of until a month ago.

Of course they wanted me to stay on. Glynne was going to work every day, as I should have been. He could not leave the club in the hands of these two, who clearly hated his guts.

Rowan and Friar needed me involved because of the promises I had made them. If I went, they would be back to square one, apart from Neil's five grand, of course. Catch 22? If ever I have made myself indispensable, it was then. I promise you, I am not that clever.

Given Dutch courage by their words of support, I seized my chance. 'We have to reach a solution here and now to this problem. If not, I'm out.' I think it was convincing.

After four hours, during which Rowan walked out twice, we had not reached an agreement.

I was still in, obviously it wasn't convincing. What we were trying to agree on was a suitable temporary arrangement with regard to the shares. Stephen Glynne was in a difficult position, I understood that. He was the custodian of the Flashman majority but Rowan had held on to the 5000 shares I had given him. This was his security against a U-turn by either Glynne or myself. What he wanted was some recognition of both the debt owed him and the fact that he, along with Neil Friar and myself, was attending the club daily while Stephen attended his business. We all accepted that until a serious buyer came along, there had to be some kind of arrangement that was fair. The situation wasn't helped by the fact that the three men sitting in front of me hated each other's guts.

At 11.30am we went our separate ways, very depressed. Within twenty minutes, via mobile phones, we finally came to an acceptable solution.

The shareholding would be as follows:

Marc Rowan - 20% and no enforcement of the debt owed to him until such time as the club would be sold to a third party acceptable to all.

Neil Friar - 10% and no enforcement of the debt owed to him until such time as the club would be sold to a third party acceptable to all.

Stephen Glynne - 28% to be held in Trust until such time as a suitable buyer for the club would emerge to purchase the majority shares and be acceptable to all.

Ricky George - 10% in recognition of the work done and to be done.

There were two board meetings held at Underhill that night: Barnet FC and Keybay Limited. Stephen Glynne chaired both, I sat to his right. Also present were Rowan, Friar, Kasmir, Liz Ashfield, Dick Hebberd, (security), Michael Kennedy (solicitor), Steve Percy, Derek Scott, Brian Lowy, George Gilson, John Skinner, and John Motson.

The meetings lasted six hours.

The share agreement was put to the meeting of Barnet FC to be ratified. Those eligible to vote were Stephen Glynne, Alan Kasmir, Ricky George, Marc Rowan, Neil Friar, John Skinner and George Gilson

Kasmir was bitterly opposed to the share division, as was Gilson. The vote was carried four to two and Stephen was congratulated by everyone for sorting it all out – everyone but Kasmir and Gilson. In front of everyone there Marc Rowan tore up his share certificate for 5000 shares. No-one was prepared for what was to come next.

Liz Ashfield was bit of a mystery. Married to Mark Ashfield, but apparently in love with Barnet Football Club, Liz had devoted the last four months of her life to the cause. As secretary of the Supporters Association, she had gone in to assist the club in its fight for survival. When Robert Woolfson and his team came in soon after Flashman's departure, she pledged herself to the new chairman.

After Woolfson's swift exit the next major player to surface was Stephen Glynne. As the front for a group of ten businessmen, Stephen was the next focal point for Liz. He appealed to her in two ways. Firstly, it seemed that Mr Glynne would lead the club to a glorious rescue. Secondly, he paid some attention to her. By that I do not mean anything other than respect for the work she had put in for the good of the club. She was also doing it for nothing.

Liz became Stephen Glynne's devoted servant. On the night of the marathon meetings Liz had sat quietly and made notes of everything that happened.

She did not like Marc Rowan at all. She was opposed to Neil Friar because of Neil's threat to wind up the club, and remember it was Liz who went to Gilbert Brothers. She did not get on with Brian Ayres and they gave each other wide berths most of the time. That night she was in total agreement with Alan Kasmir's view, although as a devotee of Stephen Glynne she couldn't say so.

Although they didn't realise it, a seed was planted that night that was to grow into a bond between Liz, Kasmir and Glynne. That bond was to strengthen and ultimately strangle the flower of knighthood that I thought was my destiny.

At this stage, I think she probably liked me but her loyalty to Stephen would turn her against me in the long run. Hell hath no fury like a woman scorned.

Read on.

The day after the day and night of the marathon meetings and pumped-up egos, Alan Kasmir made his move. In a letter to Stephen Glynne he outlined his disgust at what he considered to be a hijacking of the club. Interestingly, he didn't blame Stephen but singled me out as the prime architect of the whole sordid business. He warned Stephen in the gravest tones about what he felt the chairman had been duped into agreeing to. He was resigning as director, and urged Glynne to rethink what *he* had agreed to.

He also wrote to several newspapers, complaining of the alleged 'hijacking'. *The Barnet Press* printed his letter with one or two libellous omissions.

The campaign had begun and Alan Kasmir would stop at nothing in his determination to turn the world against me, Rowan and Friar.

He had his supporters already. Liz was one and she joined with him in persuading Glynne that he had made the biggest mistake of his life and should declare the share division null and void, claiming back the 6868 shares he had held before his holiday.

Another supporter was George Gilson. This very charming individual had given £15 000 to the survival fund. In return for this very generous sum he had requested a directorship, which I had been happy to give him.

Kasmir enlisted him along with Liz, Steve Percy and Derek Scott, none of whom were happy at this latest turn of events.

I must say deep down inside I felt a little uneasy at accepting any equity. I made myself feel better by reminding myself of the effort I had put in and was continuing to put in.

Then came another twist.

On the Friday evening following I received a telephone call from Kasmir. I remember it very well because I was just about to take Rebecca to the cinema to see the new movie 'Jurassic Park'.

His call was to tell me that Terry Brady had made a firm offer to buy the club. The offer, in writing, was for £100 000, to be distributed amongst creditors and a further £200 000 for players. I thanked him for the information. He then asked me if I had read his letter of resignation; I hadn't. He read out the letter, addressed to Stephen Glynne and dated 26th August. In it he gave his reasons for resigning and commented that he felt Glynne had been placed in a difficult position by my and John Skinner's actions, with regard to the share transfer to Rowan.

Kasmir then went on to say that as I had overspent on the wages budget, it was questionable whether I was fit to take part in the running of the club. I thanked him for reading the letter to me. He then asked me to give up my shareholding in the club and suggested that I persuade Marc Rowan and Neil Friar to do the same. I asked him why he thought I should do this and he replied that if I did, I would be seen as a shining white knight. I said that as he had, only the day before, questioned in writing my competence to take part in the running of the club, his evaluation of my position was inconsistent.

It got worse. He was going to humiliate me publicly. I asked why and he said that he believed I had taken part in a carve-up of the shares, which had been, he felt, my intention all along. He referred to my meeting with Terry Brady on 25th July and explained that Mr Brady was about to tell *The Sun* that at that meeting, I had wanted to know what was in it for me if I sold the club to him. I replied that if Mr Brady wished to defame me in a national newspaper, I would most certainly take legal action against him.

I asked Kasmir to go away and leave me alone.

Later, as I sat in the cinema with my daughter, my thoughts wandered to the man who had threatened me. At that moment, a velociraptor attacked on screen and I jumped out of my skin. In my dreams that night, Alan Kasmir was stalking me with the head of a tyrannosaurus rex.

The following morning, we had yet another board meeting before the home match against Scunthorpe. Present were Glynne, Friar, Rowan, Brian Ayres, George Gilson, John Skinner, Liz Ashfield, Steve Percy and Derek Scott.

I related to them word for word my conversation with Kasmir, then offered to resign immediately from both companies, the football club and Keybay, if any one of them present agreed in any way with Kasmir's actions and, more importantly, his opinion of me.

To be honest, I was becoming heartily sick of the whole business and wondered which one of them would have the courage to agree with him. I was half hoping one of them would.

I received yet another overwhelming vote of confidence – to my face.

As if things were not dramatic enough, the following week there came yet another twist in the tale.

My longtime friend, mentor and supporter, Jeffrey Zemmel, had come into the sportswear business to assist me while I spent every waking moment on Barnet FC. Prior to my involvement with Barnet, we had decided to go after the new market in Eastern Europe. We had travelled to Hungary together, then he had gone to the Ukraine and I to Bucharest, Romania. There was great demand for certain products in the sports and fashion area. On our return, we contacted several famous brands, amongst them Umbro and Timberland.

The big Sports Trade Fair, ISPO, was due to start on Wednesday 1st September in Munich. I absolutely had to be there. That evening, we were due to play Reading away. I absolutely had to there too, so I asked Jeffrey to go on ahead of me and I stayed near Heathrow that night, arriving in Munich the following day. We had our meeting with Umbro in the afternoon and one with Timberland Deutschland on the Friday at midday. In between, there were several other appointments to keep.

The individual from Umbro responsible for the Eastern European market gave a new meaning to the word indifference. His complete lack of interest in anything we had to say stemmed from the fact that he was about to leave the company and start out on a brand new venture. The person taking over from him was not due to begin his duties for another month, and he suggested we contact that person in due course.

That night we dined with an Austrian customer and his

wife. The following morning, we had a breakfast meeting with Barry Smith from Los Angeles, followed by a ten o'clock with two Italians and an hour later we were having coffee with the silver-haired doyen of the European sports goods grey market, Señor Sergio Vedovatti.

The midday meeting with Timberland Deutschland was one I could not attend in view of my previous relationship with their US and UK counterparts. I waited with Vedovatti while Jeffrey sat down with Herr Hans Martin Goetz. The brief background to this particular transaction was that Timberland had accepted an order from our customer in Kiev. Our new Company, not known to Timberland, was to finance the deal, worth £280 000. Our commission was around £42 000. Timberland, as they were dealing with a new customer, had requested $50 000 deposit. This had been sent by us as far back as June. The goods, scheduled for delivery in the first week of September, were due to be shipped from San Juan, Puerto Rico. The balance of the monies was to be paid upon their arrival in Rotterdam.

For the sale of these shoes, we had received a letter of credit which was due to expire at the end of September. Jeffrey's meeting with Goetz was to establish that the goods had been shipped and to collect documents that would enable us to clear the merchandise when the ship docked in Holland. The consignment would then travel overland to Kiev – in time, hopefully, for us to recoup payment under the letter of credit.

He returned all too soon and the look on his face spoke volumes.

Goetz, by all accounts, was an unfriendly and suspicious individual. He had stopped the shipment and changed the terms of the contract without reference to anyone, particularly Jeffrey Zemmel. He now insisted on Timberland shipping the goods directly to our customer in the Ukraine. This was out of the question. No-one would ever agree to that. Jeffrey told Goetz he thought this move, at the eleventh hour and when he had held our deposit for nearly three months, was outrageous.

Goetz, tall and thin with cropped hair, gazed down contemptuously at the portly figure standing before him. He took a long drag of his cigarette and, blowing the smoke directly in my friend's face, said, 'They are my terms, take it or leave it.'

Jeffrey kept his cool and told him in no uncertain terms we would sue him.

'At Timberland we have long pockets,' came the unforgettable reply.

We left the Trade Fair and took a taxi to the airport. We were both worried and depressed. I was taking a Lufthansa flight to Manchester to meet up with the team at their Preston hotel before the following day's match at Blackpool. Jeffrey was flying back to Heathrow.

As we walked silently through the terminal he suddenly stopped, put his case down and held his chest. The look of concern on both our faces was evidence of the fact that there could be a big problem here. I begged him to consult his doctor immediately he returned. Ten days later, he had a double heart by-pass operation.

We could not blame Hans-Martin Goetz for Jeffrey's heart problem; clearly that had been coming for a long while. We could even thank him in a bizarre way for exacerbating the problem and creating the warning that possibly saved Jeffrey's life. Herr Goetz is not, however, on the corporate Christmas card list.

For the time being, then, I had no partner and no business to speak of. And I still had Alan Kasmir to deal with.

This, as I was to discover, was only the beginning of his campaign. He addressed the Supporters Association and played out a charade to discredit me further that was so fantastic, even now I find it hard to believe.

One of the time-wasters who had contacted me about buying the club was Steve Wicks, an ex-player at QPR, Chelsea and Derby. Initially, he spoke to Glynne at his London office and Glynne told him to phone me at the club. I invited him to come to Underhill.

Wicks' proposal was basically a red herring to get himself the manager's job. He said he had a friend who was willing to put £½ million into the club with the proviso that he, Wicks, became manager. To me it was simple, and I told him that if his friend wished to buy the club he could then appoint whoever he wished as manager. If he wanted to pursue the matter I would be happy to meet his friend.

As with so many other potential 'buyers', I assumed that would be the last I would hear from Steve Wicks. I was right, he went back to Glynne. His proposal remained the same, except he suggested to Glynne that his friend would only put in the money once he (Wicks) was installed as manager. Stephen Glynne telephoned me to say he thought that was a fair offer. I told him that as far as I was concerned, Gary Phillips was manager of Barnet while the present situation existed. How could you give a man somebody else's job on the basis that his backer might then decide to invest? I didn't even consider it worth further conversation. I put the phone down on Glynne and forgot about Steve Wicks.

Mr Wicks then met with Glynne and, surprise, surprise, Alan Kasmir. He complained that I had rejected his offer, and Kasmir saw a golden chance to use this scenario against me.

The Supporters Association met on Thursday nights. Kasmir requested the opportunity to address them. He told them that he would prove I had no intention of selling the club to anyone. With the assistance of Steve Percy he got Wicks on the telephone. He then asked Wicks to tell Percy that I had turned down an offer of £½ million, which Wicks, of course, confirmed. Even some very old friends began to turn against me.

While Kasmir's campaign gathered momentum, I continued to attend the club daily. I had been neglecting my business badly. On Thursday 23rd September I left home to drive to Heathrow. I was due to make a hurried trip to Glasgow to meet some customers and en route along the M25 as usual, I took a call from Brian Ayres. It was 9.15 and there was no mail at the club. He had telephoned the local sorting office and was told that the mail had been redirected to Connaught Road, Barnet, the home of Liz Ashfield.

At the M4, I turned around and went straight back to Underhill.

Liz had not been quite so visible at the club recently. There was a great deal of friction between her and Brian Ayres, they didn't get on at all. What I hadn't guessed was that Stephen Glynne, marooned in his London office, had been using Liz to report back to him on every little thing. The obsessed Kasmir had finally convinced him that, having hijacked the club, we were robbing it as well.

Glynne, prompted by Kasmir, had used the poor girl to do their dirty work. She had been instructed to redirect all Glynne's personal mail to her home but the sorting office cocked it up and redirected everything!

Ayres, Rowan and Friar stood in the tiny office under the stand and demanded swift action. I called Glynne and asked him to confirm that he had indeed instructed Liz to redirect mail. He protested it was only his mail. There was no explanation but what we all knew was that any semblance of trust was now gone. It was time for decisions.

The situation, always difficult, was now intolerable.

I had tried to do the impossible: bring together a group of people who neither liked or trusted each other. For whatever reason, Marc Rowan and Neil Friar were at the club every day working for nothing. Stephen Glynne was attending his office every day, looking after his business. Nothing wrong with that, but having been more than happy to leave me in charge he should then have let me get on with it. He had succumbed to the bitter representations of the dangerous Kasmir and tried to play both ends against the middle, using Liz as his eyes and ears.

I called an emergency board meeting and invited Glynne and Liz to attend. He declined and, via an exchange of faxes, resigned as chairman, wishing me luck in carrying the club forward.

Sadly, Liz Ashfield had to go. All the good work she had done had now been swamped by a tide of bitterness and recriminations. The dismissal of Liz Ashfield was another stepping stone for Kasmir and Glynne in their ferocious desire to ruin my reputation.

We were away to Wrexham that weekend. I took Pat and Rebecca to North Wales for two nights and we spent the weekend with an old friend, Richard Bernard, whose nephew, Wayne Phillips played in midfield for Wrexham.

The team lost 0-4 in a dismal performance. We had played five league matches and were bottom of the league without a point.

As I was to learn, Keybay Limited held a board meeting at Liz Ashfield's home on the Sunday morning. In a tit-for-tat measure, I was dismissed as a director of Keybay along with John Skinner. Another measure adopted by the majority of the Keybay Board was the withholding of the remainder of the survival fund money, some £50 000.

I was advised of this by a letter which arrived at my home on the Tuesday morning. John Skinner and I were also removed from the bank mandate of which we were both signatories and Kasmir and Derek Scott appointed in our place.

In a dramatic move, they had taken away all the funding available, leaving us without any money or bank account.

This response to her dismissal and the forced resignation of Glynne was only the start of Liz's fury. A banner headline appeared on the back page of the *Barnet Press*: 'Barnet FC Stalwart Liz Sacked'. It then went on to describe how those now running the club had adopted a 'hard nose' policy. The publicity was damaging and, I repeat, unfair. Graham White, the sports editor and author of the article, made no attempt to contact me for a response. All along, since the Kasmir campaign began, I was advised to keep a low profile. Angry responses and tit-for-tat articles in the press would not be the way to handle this. I kept a dignified silence, but it was a bit like getting kicked every time I got the ball, having a referee let everything go, and not once retaliating. I was beginning to doubt the wisdom of this advice.

One of the ironies of this bizarre situation was that two of our closest personal friends had known Stephen Glynne and his wife socially. For some time they had been trying to arrange for all of us to have dinner. This date was set for Friday (after the supporters' club meeting) and ten of us sat down to eat at the Villa Rosa Restaurant in Brookmans Park: Patricia and me, Stephen and his wife Sukie, Dave and Tish Hannington, Jan and Nelson Moody and Steve and Anneke Mangion. It was an enjoyable evening and the situation at the football club was not mentioned.

The following morning I received a letter from Keybay Limited. It was a circular to all survival fund investors advising of the meeting to be held at a local primary school to debate the actions of the people currently running the football club. The letter made some very forceful comments concerning individuals and I was singled out for particular criticism. The point of the meeting was for the survival fund contributors to decide who should be running the club. There was absolutely no precedent to such a situation, but in spite of the attack on myself, I could see the point of the idea. After all, the club had survived because of the fifties, hundreds, five hundreds and thousands of pounds that around 300 people had contributed. There had been no meeting of those people to hear what they thought of it all. The unfairness, from my point of view, was that everyone who received a letter had been given the case for the prosecution and not for the defence.

After our dinner the previous night, I had arranged to meet Stephen Glynne on the Saturday morning at Barnet Cricket

Club, where his youngest son was playing in an under-elevens football match for Barnet Youth. I took the letter with me and showed it to him. He read it as if he had not seen it before, saying he knew about the meeting but not the contents of the letter. I pointed out that as he was a director of Keybay Limited he must have known, but he insisted that the letter came from the secretary, Liz Ashfield. 'She's very bitter you know, you should understand that, Ricky.'

It was a bad weekend for me. We were due to play Cardiff City on the Sunday at Underhill. I had taken complimentary tickets for the game to the Barnet Youth matches and distributed them. I did the same on the Sunday morning and arrived at Underhill around 12.30 pm. Big Dusty Rhodes, a major supporter who ran the club shop, told me about the Kasmir/Steve Wicks/Steve Percy charade enacted on the Thursday night for the benefit of the Supporters Association. 'He speaks very well, he was very convincing,' said Dusty of Kasmir. I was angry and depressed but could do nothing.

The club was approaching an unwanted record of six successive defeats. The crowd was near to capacity of 2800 and a new character in the drama took his seat in the directors' box next to me. My next door neighbour and friend, Bedros Kazandjian, was not a football man but the story had fired his imagination. We had several meetings about the financial input required. He certainly had the money, many times over, and this seemed to be a possibility, so I invited him to the Cardiff match.

At the end of the nil-nil draw, the crowd saluted the team as if they had just won the FA Cup and the players walked off to thunderous applause. Bedros was totally confused; he looked at me in panic as if he had missed something, like a goal. I explained that this was the team's first point of the season and that the supporters' reaction was typical of them. They had been fantastic through each defeat, understanding the difficulty of Gary Phillips' task and never resorting to the abuse that football supporters can dispense so readily.

I seized my chance with Bedros. 'You must be a lucky mascot.'

He smiled, delighted with what he had just witnessed and understanding immediately the significance. 'Can I meet the players?' he asked.

I took him into a steamy, happy dressing room. He looked

the part. Big cigar, expensive camel-hair overcoat. I introduced him to the player-manager as a possible new owner of the club. Gary called for quiet and Bedros went around the room, shaking hands with each player.

Here was a golden opportunity to solve everyone's problems. I invited him to travel with me to Huddersfield the following Saturday. Incredibly, the team recorded their first win in division two and on this occasion Bedros was lifted off his feet by a jubilant Gary Phillips as we entered the visitors' dressing room at the Old Leeds Road Stadium.

On the journey back from Huddersfield Bedros put a proposition to me. He was prepared to put in an initial £150 000 to secure a major shareholding in the club. He wanted me to put up a minimum of £50 000 so that between us we would hold the majority shareholding.

I put the scenario to Rowan and Friar. They were happy with Bedros and I was so involved in the thing that I could think of nothing else. Bedros wanted to be chairman but wanted me to run the club.

Even though on the surface a financial backer such as Bedros Kazandjian, plus my continued involvement and Jeffrey's help in the business, seemed to be a solution, I still had to face the Keybay-instigated survival fund meeting. My friend and business partner was now recovering from his by-pass operation.

The meeting was scheduled for a Monday evening at Trent Park Primary School in Cockfosters. On the Sunday before, I received a phone call from Alan Kasmir requesting an urgent meeting. At 7am the following day I met him and Stephen Glynne at Glynne's house in Finchley. The meeting was an attempt by the two of them to reach an agreement with me before the meeting that night.

This was clearly a forewarning that they were going to crucify me publicly and were giving me a chance to avoid the humiliation they were certain I would endure.

In the wake of the Keybay decisions to dismiss me and withhold the remaining £52 000 of the survival fund, I had been forced to open a new bank account for the club at Barclays in Whetstone. Gate receipts were now banked at Barclays, but the loss of the £52 000 was a bitter blow. There was still a schedule of payments to be made to the PFA and the players. The club was back in danger so soon after the heroic rescue act, and it was all due to the egos and hurt feelings of the very people who had worked so hard to perform the rescue.

Glynne, Kasmir and the others clearly felt that they could now manoeuvre themselves back into control of the club. The meeting of the survival fund investors was to obtain the endorsement of those good people for the actions Keybay's officers had taken. Slaughtering Marc Rowan, Neil Friar and me was one sure way of getting what they wanted.

What Glynne and Kasmir asked me to do was relinquish control of the finances of the club and to allow the receipts to be deposited once more at the Keybay Bank. I refused but told them quite openly that I had a backer, finally, in the shape of Bedros Kazandjian. As the pair of them stared blankly at me, I asked if either of them had found an alternative to what I now proposed. There was no-one.

The meeting was a complete farce, although it lasted three hours. Several agreements were reached but never adhered to. Kasmir chose to tell the 300 or so gathered that I was planning to sell the club to myself, cleverly rearranging the information I had imparted to him and Glynne earlier in the day.

At some point in the marathon, a man called Tony Thornton stood up and offered to form a steering committee which would include Stephen Glynne and myself. His role was to be one of mediation, an independent arbitrator.

There were two principal agreements voted on by the audience. The first was for the £52 000 held by Keybay to be returned to the football club immediately. The second and equally important agreement reached was between Stephen Glynne, Marc Rowan, Neil Friar and me. This was that the disputed 6868 shares in the club would be placed in the care of a neutral solicitor. They would then be available to any investor willing to inject a six-figure sum into the club. The following day Glynne contacted Andrew Gilbert, a lawyer who was also a supporter of the club, and asked him to draw up an agreement, whereby Glynne would grant me an option to dispose of the 6868 shares to an investor prepared to meet the conditional six-figure sum. The agreement was faxed to each party's solicitor for approval.

On 22nd October, I received a fax from Glynne withdrawing his agreement to everything.

The steering committee met just once. Thornton asked me to make all kinds of concessions, including restoring Alan

Kasmir to the main board. The main question I posed to Stephen Glynne was when were Keybay going to pass over the £52 000 that the survival fund contributors had voted for at the meeting?

It never happened and the 'independent arbitrator', Mr Thornton, departed as swiftly as he had come.

Interestingly, I discovered later that, far from being impartial, Tony Thornton was in fact a friend of Kasmir and the steering committee idea was a plan worked out some days before the meeting.

In July 1994, Tony Thornton published a book called *The Club That Wouldn't Die*. It was a record of Barnet Football Club's triumphs and troubles during the Flashman era. Curiously, I received no credit for my role in the club's survival. On the contrary, I was roundly criticised for challenging David Buchler (later in the story) in what Thornton described as a 'cynical move'. It didn't read very impartial to me.

Now things were critical again. I could not get Bedros in without Glynne's agreement and the club were heading for more serious cash-flow problems.

But then the team's fortunes took a turn for the better and progress was made to the second round of the FA Cup.

I was now in constant contact with my own solicitors and the days grew even longer. We obtained the statutory books of the company which showed an amount of shares, as yet unissued. To issue these shares we needed approval from the existing shareholders. As complicated as things were, the division of shares as at the August 24th board meeting was the position I was advised to adopt when calculating what we would need for a majority.

To implement any or all of what we were trying to achieve we needed to call an AGM. Statutory notices advising of the AGM were sent out fourteen days prior to the date set, November 26th, 1993.

Around this time, I received a fax from Alan Kasmir. He told me he had spoken to a man who wanted to buy the club immediately. He was very wealthy, high profile and had previously been a director of Tottenham Hotspur. He was prepared to pay the sum required for the majority shareholding. Mr Kasmir added that if I refused to meet this man he would write to the *Barnet Press*. I actually had to smile at that. Here was a man who had resigned weeks ago, sent formal demand to Keybay for the return of his £1000, embarked on a vicious campaign to discredit me, but continued to work tirelessly to find someone other than me or anyone to do with me to take over the club.

I called him and said if he would kindly give me the name of the gentleman I would certainly call him. He offered to make the appointment in his (Kasmir's) office. I declined this offer and asked again for the gentleman's name and details. After a pause, I was given the name of David Buchler and a telephone number,

David Julian Buchler is a partner in the firm of licensed insolvency practitioners, Buchler-Phillips. The firm is very high profile, having administered part of the Maxwell Estate. David Buchler was also involved in the restructuring of the finances of Tottenham Hotspur PLC and was indeed a director for a short period prior to the arrival of Alan Sugar.

We met at his Grosvenor Street offices on 3rd November. He was courteous and businesslike, but just a little unprepared for my visit, explaining that he had only just been made aware of the situation by Alan Kasmir.

Confirming his interest in Barnet Football Club, Buchler made it quite clear that he would not be putting any money in initially. His intention would be to take complete control of the club before any injection of funds. Once in control, Mr Buchler would have funds available as and when they were needed. I told him that I could not accept his proposal as there was already someone prepared to pay for control of the club.

Before I left, he said something to me which, if I had been more attuned to his way of thinking or he had chosen to be more forthcoming, could have saved us all a great deal of time and money

I had been told by the Football League that under no circumstances would they accept a liquidation or any formal arrangement with creditors. That had been the suggestion my own accountants had made on day one. As I was leaving his office, Buchler mentioned CVA, Corporate Voluntary Arrangement. I told him it wasn't possible. He looked at me and smiled.

Looking back, it was so obvious that, as an insolvency expert, Buchler would put the club into administration. He wasn't interested in buying it, or being the fairy godfather we had all been waiting for. Had he told me that was his intention or had I been bright enough to have realised it, a lot of heartache could have been avoided.

I wrote to David Buchler on 15th November to ask him to put any offer he wished to make for the club in writing. That same day, he phoned me to inform me that on November 11th Stephen Glynne had signed over 6868 shares to him and that as he now owned the club, he wished to take control. I asked him if there had been any financial consideration for the shares and he confirmed that there had not.

Our solicitors now took over and we were advised to revert to the 5000 share transfer to Rowan in August. Marc Rowan and I were now at war with the powerful David Buchler. On 16th November, John Bailey, the solicitor specialising in company law, wrote up the statutory books. On the same day, upon advice, Marc Rowan transferred 2500 shares to my name.

The AGM had been called for the 26th November. Notice was also given of an EGM (extraordinary general meeting) to be held at the same time to seek approval from the shareholders to issue 39 000 unissued shares in the club.

On the afternoon of 26th November, Stephen Glynne was granted an injunction in the High Court preventing the AGM and the EGM from going ahead. On the night of the long-awaited AGM, Stephen Glynne and others arrived at Underhill and distributed copies of the injunction, which prevented the club holding any meetings until the share dispute was resolved at trial.

A disappointed and dejected group of shareholders, some shaking their heads in utter bewilderment, drifted away into the night. But there were lots of other people at Underhill that night, including David Buchler and a very famous ex-player, Arsenal and Eire International Liam Brady. The Kasmir/Glynne machine had been at work again and a meeting of the Supporters Association had been called for the same evening. Incredibly, at this meeting David Buchler was to be introduced to the supporters as the new owner of the club and, even more incredibly, Liam Brady was to be presented as the man who would become the new manager.

If you can remember that, under Gary Phillips' managership, the club had progressed to the second round of the FA Cup, it was a totally bizarre move by the protagonists to suddenly introduce a new manager. In the event, Brady was never seen again at Underhill.

202

None of this nonsense did anything to deter me, in fact it made me even more determined to ensure that these people would not succeed.

Once again, urgent calls were made to solicitors. We were now seeking advice on the injunction. It was *ex parte*, of course, so the court had only heard one side. Our solicitors were supremely confident that the injunction would be lifted once the judge had heard of the club's parlous financial state. After all, here we were trying to inject money into the club and Stephen Glynne was laying claim to the shares on David Buchler's behalf but with no promise of any money at all.

The second round cup-tie, away at Crawley, was won in stylish fashion and the team's reward was a home tie against one of the country's most famous clubs, Chelsea, then managed by Glen Hoddle, whose brother Carl had scored a tremendous goal in the second round victory.

Upon police advice the game against Chelsea, due to be played on January 8th, was switched to Stamford Bridge. Gate receipts would be shared as it was a cup-tie and we estimated that the club might benefit to the tune of £100 000.

One of the first things I did upon becoming acting chairman at Barnet was to offer the late Lester Finch the life presidency of the club. Lester had been Barnet's greatest ever amateur player, and had made over a hundred representative appearances for England, Great Britain (1936 Olympics) and the Football Association as an amateur. In 1941, he played for the full England team in a wartime International against Wales at Cardiff. In 1946, Lester Finch captained Barnet in their first ever FA Amateur Cup final and led them to a 3-2 win over the mighty Bishop Auckland at Stamford Bridge. This game was watched by 53 802 spectators. Two years later they were back at the Bridge, this time to lose 0-1 to Leytonstone in front of nearly 60 000.

This was a golden period for the club and Lester Finch's name will be forever associated with the elevation of Barnet Football Club to the pinnacle of amateur football.

I had known Lester well for many years. His enthusiasm for cricket equalled his passion for football and he was greatly admired by many Barnet folk. I decided to mark the cup tie at Stamford Bridge by inviting him and as many of his former team mates as we could find to the big match. This was, after all, the first time a Barnet team had played at the Bridge since the '48 final.

We managed to find eight players from the two finals and there was a tear in Lester's eye as they all met up again, nearly fifty years on.

This gesture turned out to be one of my last as acting chairman.

Before all that, however, Jeffrey Zemmel returned to action in time to sit alongside me once more in yet another courtroom.

On December 16th 1993, Mr Justice Evans Lombe turned back the hands of time and returned us all to 25th July 1993, the day Stephen Glynne went on holiday.

I won't bore you with the details of the hearing, suffice to say it was a complete fiasco from our point of view. My solicitors had engaged a bumbling fool as counsel and the court was treated to some theatrical performances from the other side. At one point, proceedings were interrupted by an excited Alan Kasmir rushing into court brandishing a banker's draft for £100 000. The judge didn't even look at it. Our stupid barrister didn't even have the wit to ask who it was in favour of, and it was never seen again, ever.

I have never understood the order that the judge made. I still don't. Our application was simply to ask the court to lift an injunction. Either he would or he wouldn't.

I asked my solicitor several times prior to the hearing what the worst-case scenario was. His answer was always the same: 'The judge would refuse the application and the injunction would remain until trial, when the share dispute would be decided once and for all.'

A refusal would be a blow as it meant the loss of a potential investor. But we would still have control of the club and although cash was desperately needed, we had Chelsea coming up on January 8th.

Mr Justice Evans-Lombe decided otherwise. He didn't rule on the question he had been asked. He ruled on something that had nothing to do with him. The immediate reaction from our flustered and totally inept barrister was to appeal. He had no explanation for the judge's actions, so to me and my colleagues he remained as useless as he had been in the courtroom.

Standing behind the barrister was a very sheepish solicitor. For the first time I let my anger show. 'How many times did I ask you if this could happen?' I turned on him. Like the brief, he had no answer.

So there we stood outside the courtroom, like complete fools. Marc Rowan and Jeffrey Zemmel were with me and as we stood contemplating God knows what, the solicitor came as close as anyone had during this entire business to receiving a right-hander from me. He asked me for a cheque for £12 000, there and then, no longer than ten minutes after I had heard that the last four months of my life had been a complete waste of time and money.

Jeffrey had a quiet word with him while Marc calmed me down. Mind you, it was me who had to calm Marc moments later as Alan Kasmir passed by in triumph.

The only people in court for the 'other side' were Kasmir and Liz Ashfield, still campaigning tirelessly for Stephen Glynne and now for David Buchler.

The three of us walked up the Strand to the Waldorf Astoria Hotel and, still in a state of shock, sat in the cocktail lounge and sank a few vodkas while the events of the day sunk in. The hearing had lasted two days and absolutely no-one had legislated for this scenario. After an hour or so, I suddenly realised that the club now no longer had anyone at the helm. It was a Thursday, and the following day the team were due to leave for an away fixture at Hull City. The wages needed to be paid and a million other things needed to be attended to.

I called Michael Robin from the hotel phone. Michael is my solicitor, although not the one that acted for me in this matter. To his credit, he had advised me from day one not to go forward with the share dispute. He correctly predicted it would end in misery, but knew I was on a crusade. With the best of intentions, he decided his fees would be too great, so a lesser light in the firm was engaged.

Michael, of course, knew of the outcome and also of the unfortunate incident outside the court. He was furious that one of his colleagues should have been so insensitive and for the moment the subject of the £12 000 was put to one side. Good friend that he is, he was sensitive and sympathetic. He had spoken to the other side's solicitors, and they were all as surprised as we were at the judge's ruling.

However, the ruling meant that Stephen Glynne was once again the custodian of 6868 shares in Barnet Football Club until trial, when the whole matter would be determined. As Glynne had promised the shares to Buchler, it was he who now had control of the club.

There was a request via Michael Robin for me to contact Buchler. I was now composed and clear-headed in spite of the vodkas and realised I had one more duty to perform at Underhill.

I phoned Buchler and we had a polite conversation, during which he expressed his surprise at the ruling. I mumbled something about the referee's decision being final and arranged to meet him at nine the following morning.

At the appointed hour two other men joined us. I had never met or heard of either. One was introduced as Colonel Brian Williams and the other as a Mr Fenton Higgins. Buchler explained that they had come in to help him take over.

For the next three or four hours, with the help of secretary Brian Ayres, we went through in fine detail every aspect of the day-to-day running of the club.

At around midday, the entire playing staff and non-playing personnel were gathered in the boardroom. I addressed them briefly and introduced them to their new boss. The team left for Hull, but not before the captain, Brian Marwood said a few complimentary words and each of them shook my hand. This was the worst of it for me, by a long way. The squad that Gary Phillips had put together had been magnificent in the worst possible circumstances. With Terry Bullivant and Roger Thompson coaching and Brian Marwood's influence on the pitch, they had suddenly hit form. Bearing in mind Phillips had only six players on the day I walked into Underhill, his performance in signing free transfer players and creating the tremendous team spirit that existed now deserves great respect.

I had completed my task but before I left, David Buchler asked me to relinquish any claim I might still have with regard to shares. I told him if he was prepared to reimburse me the money Jeffrey and I had injected into the club while Keybay withheld the survival fund, I would consider it. He told me that he was a fair man and would act fairly. I told him I did not understand why he was so keen to own this tiny football club. He asked why I was so keen. I told him.

It was flattering in a sick way. They clearly thought I was devious, rather than simply an 'I love my club' ex-footballer. As stupid as it sounds, the latter is exactly what I was. Having fought so hard against people whose motives I never understood, I had pressed on, trying to find the right person to take over this famous little club. Bedros was a businessman and he knew there could be no profit in running a club like

Barnet. The aim is always to break even and if you can get anywhere near doing that, you have done well. Also, Bedros knew me very well and realised that my continued involvement could be of benefit to the club in some capacity.

In contrast, I never understood why Glynne and Kasmir were so involved in the first place. Neither had anything in their background to link them with the club. Glynne originally headed the ten-man consortium that sought to buy the club in June. But that was purely a business deal. The squad of players from the '92-'93 season had been valued at close to £1 million. One player, Gary Bull, was rumoured to be worth £½ million on his own. The consortium were prepared to put up £250 000 to pay the players' back wages. It would then have taken a charge in the form of a debenture over the club's assets. The only assets of Barnet Football Club were its players. Effectively, for £250 000 the consortium would then own assets of £1 million. With the sale of one player they would have shown 100 percent profit on their investment. The Football League's draconian attempt to get rid of the club by imposing two £250 000 bonds scuppered the consortium's plan. Nine disappeared without trace; for some reason Glynne didn't.

Stephen Glynne was never a supporter of Barnet Football Club. He is an Arsenal season ticket holder and has been for some years. When it seemed likely that the football club would go into liquidation and a new club would begin again in Diadora Three, he made no secret of the fact that he would not be interested in the club outside the Football League. Therein, in my opinion, lay the answer. When he arrived to head the consortium, he was welcomed as a messiah by some of the staff at Underhill. He acted as chairman for a while because there was no-one else. This entry into the world of professional football, and the kudos that went with it, appealed to his ego. In the anonymous backwater of the Diadora League there would be no kudos. It certainly would not be worth sacrificing seats in the North Bank at Highbury.

After the consortium fell apart, I don't think he realistically felt there could be a profit made at Barnet, although when asked if he would have stayed at the club if it lost its league status, he replied, 'No, because it wouldn't be viable.' Viability obviously comes in different forms.

Alan Kasmir had been a recent supporter of Barnet Football

Club. Living in North Finchley and not having a season ticket at Highbury, he was one of many new supporters who came along when the club gained promotion to the Football League. When he had first introduced himself to us before the survival fund meeting at Underhill on 22nd July, he told Glynne and myself he could raise £½ million on a rights issue. In all the time he involved himself the £½ million was never mentioned again. So what was his motive? A genuine desire to help the club, although a little misguided at times, would be the charitable answer. A pain in the backside busybody with a bitter and twisted side to a worrying character prone to acts of irrationality would be the uncharitable view. It think it is somewhere in between the two. He certainly could not have been in it for profit; he's an accountant and knows insolvency when he sees it. At the infamous board meeting of the 24th August he was heard to mutter when Glynne read out the share division, 'What has Ricky George got shares for, why haven't I got shares?'

My final opinion is that he had good intentions but behaved like a petulant schoolboy because he was excluded from a share of what amounted to nothing.

David Buchler was altogether a different matter. He was cleverer than all of us, including his so-called colleagues, Glynne and Kasmir. His motive was purely business. He is by profession a licensed insolvency practitioner. He calls himself a company doctor and he is good at what he does. Of course he was not going to pay for any shares. What he would have liked ideally would have been for a director to appoint him as administrator. He would then get full control of the business. What he got from Glynne was nearly as good so with Glynne doing anything he was asked to do, Buchler became chairman. Why become chairman? The club was due to play Chelsea in a high profile FA Cup tie. The Buchler public relations team saw this as good PR for him. It got his name in the newspapers and in one fell swoop he became the new saviour of Barnet Football Club. In his zeal to grab as much publicity as possible he tried desperately to link himself to a famous football name. Hence the attempt to bring Liam Brady into the fold, ignoring the presence of the manager who had fashioned a team out of nothing against the non-existent track record of the Irishman.

Ultimately, and I found this move the most distasteful of

all, on the day Gary Phillips' team held Glenn Hoddles' premier side to a nil-nil draw at Stamford Bridge, Buchler announced the appointment of former England Goalkeeper Ray Clemence as the new manager. Instead of the Sunday papers praising Phillips and his team, Clemence and Buchler took the plaudits for the amazing result.

David Buchler did not become involved in Barnet because of a genuine sympathy for the plight of the club and its loyal supporters. By taking over at Barnet on 17th December 1993, he was breaking two rules that both the Football Association and Football League had recently introduced.

As a result of the late Robert Maxwell's attempt to own more than one football club at once, the two ancient institutions had decreed that no person or member of the same family could hold shares in or control more than one club. When David Buchler took charge of Barnet Football Club he was still the administrator of Wealdstone Football Club. To show how much he cared for the supporters of Wealdstone, he had sold their stadium in Harrow to Tesco, leaving an old and much respected club with no stadium.

When I spoke to the Football League regarding the financial plight of Barnet FC I was told in no uncertain terms that liquidation or any formal arrangements with creditors would mean loss of league status.

David Buchler's expertise is dealing with insolvent companies. To deal with the creditors he appointed David Rubin, a local accountant, to instigate a CVA (Corporate Voluntary Arrangement). The CVA offered the creditors 10p in the pound to be paid sometime in the next three years, conditional upon several things, including the successful resolution of the share dispute. The acceptance of the CVA by the creditors meant, of course, that the debts were crystallised in one fell swoop. It is as near as you can get to flushing the old company down the loo and starting again with a brand new one. It is a wonderful way of dealing with an insolvent company.

The joke about this particular situation is that it was the first thing my own accountant suggested to me on day one. As I have said, when I phoned the Football League to suggest this, I was met with a firm and absolute refusal. They even sent me a copy of the rule stating the fact.

For David Rubin to get approval from the creditors to

implement the arrangement, he needed the majority to vote for it. The majority, measured in money, was to include some interesting names.

The day after Justice Evans-Lombe's infamous decision, even as I sat patiently giving the Colonel and Mr Higgins the information they needed, the remaining £52 000 of the survival fund was released to David Buchler.

When the creditors' list was published, Keybay Limited (the survival fund) was high up there with £140 000, as were the Football League, the players, the Flashman family and the Inland Revenue.

The reason I make these points is to highlight once more the behaviour of the Football League. They actually publish a rule then actively support the breaking of it. Incredibly, in 1992 a premier football club actually went into liquidation with debts of £2 million. The League and the FA allowed it to happen right under their noses. That club today is worth several hundred million.

The other significant aspect of the CVA is the appearance of Keybay Limited. The £140 000 was, of course, the survival fund, put up by the supporters. For some time, members of the Keybay board had been lobbying for recognition in the form of a shareholding that would reflect what they had done to keep the club alive. In fact without the survival fund the club would never have kicked a ball in that '93-'94 season. Now those same Keybay directors were going to vote acceptance of the CVA proposal of 10p in the pound sometime in the future.

David Buchler, by courtesy of Kasmir, Glynne, Ashfield and others used the £52 000 as his start-up fund when taking over. He never had to spend a penny of his own money. You may remember that the players from the previous season were due another payment via the PFA. One of Mr Higgins' first tasks was to write to the PFA and other creditors, stating that an injunction prevented the club making any payments to anyone for the time being. It was clever but untrue.

So Buchler's plan was to implement the CVA, thereby crystallising the debts.

Having established that the Football League would not now oppose it, a creditors' meeting to advise them of the intentions of the new board was called.

Between December 17th and the first creditors' meeting

in January, I had several conversations with David Buchler. His manner went from amicable to threatening when he discovered that I was not going to lie down and accept the inevitable. I was still receiving advice from all quarters and stupidly my ego forced me to continue down a road that lead to nowhere.

The outrage of those on my side of the fence at the way Glynne and Kasmir had manipulated David Buchler into the position he now enjoyed became the prime motivation behind the challenge I now mounted to regain control of Barnet Football Club.

'Mad', 'foolish' and 'cynical' were just three of the adjectives used to describe the path I took to convince the world of the gross unfairness I had suffered. Mad and foolish I would agree with now; cynical I most certainly was not.

During the creditors' meeting in January, the 'independent' Mr Rubin, administrator of the CVA, offered the creditors 10p in the pound dependent upon a successful resolution of the share dispute. Successful resolution in this instance meant a win for the Glynne/Buchler team. With the assistance of another firm of accountants from Manchester, I challenged the offer, countering with a much larger one that was not conditional.

The meeting was adjourned for two weeks while both sides regrouped. Backed with Bedros' funds still available, plus a further £350 000 from a third party who wished to remain anonymous, I returned two weeks later with the firm proposal of 25p in the pound and 100p in the pound for the Inland Revenue, who up until then had remained very quiet.

Meticulously prepared and briefed, the opposition now proceeded to character assassinate me before a packed clubhouse, the very building whose construction and non-payment of lay at the heart of so much of this mess. Stephen Glynne referred to the fact that I had been director of two companies that had gone into liquidation. He now openly accused me of abusing the power of attorney he had signed back in July. I was labelled at best a 'chancer', at worst, a devious and cynical individual bent on personal gain. In the 'audience' on this occasion were a couple of 'plants' – friends of David Buchler, representing tiny and almost forgotten creditors.

One of them, a Mr Snook, an employee of the giant firm of

Touche Ross, took the opportunity to assist Buchler by standing up and attacking the credibility of my offer, citing the fact that I would not divulge the identity of my third party backer. He then went on to tell the gathering that as far as he could see there was only one person who had put any money into Barnet Football Club and that was David Buchler. I was able to score my only point of the day by asking Mr Buchler to tell everyone just how much he had put in so far. The answer of course was nothing.

Ultimately a vote was taken and unsurprisingly, the majority went for Buchler's deal, undoubtedly on the grounds that he did have the funds available to pay the 10p in the pound and we had not been able to convince them that if they accepted our higher offer, we would indeed be in a position to respect it.

It remained to be seen which way the Revenue would go and after a brief recess, they too voted for David Buchler's package.

Mercifully, in hindsight, it was the end of the road for me and my consortium. There was still the matter of solicitors' and accountants' fees and Mr Buchler and I were destined for another meeting, at which I relinquished all claims to any shares.

It was now approaching the end of February. Seven months of my life had been taken up trying to win a battle that in the end was more about personal feelings and bruised egos than anything else. The only consolation I have, looking back, is that the original purpose was achieved and a great deal more. I was asked to be chairman of a new Barnet Football Club in non-league football, light years away from the Football League. Today, as I write, Barnet stands proudly at the top of the third division of the Nationwide League. I am proud of the part I played in that.

As so often in life, you discover your true friends in times of adversity. Apart from those I have written about in the next chapter, I still had Earth Summit.

Chapter Twenty-Seven
Friends

Things often go wrong in people's lives for a number of reasons. A poor decision is often the main factor. My experience at Barnet Football Club will go down as a particularly bad period for me and those close to me. In particular, I put my family through a very worrying spell and my relationship with Patricia was at times very strained. We have come through it OK and Barnet Football Club is rarely mentioned these days.

Upon reflection, the whole affair was a catalogue of poor decisions on my part and in spite of the disgraceful behaviour of some of the individuals mentioned in the previous chapter, I accept total responsibility for the misery it caused.

During the bad times, as the old saying goes, you get to know who your friends really are. The greatest friend I have in the world is my wife. It is when things go against you that you appreciate a friend most of all. There have been times in the last twenty years when I have been badly in need of moral support. There have been occasions when to lean on Patricia would have been unfair to her, there have been situations I could not discuss with her. Barnet Football Club was one of those situations. There have been others.

In 1977 I went to Israel to take part in the World Maccabiah Games. I was in a squad of footballers who were to represent Great Britain in what is a glorious gathering of Jewish sportsmen and women from all over the world. Some of the competitors, particularly in tennis and athletics, perform to very high standards. Soccer is not so high on the scale and the host country always wins the tournament. Not surprising, as Israel is a Jewish state, but to be fair it is not the full national side that takes part, it is generally the under-21 squad.

The opening ceremony was something I will never forget. It was a happy occasion, but very emotional. Sixty thousand people filled the Ramat Gan Stadium in Tel Aviv and 200 athletes paraded in front of Israel's first lady, President Golda Meir and Prime Minister Monachem Begin. When prayers were said in remembrance of the victims of the Holocaust and the Israeli athletes slain at Munich five years before, all the lights went out in the stadium except for 1000 candles, lit in honour of those who had gone, and a choir sang softly. I felt the tears streaming down my face and glanced either side of me to see I wasn't alone.

We beat Italy, Peru, Uruguay and Argentina before losing 1-5 to Israel. I played in a team with a group of guys I had met barely two months before. They were a fantastic bunch and some good players as well. Two of them had spent spells at Barnet.

Mark Tucker, a big energetic nineteen-year-old, was the reason I was there. He had joined Barnet in the 1976-77 season. Once he realised that I had been born of a Jewish mother, he informed the selection committee. Although I had not been raised in any particular religion, in Judaism you follow the female line. It is simple enough: there can never be a doubt as to who your mother is. My mum, the youngest of ten children born to Solomon and Golda Berlinner, was definitely Jewish.

I hadn't seen Mark Tucker for thirteen years when I took over at Barnet. He lives in Canada working for a major oil company or something. He wrote to me in 1993 offering £25 000 to the cause if it would help. Thankfully, I didn't accept it but I'll never forget the gesture.

Captain of the team and a very talented midfield player was Jeffrey Bookman, who also came to Barnet in the late 70s. He and I got on brilliantly in Israel, so much so that upon our return, we went into business together. He introduced me to Jeffrey Zemmel, at that time an accountant with offices above Blooms restaurant in Whitechapel, about half a mile from where my mother was born.

Our idea so fired Jeffrey's imagination that he came into it with us. He obtained banking facilities and serious funding for the new company at Bank Leumi in Great Queen Street EC1.

Our business was an extension of what I had been doing for three years, albeit in a fairly small way: buying and selling sports shoes and clothing. With two new partners and a helpful bank manager, the plan was to greatly increase an existing turnover of around £200 000 per year. I would sell abroad in Europe, Jeff Bookman build up the home market, and Jeff Zemmel would ensure the pennies grew into large pounds.

It went so well in the beginning it was almost to good to be true. The three of us would take the odd trip together to see suppliers in France and Sweden and we found a mutual sense of humour that carried all before it. Sometimes something really small would start us off and I wonder now, twenty years later, what some of the foreign partners thought of us. Jeff Bookman is one of the funniest people I've ever met in my life. Sometimes I only had to look at him to start laughing. There were some classic meetings with serious people that had to be abandoned or at least adjourned until we had composed ourselves.

In Sweden, our supplier was a very old and famous tennis ball company call Tretorn. They had invited us as their UK distributor to view a brand new range of jogging shoes. As Scandinavians often pronounce 'J' as 'Y', our host kept referring to 'yogging shoes'. Initially this just produced a tiny smile from all three of us. Not daring to look at each other, we remained on our best behaviour. Finally, I was asked by the gentleman what I thought of the new shoes. Unfortunately, 'G' is also pronounced 'Y' and when I told him I thought we could sell upwards of 30 000 pairs of the shoes his response was too much for us to take. 'Mr Yeorge,' he began, 'if you can sell 30 000 pairs of our yogging shoes, I will yump for yoy!' It was Bookman who cracked first and it was nearly half an hour before we could resume. The poor man was completely bewildered at our behaviour and Jeff Zemmel gave him some stupid explanation concerning an old joke.

On another occasion, the big boss of our French supplier, Noel Football Boots, came to London to visit us. We met in the Whitechapel office. This man, whose name was Xavier Noel, was a portly, distinguished-looking man in his 60s. He was not unlike the late General de Gaulle in some ways, particularly his nose, which was one of the biggest I had ever seen. He didn't speak a word of English so the meeting was conducted with the help of his sales manager, who translated. Monsieur Noel practically never smiled and everything we said was then relayed to him in detailed terms as he sat and pondered a reply.

We were discussing pricing and terms and Jeffrey Zemmel was doing most of the talking for us. He had just finished a rather lengthy speech on the terms we would like, which took an age to translate, and as Monsieur Noel sat listening he absent-mindedly began to pick his nose. At first it was no more than a gentle tickle but, as he concentrated more on what was being said, he began to forage deeper and deeper. I could feel Bookman fighting the urge to laugh as he sat next to me. I was praying that the Frenchman would stop but he had obviously located something and the digging became even more concentrated. Finally, he located whatever it was he was digging for, removed it, studied it for a couple of seconds and stuck it under the desk in front of him, which happened to be Jeffrey's. It was me who cracked this time, releasing the other two into absolute hysterics. Monsieur Noel stopped digging and looked at us in astonishment as we wiped our eyes. Again, Jeff Zemmel tried to explain it away to the sales manager, who by this time was nearly laughing himself.

There were many funny times, too many to recount here, but it *was* too good to be true and we came down to earth in spectacular fashion when, in July 1979, Bank Leumi pulled the plug on us and about thirty other companies that JB Zemmel had introduced to them. It happened while he was on a family holiday in California.

It remains, to this day, one of the most despicable acts of sabotage that I have ever experienced from a bank. They gave no reason and have never offered one but on the day we came to call the 'Day of the long Knives', they withdrew all facilities and closed all accounts associated with one JB Zemmel.

I will never forget the morning, 6am Jeffrey's time, that I woke him to give him the awful news. How can a company operate without a bank account? All our money was tied up in stock and debtors.

He cut short his holiday and flew home alone from San Francisco. His opening words to us were 'Someone is going to pay for the look on the faces of my kids.'

The Leumi act very nearly ruined us all. We had taken an office and warehouse in Garston, near Watford. We had a small staff and mouths to feed.

While Jeffrey Zemmel tried without success to elicit a reason from Leumi, we rushed to open an account at the Allied

Irish Bank in Watford. Our largest debtor was a Belgian multinational, Makro BV in Antwerp. We telexed them urgently to request them to wire the seventy odd thousand pounds they owed us to the new account. They complied and we felt we had some breathing space. Within twenty-four hours and before we could touch a penny, Bank Leumi had served Allied Irish with an injunction, forbidding them to release the funds to us. Allied Irish, not knowing or understanding any of what had happened, washed their hands and complied with the injunction.

We had no choice but to make application for the injunction to be lifted. Again it was *ex parte* and we were advised that we had a good chance of success. Our solicitors, a local Barnet firm, took us to a barrister whose chambers in the ancient temple were straight out of Dickens. We sat in front of this man, quite young but incredibly scruffy, in the most serious situation of our lives. We were in no mood for laughing.

Unbelievably, the barrister, as we outlined this terrible problem, proceeded to make every effort, unwittingly, to bring the briefing to an end. Barrister's bundles of papers, their briefs, are always tied up with something that looks like a faded pink shoelace. Our scruffy young man persisted in twirling this bit of tape around his fingers. Several times he tied himself up so tightly, he had to yank his fingers loose before the blood stopped flowing. We all noticed this of course, but were not about to laugh at anything. However, it couldn't last because, having stopped twiddling, he then leaned on the arm of his chair. It fell off and he picked it up and replaced it. We had to laugh a little at that but when he did it again five minutes later and this time fell with it, the tension inside us burst and we all left the room in separate directions.

The injunction was heard in front of a second-rate judge, Master Warren. Our young eccentric counsel argued our case eloquently, but Master Warren came out with one of the classics of all time: 'I'm sure it's not the end of the world if you don't have a bank account for a few weeks.' Enough said, the injunction stood, our lifeline frozen at Allied Irish until trial. There would never be a trial; effectively Bank Leumi finished our business. The matter rumbled on for many months, years in fact, but there was never an explanation and at the end of the day all they wanted was their money back. What a way to go about it.

We hung around for a while at Garston but with no money to pay suppliers or staff it was a hopeless case. Jeff Zemmel did his best to keep things going and it cost him personally. But things were never the same again and eventually, we went our separate ways.

Maybe we had just had it too easy but for many nights afterwards I went to bed cursing the name of Bank Leumi.

I started again from home and renewed my contacts with people like Makro Belgium. After a while things picked up again, but not before a famous meeting Patricia and I had with our Barnet solicitor one morning. His name is Kevin McMeel and I still use him.

McMeel is an unusual name and could easily be mistaken for McNeil. There was a famous centre-forward who played for Wrexham and Hereford by the name of Dixie McNeil, and Bookman, Zemmel and I always referred to Kevin McMeel as Dixie. Twenty years on we still do. Of course, he doesn't know this and if he did he would think it as stupid as it probably sounds.

Anyway, shortly after the Leumi episode I found myself in financial difficulties with National Westminster Bank. They had taken a charge over our house in New Barnet. It was worrying because they had made formal demand for the money I owed them. We knew roughly the value of the house at the time and it wouldn't have taken a genius to work out what equity there may have been after settling with NatWest. So we decided to consult our friendly local solicitor, Dixie. He did the sums and advised us to sell the house and pay the bank. After costs and legal expenses, he estimated, we would be left with £2000. We had been married twelve years, had two very young children.

Patricia, naturally, was upset as we left Dixie's office. We sat in the coffee shop in John Lewis in Brent Cross and discussed it. I told her there was no way we were selling the house, whatever happened I would make sure that didn't. For advice of another kind, I turned to my ex-partner Jeffrey Zemmel.

It was not the first time, nor would it be the last, that his powerful and optimistic personality would motivate me when I needed it most. It wasn't money I wanted from him although I'm sure I could have requested a loan.

'What are your prospects, dear boy?' he asked me. I told

him my plans to travel to Belgium and pick up whatever I could, perhaps on an agency basis. 'Brilliant, phone NatWest and make an appointment, I'll come with you.'

And so he did. He convinced the bank manager to give me two years to straighten things out by telling him I was the best salesman he, Jeffrey, had ever met. He had bought me something money could not – time.

We eventually sold the house, in our own time, in 1982, to move to a larger one.

We stayed in touch, Jeffrey Zemmel and I. Jeff Bookman went into retail with a friend in the East End.

In 1981 Jeff Zemmel went on trial with a leather merchant by the name of Victor Mellik for VAT fraud. Jeffrey, as the firm's accountant, was accountable and he went to prison for two and a half years. (Mellik got seven.) When he came out in 1984 I had re-established myself in the sports goods business. His days as an accountant were over and he came to see me.

Now it was Jeffrey who needed help. For one of the few times in his life, it was he who required motivation. I directed him to several suppliers of goods I had been trying to obtain. He did the job brilliantly and we both benefited. I was glad to be able to play a small part in getting him back on his feet.

In 1988, I expanded my activities and took on a new distribution company to sell American World War II leather bomber jackets, among two or three other brands I had discovered. This operation necessitated huge expense and I needed more people around me. Jeff Zemmel and I, although not partners, were seeing a lot of each other and he was becoming more involved in the trading side of the company.

I was constantly meeting new contacts and during 1988 I had been introduced to a huge German who lived and worked in Dublin. This man offered me a big parcel of Nike shoes. What possessed me I'll never know, but in the autumn of that year I sent £80 000 to Dublin in advance of receiving the shoes. The shoes never materialised and I sued, not through Dixie but through Michael Robin, who in turn engaged Dublin lawyers.

Apparently, my giant Bavarian friend was well known to the firm of solicitors that acted for me and they moved swiftly. They were aware of a freehold property owned by the organisation run by the big man. They secured a lien on the property. It seemed a cut and dried case. All I had to do was sue in the Irish courts, obtain judgement and, if he couldn't pay, enforce the sale of the property. As the months went by, the eighty grand crept nearer to 150. Legal costs, loss of profit, etc etc were all mounting in my favour. I had been brainless sending the money in the first place, but it seemed this time I was going to come out OK.

The trial was set for a date in late November.

For some time I had been aware that my mother was very ill. She had been in and out of hospital since September and just a few days before I was due to go to Dublin for the trial, my brother and I received the awful news that she had only months to live.

She suffered a small stroke and was due to go back into hospital on the day before I was due in Dublin, a Tuesday. On the Sunday afternoon I was at home when the telephone rang. An Irish voice asked me if I was Ricky George. I knew immediately what was coming. I was warned not to set foot in Ireland, the threat was implicit. I thought my head was set to burst.

I really didn't know which way to turn.

When I called Michael Robin and told him, he immediately contacted Dublin. It was not unusual, we were told; people use the threat of terror regularly in such cases, particularly in Ireland. They advised me to go.

Patricia was absolutely positive about what I should do. 'Forget the money, no way must you go, you have three children and a very sick mother, don't go.'

I took her advice.

Michael Robin and the Irish solicitors handled it brilliantly. They proceeded as if I had gone and on the steps of the court, the German's solicitors offered £70 000 in settlement. A quick call to me and I told them to accept it immediately. They didn't want to but by now they all understood how much I wanted this out of the way.

At 11pm on January 1st 1989, my mother, May Victoria, passed away peacefully in her sleep at home in St Albans. I shall be ever thankful that I was at her bedside and held her hand as she left this world, having graced it with her presence for seventy-four years.

I had never had to deal with grief before. We never know how we will react. My dad, now alone, had to be taken care of. He and I waited for the doctor to arrive and then at 6am the funeral directors came. I have never known a colder, bleaker dawn.

I took Dad home with me but we all knew that was not the short-term solution, so we went back to his house and I told him to pack a small suitcase. Later that day I checked him into the West Lodge Park Hotel. We sat at the bar for a couple of hours before he announced he was tired and went to his room.

I went home to my family. Pat had lit the fire in the front room and she held me as I cried like a little boy before falling asleep on her shoulder. The first of my close friends to come round was Martin Webb, and I cried on his shoulder too.

Jeffrey Zemmel was once again a tower of strength. He had suffered the loss of both his parents and was quickly by my side.

Kindness is so important and it comes in many different shapes. In this case it came in the form of letters from those who knew my mother and from those who didn't. I cherish every one of them, and I cherish the memory of a wonderful mother.

Chapter Twenty-Eight
Timberland

In 1986 I started buying a brand of shoe called Timberland from a tiny company in West London with the ingenious name of ATOC (A Touch of Class). The two directors were Rod Williams, an Australian, and Simon Glasgow from New Zealand.

My customers were mainly Swiss and Italian but whoever wanted to buy these shoes ultimately would sell them to Italy.

Between 1986 and 1992 I bought and sold over £20 million of these shoes. The business was good for all three parties (Timberland, ATOC and me) in the beginning.

After three years ATOC sold out to their American parent company, Timberland USA, and Timberland UK was created. A new managing director was appointed, Richard O Rourke, who had been a buyer at Harrods. The relationship continued to flourish.

However, in early 1992 I became aware that my suppliers, now Timberland UK Ltd, wanted to ditch me as a customer. I was not told this directly but through Rod Williams, who now worked for the parent company in the USA

Sure enough, in the summer of '92 I received a letter from O'Rourke. It didn't mention not supplying goods any more, only a list of new trading conditions that would have been impossible to comply with. He was assisted in this regard by Mr John Ranelli, described by Williams as a 'tough Yank'.

Several meetings and telephone conversations later, it became clear that after six years of profitable business, they were indeed closing me down. The conditions they imposed were so ludicrous that no one in their right mind would have agreed to them. I consulted solicitors but with no written contract in force, there was very little I could do.

I tried to be philosophical. Looking back, I was grateful for the good years. However, I wasn't the type of person to just accept the situation and I was determined to give it one more try.

The Timberland Company is owned by the Swartz family. Sidney Swartz, one of the founders, has a son called Jeffrey. During my relationship with them Jeffrey became CEO. I met him a couple of times in London and he was absolutely charming. A man in his late twenties, Harvard-educated, Jeffrey Swartz was groomed for the job. Sidney became President.

I had always got on well with Jeffrey, though I had never met his father, and I decided to go and see him. I had no idea what could be achieved, but I guess I needed something to satisfy this unpleasant feeling of being a lost soul. I needed to be sent on my way forever, like the poor souls whose time on earth had been traumatically interrupted. I needed an exorcist.

I faxed the Timberland HQ at Hampton, New Hampshire, requesting a meeting with Jeffrey Swartz and suggesting a time and day that I planned to be in the Boston area. I had no other reason to be in Boston, but to my surprise I received a reply stating that we had an appointment in Mr Jeffrey Swartz's office at 9am on Tuesday 3rd November 1992.

I confirmed by return fax and made plans.

A positive result was not what I expected; I didn't know what I *was* expecting, but I decided to make the trip worthwhile by seeing a contact in New York and then going on to Montreal after Boston, returning direct from Canada to London. My contact in New York suggested we had dinner on the Sunday night. I could then take the 6.30am shuttle up to Boston to be in good time for my 9am appointment.

In those days, travelling alone to the North-East US and in a hurry, I would take the Concorde. I chose the Sunday evening supersonic which left Heathrow at 7pm, arriving in JFK at around 5.30pm New York time. I had booked in at The Pierre and my Manhattan-based contact would pick me up at 8.30 for dinner. It was this man who had first taken me to Sammy's Roumanian restaurant on Christie Street on the Lower East Side, and I could almost taste the chopped liver and onions as I drove to London's Heathrow Terminal 4.

Sammy's is basically a dump, at least that's what it looks like from the outside. Inside, the decor is deliberately tacky. Bright lights, checked tablecloths and walls plastered with thousands of business cards from all over the world. The food, described as Eastern European, kosher style, is wonderful. From the chopped liver and chicken soup your mother used to make to the gigantic veal steaks they call tennis rackets laced with Schmaltz (chicken fat), Sammy's cuisine is utterly unique. However, once a year is more than enough if you want to keep your cholesterol below the body equivalent of the World Trade Centre.

There's always entertainment, from the brilliantly talented violinist Rubin who sadly passed away recently in his late eighties, to Michael the pianist who plays everything from Yiddish love songs to Elton John. Sammy's is indeed an experience.

It had been particularly windy in the UK for some days and I felt the car being blown from side to side as I sped down the M25. It was Sunday afternoon.

Like most people, I still feel the trepidation that precedes air travel. The thought of flying back in time to New York on a very windy Sunday evening gave me a few butterflies, but nothing could compare to the excitement of the Concorde. The mere idea of its take-off speed of 250 mph, the height it reaches of nearly 60 000 feet, plus the incredible in-flight experience of breaking the sound barrier at Mach 2, is something that still makes the goose bumps break out.

It was still very windy outside as I took my seat by the window. I have always chosen window seats so that I can see what is happening. Hysterical, isn't it, when most of the time you are six miles or so above the earth!

Most Concorde flights I have taken have been full and that night's flight was no exception. The pre-flight information given by the British Airways captain increased my feeling of butterflies, fear and thrill. Take-off manoeuvres at Heathrow were similar to those in New York as far as Concorde was concerned; the engines would be cut back seventy-two seconds after take-off. It always felt as it the engines had stalled because the dramatic difference between the roar of take-off and eerie silence was very weird. So the captain always warned his passengers about this, while casually outlining our intended height, speed and route, and ETA into Kennedy. I admire lots of different people in many different ways. Airline pilots are right up there.

I had good reason to admire this particular captain, even

though the actions he was about to take terrified the life out of me.

'We're number one for take-off, cabin crew please be seated.' The engines roared to a deafening sound and he released the breaks. As we sped along the runway, I could feel the wind buffeting the sleek, aluminium capsule I was strapped into.

You do get to know roughly when an aircraft is going to lift off. I braced myself, then, at the most crucial point of any flight, the point of no return, the captain shut down the engines and stepped on the brakes. We were returning from nearly 250 mph to nothing. In a few seconds we had slowed, and I breathed again.

The captain, true to form, came straight on the address system. In the same calm, reassuring voice, he explained that there were two computers on the Concorde and they did not agree at the point of no return. This might have been caused by wind shear and could have been nothing, but he had made the split-second decision to abort the take-off. While the passengers may have been scared, there was no harm done, only the loss of several thousand pounds' worth of fuel and a disruption to the airline's schedule. It is precisely the ability to make those crucial decisions that make these guys special in my book.

We went back to the stand and waited while the engineers checked out the problem. Several people left the plane, not to return, and after a delay of 2½ hours we took off from a still very windy Heathrow Airport. During the delay, I was able to get a message to my friend in New York to cancel our date. I decided to go straight to Boston on my arrival.

I took a cab to La Guardia and caught the 10.15pm Eastern flight to Logan airport, from where I called an old friend from New York who kindly collected me around 11.30 in Boston. This was an ex-employee of Timberland, still living in the Hampton area. He drove me to a local hotel where, very tired, I finally got to bed around 1.30am, nearly eighteen hours after leaving home. So much for saving time, but I reasoned that the BA captain knew best, and we were all safely at our destinations.

Paul Crawley, the guy who picked me up, had worked for Timberland in London and moved to Hampton with Rod Williams. I like him and on the way up to Hampton, he gave me his view of the company, the Swartzes, Ranelli and

O'Rourke. It may have been for my benefit, but he confirmed everything I knew to be true. They took my business when it suited them, but their Italian distributor was threatening to expose them as cheats to the rest of the world. This they couldn't risk, and some very large corporations were looking in the direction of the Hamptons.

'Jeff's an asshole,' Paul said, 'he'll be crapping himself at the thought of meeting you tomorrow. Good luck, sue the bastards for everything.'

I was encouraged by my chat with Paul and looking forward to seeing Jeffrey Swartz squirm as I took him to task about the real reason Timberland had blown me out.

I was in the entrance hall of the main offices at precisely 8.55 the following morning. I announced myself to the receptionist, a young woman who did not smile but politely asked me to take a seat while she checked; she wasn't sure if Mr Jeffrey was in today.

'I have an appointment for 9am,' I said.

She ignored me while she spoke to someone. 'He's not well, Miss Owers will see you.'

'I'm sorry, who's Miss Owers?' I asked, my anger rising.

'Miss Owers will see you, Sir, and possibly Mr Sidney Swartz.' She spoke firmly, unsmiling. I saw it all immediately and realised that this was the final *coup de grâce*. I could not possibly have been made to look a bigger fool if I had tried.

Sidney Swartz did actually show his face. He barely spoke, I only remember him saying, 'Jeffrey is unwell, he has a cold.'

Miss or Ms Jane Owers was Timberland's in-house lawyer. With a carefully prepared bland and meaningless statement, she confirmed that Timberland prided themselves on their honesty and integrity, and expected anyone they worked with in the world to behave the same way. When they did not, Timberland would decline further business. I can only assume that they were referring to the fact that I was selling their product into an already existing market, ie Italy. They had been very happy with that at the beginning.

'What about the £20 million of business I gave you and my influence on you capturing precious Western European markets?'

No comment, neither of them spoke.

I told Swartz, the sound of my own voice magnified a hundred times in my ears, that I had taken legal advice and

226

considered them to be in breach of contract. 'More to the point,' I continued, 'you have shown a remarkable lack of good faith towards me in the circumstances.'

Silence.

It was over. For them there was relief, for me acute embarrassment and frustration that Jeffrey Swartz couldn't face me. I had travelled 3000 miles to keep an appointment he had agreed to. All totally meaningless.

I went back to my hotel and called Paul. It was just after 9.45am. My audience had lasted about ten minutes. I had a light lunch with him and his wife Victoria, who still actually worked for Timberland but was working out her notice. They weren't in the least bit surprised that Jeffrey had failed to show. Paul and Vicky dropped me at Boston's Logan. They were a smashing couple; I didn't know if I would ever see them again.

I flew up to Montreal and spent a day with a customer who had previously bought a £½ million worth of skiwear from us. We had taken export credit insurance when shipping the goods but he had yet to pay us. I was given a thousand promises. They don't pay the mortgage. Why did I feel this trip was becoming a waste of time?

Instead of flying back straight to London as planned, I had rearranged my New York appointment and stayed the Tuesday night in Manhattan. That meeting, at least, made some of the trip worthwhile, because he told me he was working on a huge close-out of...Timberland clothing.

I caught the 9am Concorde out of Kennedy Airport. It was a bright, cloudless, cold November day and I experienced the same incredible excitement flying that super bird.

The UK was still windy, and we were buffeted quite badly as we made our approach. With the landing gear down and the display at the front of the cabin which gives you height, speed, temperature and miles to go throughout the 3½ hour flight, showing in bright green, we waited silently for those wheels to touch down. I really couldn't see very much through the low cloud, but as the airport lights and the runway beneath us came into view, the engines suddenly roared into full crescendo and we climbed steeply away from the airfield. Everyone stiffened in their seats as we climbed up into the turbulent sky, the aircraft still bumping around uncomfortably.

The captain came on to tell us that at 200 feet he had noticed an aircraft that had been slow to clear the runway.

He was sorry that we would have another uncomfortable ten minutes or so while we went around one more time.

What a trip! One aborted take-off, one aborted landing, a terrible first and last meeting with Mr Sidney, waffle in Canada and chicken soup with huge matzo balls in Sammys. Mind you, I thought as I drove back along the M25, I'm home safely to see my family, they love me...and, who knows, maybe I'll write about this one day.

Although Timberland didn't know it, our paths were to cross again.

Chapter Twenty-Nine
Hereford Reunion 1997

After the 1972 season, Hereford gained a historic entry to the Football League. The team actually finished second in the Southern League Premier but in those days there was no automatic promotion for the side who finished first. You had to be elected and the vote was cast by the chairmen of the ninety-two league clubs.

The incredible cup run – four games against the highest opposition watched by 110 000 people, yielding one win, two draws and a defeat – undoubtedly helped in their quest for league status. And there was a lot more in Hereford's favour. In terms of league football they were isolated, geographically; Newport County some fifty miles to the southwest was the nearest league club. Hereford United had another, priceless advantage: wonderful supporters. Throughout the 1971/72 season attendances averaged 5000, more than most fourth division clubs, particularly poor Barrow, who dropped out of the Football League to make way for the Rampant Bulls.

For the club, the manager and the players that stayed after the historic season, the fairytale continued. Incredibly, the team won promotion at the first attempt. Neither Billy Meadows nor myself experienced this amazing feat. At the end of the season we were given free transfers which, believe it or not, was no surprise. Colin Addison, the manager, was as ambitious as the chairman and the club needed full-time players.

Had the club wanted us to stay, we would have had to consider leaving London and moving to Hereford. It was never going to happen.

Billy went to play for AS Ostend in Belgium. He trained at Barnet and flew over for matches. I went to Stevenage Athletic briefly and then back to Barnet where, as you can imagine, I was very happy.

A lot of the team stayed at Edgar Street. Dudley Tyler famously went to West Ham United for a couple of seasons to play alongside Bobby Moore. Dudley still lives in Hereford and works as a sales rep for a local engineering firm. Fred Potter is now semi-retired, living in his native West Midlands. Roger Griffiths lives and works in Hereford and was the one Giantkiller to take the pitch in the recent FA Cup tie against Leicester City. He and a group of supporters performed the ritual of kicking a black and white swede (the vegetable) into the bottom goal where our goals against Newcastle were scored. Ken Mallender lives in Hereford and works for the sport shoe giant, Nike.

Mike McLaughlin lives in Atlanta, Georgia and runs a shipping company. Alan Jones is a prison warder in Swansea. Tony Gough lives in Bath and runs his own engineering company. Brian Owen also lives in Bath and has his own electrician business. Colin Addison is manager at non-league Scarborough, having managed Derby County, West Bromwich Albion and Atletico Madrid, among other Spanish clubs. Ronnie Radford lives near his birthplace, Leeds, and is a joiner. Billy Meadows drives for a living.

In the intervening years, there were a series of reunions highlighted by a game at Edgar Street. We were known simply as 'the Giantkillers' and will be forever more.

February 5th 1997 would be the 25th Anniversary and Colin Addison, helped by his wife Jean, daughter Rachel and a committee of hard-working and committed supporters, arranged a reunion that would cover a weekend but this time no football match. After all, we were all in our 50s.

About a month before the reunion I went into Princess Grace Hospital in Marylebone to have a total hip replacement. Nothing that would stop me making the weekend, although I was warned not to dance too much.

It was brilliant. We all met up on Friday night and had dinner in the Green Dragon Hotel where, 25 years before, Motty and I had encountered Jackie Milburn. This was a function for just the players and their wives and the greatly-loved physio Peter Isaac.

On the Saturday afternoon, we all attended the Hereford versus Northampton division three game. Before the match we walked on to the pitch to emotional applause.

Hereford lost 1-2 and unbelievably dropped into second

from bottom place, perilously close to the danger zone. Today, if you finish bottom of division three, you're out!

The Saturday night was memorable. Over 400 people crowded into the Three Counties Hotel as we all relived the cup run. There was footage of our second round replay victory over Northampton at West Bromwich, as well as the big games. The evening was one of glory and nostalgia, I do not expect to experience anything like that again. Motty arrived from the FA Cup tie between Derby and Middlesbrough and made a great speech, remembering fondly what Hereford United and Ronnie Radford had done for his career.

I grabbed the opportunity I had been waiting twenty-five years for, to pay tribute to my team-mates. It's always Ronnie and me who get mentioned in the media because of the goals, but that team were a magnificent bunch of men. My role was tiny, I just happened to pop up when needed, but my memories of those players and what they did are as clear today as then. I've only got to hear one of their names and I can picture his face, hear his accent, remember the way he kicks or heads a ball. They will be a part of my life forever.

Sadly, Hereford finished bottom of the league in 1996-97 and, exactly twenty-five years after their historic victory, they found themselves a non-league club once more.

Over the quarter of a century since 'the goal', I have told countless stories about that period in my life. Some of them are in this book, of course. Every now and then – more so these days than ever before – I meet people who have a spark of recognition when they hear my name. Some instances have been very funny.

Jeffrey Zemmel and I visited a new customer in London's East End about three years ago. He is an extremely wealthy man, the son of a famous trader who had a very fine reputation and dealt in army surplus after the Second World War.

We were shown into this man's office while he reclined in a huge chair with a telephone clamped between his shoulder and his ear. The first thing I noticed was his stomach protruding through his shirt buttons.

We were waved to our seats as he continued his conversation. When he finished, he looked up as if surprised to see us.

'Oh yes,' he began, addressing me. 'You're a footballer, aren't you?'

'I was once,' I said.

'Yes, Hertford Town or someone, wasn't it?'

'Actually, it was Hereford United.'

'Oh yes, Hereford, didn't you beat Arsenal or someone?'

'Actually, it was Newcastle.'

'Oh yes, Newcastle, in the FA Cup, when was it, late 50s?' I was thirteen in 1959.

'Actually, it was 1972 but it *was* the FA Cup.'

'Oh yes and didn't you score a goal?'

'Yes.'

'Oh yes, I remember now, wasn't it a long shot from twenty-five yards, or something?'

'Actually that was Ronnie Radford and it was nearer thirty-five yards.'

'Was it really, now I remember, Hereford-Newcastle 1972, Ronnie Radford from thirty-five yards, yes I remember.'

He paused looking up at the ceiling of his office. 'So, who are you then?'

Jeffrey and I exchanged amused expressions. Fifteen years ago we'd have been on the floor in hysterics.

I quietly told him it was I who had scored the winner. He didn't seem remotely interested after that.

On another occasion I was invited to a close friend of Patricia's whose husband was holding a wine-tasting party. Most of the guys were connoisseurs; I haven't a clue, normally I order the second most expensive on the list.

I was introduced to people as Patricia's husband, Ricky George. One guy called Terry immediately narrowed his eyes.

'Didn't you score a famous goal once?'

'Yes,' I replied truthfully.

'It was for Hereford against Newcastle, that amazing match back in 1971.' He was nearly right, so I left it.

I could see him thinking of something else to say and then he came out with a classic. 'So are you Ronnie Radford, then?'

Very late on the Saturday night of our wonderful weekend reunion, as Patricia and I were leaving the party, the DJ played the football anthem, Rodgers and Hammerstein's 'You'll Never Walk alone'. I stopped for a brief moment of reflection as I watched a few of my old team-mates, some still dancing, some just sitting and thinking like me. As the music played, I felt my eyes moisten. Patricia walked on, sensing my mood. I brushed my hand across my eyes and looked up.

We all glanced at each other in turn, gave the thumbs up and I moved on.

Chapter Thirty
John 'Motty' Motson and World Cup '98

The BBC's number one football commentator had been a great friend over the years and we remain as close as we were three decades ago.

In 1980 a Dutchman by the name of Theo Van Schie – a tennis coach in his late sixties, and a gentleman – asked me if I could ever get him a ticket for the Wimbledon Tennis Championships. In those days Motty was doing tennis commentaries for Radio Two. 'Meet me at the main entrance at 12 o'clock, I'll get you in,' was his response to my request.

John took us up to the radio commentary box overlooking Court 14, where we were introduced to none other than Fred Perry, the last Englishman to win the Men's Singles title at Wimbledon in 1936, having also won it in 1934 and '35. Theo was speechless as Perry's friendly and engaging manner put us at ease. From Box 14 we went to the commentary gantry above Number One Court, where we watched Vitus Gerulaitus playing Kevin Curren. There we met Christine Janes (née Truman) and the legendary Max Robertson. The day was a feast of entertainment and great interest. At one stage we sat with earphones on as Motty described every shot for the listeners while the producer chatted away in our ears. When I bade Theo farewell that night at his hotel, there was a tear in his eye. 'Apart from my wedding day, Rick, that was the greatest day of my life.' And he gripped my hand tightly as he spoke with great sincerity.

Over the years, that Wimbledon visit remains a memorable event and example of John's friendship. It is, however, the only time I have made such a request, as I never like to ask people like John for favours.

I have other happy memories of him. During the 1998 World Cup Finals, I went twice to the Stade de France to watch the hosts play against Italy in the quarter final and Croatia in the semi. I had placed a serious bet on *les Bleus* before the start of the finals at 7/1.

On the first occasion I just happened to be in Paris with Jeff Zemmel, visiting a supplier. It was a beautiful July day and the game was due to kick off at 4 pm. The atmosphere in the city was electric and in spite of the fact that I had been quoted 4000 francs by my supplier for a ticket to the match, I decided to stay on and take a chance. Jeff caught the Eurostar home and I took the metro to Station Stade de France, about fifteen minutes and ten francs from the Gare du Nord. Outside I waited until ten minutes before kick-off before paying 1000 francs (about £100) for a seat in the brand new stadium. France triumphed in a penalty shoot-out and, before making for home, I stood amongst the fifty-odd thousand as the home fans belted out *La Marseillaise*.

Before Motty left for the finals, he had given me a few telephone numbers where I might reach him during the tournament. The night before the World Cup semi-final, I called him at the Hotel Castille in the Rue Cambon. The hotel is opposite the back door of the Ritz Hotel, through which Princess Diana and Dodi Al Fayed had fled on *that* terrible night in August 1997. He was overjoyed to hear that I would be there and immediately arranged a room for me in his hotel.

'What time will you be there, son?' he asked me several times. I hoped to be in the centre of Paris by 1.30 pm; I was driving as I had to return very early the following day to go to Newmarket Races.

During the journey my mobile went at least three times. 'Where are you, Ricky son? What's your ETA?' When it seemed I would be at the hotel by 2 pm, John gave me the name of the restaurant where he and Trevor Brooking would be lunching. When I arrived, I was greeted like a king. 'I'm so pleased you're here,' Motty said several times as we shared two or three bottles of chilled Chablis. As pleasant as all this was, I was a bit taken aback; I mean, I knew we were good friends but, being a modest sort of fellow, I felt a touch embarrassed.

The match was due to kick off at 8 pm. I had no ticket but had not requested any assistance from Motty in that regard. However, he offered me a seat in the courtesy car, leaving the hotel at 5.30 pm. As we returned to the hotel after lunch in glorious sunshine, John had a question for me.

'What time are you leaving in the morning?'

'Around 6 am.'

'Could you do me a small favour, son?'

Of course I could.

'I've got some dirty washing that I'd like you to take home for me, I've been away over three weeks and it's been piling up.'

I laughed. 'Of course,' I said, 'I knew there was a good reason to come to Paris. I mean, forget the football, your dirty washing is far more important.'

France beat Croatia 2-1 that night to enter the World Cup Final. I paid 1200 francs (£120) for a ticket and an hour or so after the game, caught the courtesy car back to our hotel with my mate and his co-commentator. As I waited outside the Stade de France, I watched the crowds disperse. There was nothing but good humour from everyone, including the Croatian supporters. At one point an old guy riding an old motorcycle pulled up alongside me. He took off his helmet and stared at the circular structure still bathed in light as if it were an alien craft. All over Paris you could hear the sound of car horns celebrating the semi-final victory.

The old man continued to stare in wonder at the Stade de France. As he caught me looking at him he smiled; there were a few teeth missing.

'Allez les Bleus,' I said.

He grinned again, then became serious. 'Mais' – he gestured with one hand and a slight movement of the head – 'Brazil, c'est difficile, n'est-ce pas?'

'C'est possible,' I said, 'La France est une bonne équipe.'

'Oui?' he said hopefully.

'Mais oui!' I said positively.

He put his helmet back on, wished me *bonne nuit* and put-putted away into the dark. I imagined him living in a tiny house dwarfed by the huge stadium, going home to his wife, sitting down to a glass of red wine or Cognac, and shaking his head in wonder and disbelief: 'Edith, I don't know what's happening. A giant spaceship lands in our quiet little street, France is in the World Cup Final, and a spaceman just told me we could actually beat Brazil. *C'est fou*, eh?'

That night I sat in a little bar near our hotel with Motty, Trevor Brooking and Ray Stubbs. At three o'clock we all wished each other good night and John plonked a great big holdall at my feet in the lobby. It was his laundry.

I knew then that I actually had some uses in life, that it had not been all in vain.

Chapter Thirty-One
Owner

I had always wanted to own a racehorse. Earth Summit wasn't my first investment. With two others I had owned a brown gelding named Order of Merit in 1990. The only time he got near to winning was a two-horse novice chase at Plumpton in August. He finished second to a thirteen-year-old who hadn't won for nine years.

I leased a beautiful filly named Barnet Fayre from the trainer Alec Stewart in 1991. She was very well bred out of the champion miler Waajib. Sadly, she was never well enough to run, for me at any rate. She was sold cheaply and during 1992 I noticed she was entered at Brighton in a seven-furlong maiden. I jumped in the car and drove to the Sussex track high above Hove. She still looked magnificent, so I backed her at 33-1. She finished in the middle of about sixteen horses and never raced again.

Earth Summit's start to his racing career was fairly low-key. After the promising bumper at Cheltenham he disappointed a few times before romping away with a three-mile hurdle at Chepstow in March 1993. I was in Florida with the family at the time, but I always backed him and had £50 each way. My secretary Valerie telephoned me with the exciting news that I had finally owned a winner, at generous odds of 12/1. While I was going to hell and back with Barnet, Earth Summit's second season was a superb one. In seven outings he finished first on four occasions and was second twice.

After his victory at Chepstow in heavy going, it became apparent to everyone that our delightful little gelding loved soft ground like his father, Celtic Cone.

However, in April 1994, a few weeks after the Barnet Football Club episode and just when I was in need of a psychological boost to my fortunes, he pulverised a good field in the Scottish Grand National at Ayr on what was described as good ground. Even though on that day his jumping wasn't faultless, the four-mile, one-furlong stamina test suited him admirably and David Bridgwater had him so far in front at the last he slowed to a walk before finishing sixteen lengths ahead of his nearest rival.

Now everyone sat up and took notice. At only six years old he was still a novice and had proved that he loved soft ground and long distance. There is no greater stamina test in the racing calendar anywhere in the world than the Aintree Martell Grand National, the race I loved most of all.

Suddenly, Nigel Payne's dream of having a runner in the race he did so much to preserve and has been so involved in for over twenty-five years looked a real possibility.

The plan had been to aim him at the big one the following year, as a seven-year-old, but fate decreed otherwise and an injury sidelined him while Jenny Pitman's Royal Athlete gave the first lady of Aintree her second National success.

That year, the most famous Grand National horse of all, Red Rum, celebrated his 30th birthday. Later in the year, October 18th to be exact, he was put to sleep after suffering a heart attack and was laid to rest by the winning post at Aintree.

Even though, twenty-one years earlier, he had robbed me of what was then a small fortune, I, like all racegoers, loved Red Rum. When he beat L'Escargot in 1974 he was carrying an incredible twelve stone and his third victory in 1977 was again at the head of the handicap shouldering eleven stone eight lbs.

Red Rum, L'Escargot, Aldaniti, Little Polveir, West Tip, Jay Trump and in 1997 Lord Gyllene have all carried my money in the great race.

Earth Summit's appalling injury at Haydock in February 1996 put paid to any racing for nearly two years and it was his comeback race at Haydock in November 1997 that provoked thoughts, once more, of a tilt at the ultimate prize.

When we went down to Chepstow for the Welsh National on December 27th 1997, I was cautiously optimistic. The ground was going to be heavy. He had won twice before at the track and he had a handy weight.

On arriving at the picturesque racecourse just across the Severn Bridge, I was met by both Nigel Payne and Bob Sims, both of them incredulous at the odds of 25/1 being offered on our boy. It seemed that the experts had forgotten him after his long absence. Sims was uncharacteristically optimistic and it was his confidence that persuaded me to double my bet. '£100 each way will do me,' I said to myself, although the thought did cross my mind to up the wager to £1000 each way. 'Hold on,' I said again to myself, 'if he wins today, put it all on the big one.'

As Earth Summit and Indian Tracker drew clear turning into the long Chepstow straight, Tom Jenks pulled his goggles down and glanced sideways at his only challenger.

'Aye, aye,' I said to Patricia as I gripped my binoculars tightly, 'we've won this.'

'I can't see anything,' she said, 'and haven't they still got a long way to go?'

'Four fences, darling, and he only has to jump them.' I glanced at her and she gave me the famous look I'd seen a thousand times before. It said: 'Well, I hope you're right this time.'

When Tom and 'Digger' arrived at the last fence, Digger was so far in front that he virtually stopped to ensure clearing it safely.

Once he was over the cheering started in earnest and then from another county came the tiny grey, Dom Samurai, putting in a storming finish. For a second I stopped shouting as Martin Pipe's game little horse actually got to the withers of our hero. But Tom got him going again and at the line that one-and-a-half lengths was on the increase.

There were great scenes of joy and I lifted Patsy off her feet before rushing down to the winners' enclosure to greet our mud-spattered duo. Curiously, Tom and the horse reminded me of previous mud-spattered heroes, in white shirts.

Now came a memorable interview with the BBC's Jonathon Powell. 'Were you worried when you saw Dom Samarai?' he asked.

'Briefly, but our fellow stays forever, he'd have gone another circuit.'

Sims loved that one. 'Another circuit, George? Are you sure?'

Another circuit would have made five miles, just half a mile longer than the Grand National.

It wasn't that stupid.

Chapter Thirty-Two
Titanic

On Saturday, March 28th 1998, one week before the Martell Aintree Grand National, I phoned William Hill. I gave my name and account number.

'Yes, Mr George.'

'Could you give me a price on Earth Summit to win the Grand National, please?'

'Sixteen-to-one, Sir.'

'I'll have £1000 each way at the sixteens, please.'

'One moment, Sir.' Ten seconds later. 'That's RG1234, Mr George, you have £1000 each way Earth Summit at sixteens, that's £2000 plus tax, thank you, Sir.'

'Thank you,' I said and punched the air in delight.

I had promised myself to have the Welsh National winnings on the 'Big One', and I did. Immediately after Chepstow I had £100 each way at 20/1.

The total conviction I now felt, in spite of two indifferent runs between Chepstow and Aintree, I kept very much to myself.

The BBC called and asked if I would do an early morning piece with Rob Bonnett in front of the famous 'Chair' fence on the Friday before the race. Early morning was 7am, so Patricia and I drove up to Liverpool on the Thursday night. Daniel, our eldest, was trekking around Europe with Will Kolbe and due to be in Berlin on the big day. Adam and Rebecca decided to stay at home and watch on TV.

Even though no-one close to me was expecting a victory, it was incredibly exciting. My brother Michael, who never bet on horses, was beside himself with expectancy. Tony, the landlord of the White Lion pub in St Albans Road, Barnet, where we take Dad two or three times a week, was also rooting for us. Tony is a truly great guy, a typical Irishman who loves the racing game. He is also a very generous man. As soon

239

as we arrive in the pub he makes Dad a sandwich. It may sound small, but he never charges for it. The White Lion has become a happy venue in our lives. The locals are real Earth Summit supporters and his picture hangs proudly in Tony's recent extension.

On the way to Liverpool I telephoned our close friend, Richard Bernard, who lives in North Wales. I told him we were driving to the Grand National. 'I bet you've got a horse running,' he said. I laughed, as he isn't a racing man at all, and we invited him and his lady Anne to join us for dinner in our hotel.

During dinner I asked them if they wanted to come to the National. He wasn't bothered but Anne was very keen. She wanted to bring her daughter Rachel, who was nine years old. We encouraged them to come.

On Friday night we moved to the Park Hotel in Aintree and joined the other owners for dinner. Only Mike Bailey wasn't there. The only local lad, he was at home with his mum.

On the day of the race, I had a live interview with Des Lynam in the famous winners' enclosure. I told him and several million viewers the Nigel Payne/Peter Scudamore/Earth Summit story recounted in Chapter 19. He seemed to enjoy it. I also reminded the world that Motty had turned down a share in Earth Summit. At another time in our lives, thirty-odd years earlier, I had met Lynam at a party at John Motson's flat in New Barnet. Des, like John, was a Radio 2 reporter at the time. He's done okay, they both have.

I still had a £1000 to wager and as post time for the great race drew nearer the heavens opened. We went down for the parade, and Patricia and I took little Rachel along.

Nigel Payne had arranged a fantastic box facility overlooking the winning post and the six owners plus friends and family were gathered, nervously waiting the big moment.

Behind the parade ring there is a row of stalls where the runners are saddled before a race. We all stood looking at the stall where Nigel Twiston-Davies was waiting, saddle in hand. Horse after horse in the thirty-seven runner field arrived, was saddled up and left to take his or her place in the parade ring. There was no sign of Earth Summit and we could see the trainer looking increasingly anxious.

Finally, Marcella led him in. She look flustered and worried. It turned out that when she led him out of the horse box, he had stopped in front of a puddle and would not budge. Eventually, she had to get one of the other stable lads to gee him up from behind.

'If he won't go through a puddle, how the hell is he going to jump thirty fences here?' said Twiston-Davies in his own imitable fashion. We all laughed nervously.

The horse looked completely unconcerned. 'He looks half asleep to me,' said Nigel Payne.

As the runners for the world's greatest steeplechase paraded for millions, the rain poured down.

Carl Llewelyn climbed aboard, looked up at the sky and said, 'I'll stay wide, keep him out of trouble. There won't be many get round today; we will.' He winked at us and wheeled the magnificent blinkered gelding around and out of the parade.

I sprinted down to the rails in the pouring rain. 'What price Earth Summit?' I asked the Ladbrokes representative.

'Nine-to-one,' he replied.

I peeled off £500 and gave it to him, then made my way to the grandstand, stopping at the bottom of the stairs to make a telephone call. 'Nine to one, Sir,' said the Hill lady.

'I'll have £1000 to win,' I said confidently. No hesitation.

'That's £1000 to win Earth Summit at 9/1, £1000 plus tax, £1100, thank you for calling William Hill.'

I thought of the countless times I had phoned that number over the years. A £10 bet was taken in the same way as a £1000 or presumably ten grand. Everyone thinks their bet is important. I shouldn't think my 2000 win and 1000 place would have raised any eyebrows, but by the time I got up to the box in the Queen Elizabeth Grandstand, Earth Summit was down to 7/1. As the rain tumbled down, so had his price. Everything else, including Rough Quest, was on the drift.

A streaker threatened to hold up proceedings as he completed nearly 100 yards of the four-and-a-half miles.

The balcony outside our box was jam packed. I was amazingly calm as the whole world waited for the tapes to go up. Patricia went inside and watched on television. I guess she thought I would have a heart attack or something. Alongside me stood Richard Bernard who, although one of our oldest and closest friends, was the most unlikely witness to this historic event.

The other owners stood quietly amongst their own friends and family. People who have been racing with me over the years will tell you I can get very excited when a horse I have backed looks like winning. Today an inner calm possessed me. I had only one fear, the Chair fence. I don't really know why. Having stood by it during the Friday morning interview on BBC breakfast news, I suppose I had built it up in my mind. It's not the highest of the Grand National obstacles but there is a yawning open ditch on the take-off side and the horse's stride has to be perfect for it to clear the fence. It is also the narrowest of the thirty, so I suppose I was worried about crowding.

In any event, my binoculars never moved as the huge field got away to a massive roar from the crowd. Five fell at the first fence and Earth Summit, on the wide outside, had to sidestep two of them. Carl Llewellyn negotiated the famous Bechers Brook still on the wide outside and was in mid division at the canal turn. Coming back on to the racecourse, Greenhill Tare Away led from Decyborg and the French challenger, Ciel de Brion. At the fourteenth a loose horse crossed right in front of the field and another roar, this time of apprehension, went up from the packed stands. By this time Earth Summit had moved into sixth position. The fearsome Chair loomed. He literally skipped over it and the water jump right underneath us, and I felt the emotion well up inside me. The Chair and the water are only jumped once. The ground was so heavy that the leaders literally hacked down to Becher's Brook the second time. This pace was perfect for us as Earth Summit revelled in the heavy going, the ground resembling more and more the Edgar Street pitch on February 5th 1972.

At the canal turn, Suny Bay moved into third place just in front of Earth Summit. At this stage there were only eight of the thirty-seven still standing. Ciel de Brion fell at the plain fence after Valentines and Suny Bay and Earth Summit swept past the longtime leader Greenhill Tare Away, who came down at the next.

The Radio 2 commentary of the race which I keep in my car stirs emotions like only radio commentary can. As Cornelius Lysaght hands over to Peter Bromley, he says, 'And there's only two in it, Earth Summit and Suny Bay.'

Bromley takes over. 'So the Grand national has distilled itself down to a precious brew of two.'

There were still three fences to jump and the pair were a distance clear of St Mellion Fairway and Samlee.

Incredibly, this was the first time I had experienced the Grand National live. The excitement and atmosphere would have been phenomenal, quite apart from the fact that I was watching a horse I part-owned sharing an unassailable lead with one other horse out of a field of thirty-seven. With three fences to jump there were just five horses standing.

I remained calm, at least I thought I did. Not daring to take anything for granted now, I tried to hold my binoculars steady as the two approached the second last. The noise was deafening.

On the balcony above the screams, Richard Bernard's girlfriend shouted to him, 'What's happening Rick, I can't see?'

'His horse is fucking winning, that's what's happening!' Rick's voice betrayed the incredulity everyone was now feeling.

As the two brave horses drew further and further away, uppermost in my mind and everyone else's was that Earth Summit was receiving a huge weight advantage from his lone rival. Both Carl Llewellyn and Graham Bradley were acutely aware of this and Carl made his decisive move just before the last. Urging his mount into the lead, they landed a length clear of the gallant grey and gradually forged ahead as they approached the elbow to win the greatest steeplechase in the world by eleven lengths.

As our heroes crossed the winning line, I rushed into the hospitality box and grabbed my wife, who had tears streaming down her face. We raced out into the corridor and literally floated, hand in hand, down the six flights of stairs to the ground and across to the famous enclosure where the world was waiting to greet the winner. A hurried interview with Desmond, a thousand photographs, the presentation by the Princess Royal and the inevitable press conference were followed by drinks in the sponsors' lounge, where Patrick Martell, Sir Peter O'Sullevan and Her Royal Highness graciously congratulated six elated and shellshocked owners.

The time between the end of the race and where I now stood had been a blur. Suddenly, I looked out of the large bay french windows facing the winning post and noticed that Aintree was fast becoming deserted. I was still in a daze of joy when I noticed some betting tickets floating by on a sudden breeze. It was then I remembered I had £5000 to pick-up from Ladbrokes on the rails. Hurriedly excusing myself, I rushed out onto the lawn and looked left towards the bookmakers. It was still raining and there was just one umbrella left open. Two cold and wet Ladbrokes representatives were waiting patiently for me to collect the bundle of notes they had neatly bound together with elastic bands. I didn't need to count it. They congratulated me and we shook hands.

I wanted more than anything to be with my family. As I climbed the stairs Patricia and I had negotiated so speedily an hour before, I had an overwhelming desire to be holding my three children to me tightly. Daniel was in Berlin and Adam and Rebecca were at home watching on TV with about twenty of our closest friends.

We decided to go straight home to Barnet.

The choices were to stay in Liverpool and celebrate, follow Earth Summit back to the yard and celebrate with the masses in the Hollow Bottom, or go home. I knew that we would have to be in Naunton the following morning for the traditional media jamboree at the winner's stable, so at eight o'clock we began the journey down the M6. Curiously enough, there had been so much excitement immediately after the race that I hadn't actually found the time to have more than one glass of champagne, courtesy of Martell.

At exactly eleven o'clock, tired and happy, we pulled into our drive. I stopped the car and we both sat with our mouths open in amazement. The house was bedecked with black and yellow balloons and a huge sign above the door read, 'You've reached the summit.' Peter Main's sister Jill, assisted by the kids, had given us a fabulous welcome home. Before we went to bed I watched the race again.

The scenes at Grangehill stables the next day were memorable, and Earth Summit was his usual amiable self, looking a lot fresher than most of his connections. After a raucous lunch in the Hollow Bottom, we headed for home again. On the way, I called Adam and Rebecca and told them to invite all our friends to the house and to get in as much champagne as they could.

Daniel phoned from Berlin to tell us that he and Will Kolbe had been in an Irish bar during the race. There was no television but at some point they'd asked the barman if he knew the result of the Grand National. He said he didn't know the name of the horse but he was sure the jockey was Carl Llewellyn. A long way from home, my eldest son and his great friend got completely smashed with a happy but mystified group of strangers from all over the world.

At some point that evening, surrounded by friends and family, Patricia made an unforgettable speech. She likened our race down the stairs to a scene from the movie 'Titanic', telling everyone she had felt like Kate Winslet, literally floating on air.

As she described her feelings of joy for what she knew was a momentous experience for me, I looked around the room. The smiles on people's faces coupled with the tears in their eyes reminded me, once more, how lucky I am to have shared my life with this very special lady.

Chapter Thirty-Three
Aftermath Two

Three days after the Grand National, I flew out to Orlando, Florida with Patricia, Adam and Rebecca.

At Gatwick Airport I bumped into David Icke. I had not seen him since we were playing colleagues at Hereford in 1972. His life, since then had been eventful, to say the least, a large part of it well-publicised. He was the same well-mannered, pleasant individual I had known all those years before. His face lit up when we spotted each other and he warmly congratulated us all on Earth Summit's victory. He was on his way to Phoenix, Arizona to lecture on wealth distribution. I didn't go too deeply into the subject, having just won approaching £100 000, including my share of the prize money.

I was still getting used to being the part owner of a Grand National winner. After all, there had only been 150-odd people ever to have achieved the feat.

David had seen it all on the telly. I imagined everyone knew who I was as we strolled through the South Terminal. I could have flown to Florida without an aircraft.

The stories that followed the big day are worth recording.

Since the Barnet Football club episode I have been a regular at Tottenham Hotspur, with the kids when they are around.

On the day of the National, John Motson was at White Hart Lane covering the Spurs versus Everton game for Match of the Day. The race was beamed live on the jumbo screen at half-time and the Zemmel family, surrounded by thousands in the West Stand lower section, were screaming their heads off as Earth Summit forged clear on the run-in.

That night in his commentary, Motty mentioned that he knew one Spurs season-ticket holder who would be very happy at the result of the race.

Whilst we were in Florida, *The Jewish Chronicle* contacted the office. Having heard that one of the owners of the Grand National winner was a member of the 1977 Maccabiah squad, they were anxious to get a story. Jeffrey Zemmel willingly obliged in my absence. Upon hearing the names of the other members of the partnership, for some reason the reporter asked if Bob Sims was Jewish. 'No, but the horse is,' Jeffrey replied, laughing; 'he's a gelding!'

My mobile phone had gathered a mass of goodwill messages immediately after the race. I played them as we sped down the M6. One was from Alec Stewart, the Newmarket trainer, with whom I had owned Barnet Fayre, Barrack Yard and Dmowski. He was thrilled for us.

My brother Michael, who only ever bets on my horses and had told all his friends and business associates to back Earth Summit months before, was beside himself with excitement.

Russell Townsend, thirteen years my junior, who had followed me through East Barnet school into the world of professional football to also finish his career at Barnet, via Arsenal and Northampton Town, tried desperately to leave a message but was overcome with emotion. When I heard his voice I cried as well.

Adam and Rebecca had watched the race at the Mains, Patricia's younger sister and her family. There were twenty or so people crammed into the lounge and, so we were told, the excitement was excruciating. The stories were always the same. Everyone, no matter how remotely, felt a connection to this win. All over the country, it seemed there were people jumping up and down in front of their TV sets screaming as our gallant little horse battled home.

I had dozens of letters of congratulations. One was from Johnny Danter with whom I had stood watching Barnet in the 1959 Amateur Cup Final and who I hadn't seen for thirty-six years. He told me that he spends every Grand National day with his Mum, by tradition. This year she asked him to put a fiver on Earth Summit because the colours of yellow and black reminded her of Barnet Football Club. John went down to the betting shop and returned in time to see my interview with Desmond Lynam before the race. He said that him and his dear old Mum just sat there staring at the screen in disbelief when they realised who one of the owners was. She had last seen me when I was fourteen. As if that excitement wasn't enough to last a lifetime, the horse went and won!

Betting stories abound. I know so many people who had never placed a bet in their lives until that day. The stakes varied greatly.

Jeff and Elfie Jarret live three doors from us in Hadley Green, Barnet. Jeff walked to Barnet High Street and drew £100 from the cash machine. He then proceeded to walk back the seventy-five yards or so to Ladbrokes. With every step his misgivings grew at the thought of losing such a large sum. He ended up having £20 on. It didn't detract from his enjoyment, he tells us. John Botterill, a golfing and red wine expert with a sense of humour so wicked that no-one would ever guess he was a solicitor, had £100 each way and cried his eyes out as Earth Summit steamed home in the mud. Many people just had £1 on but admitted to shedding a few tears.

There's something about that race.

What I loved hearing was the story of the queues of punters at Ladbrokes in Barnet High Street. There were so many winning bets, the shop literally ran out of money.

I called my dad straight after the race. 'Didn't Carl ride a fantastic race, Dad?'

'Yes,' he replied, 'and so did the horse!'

Chapter Thirty-Four
Finale

Earth Summit had a good long summer break after his Grand National win, then in November of that year he returned to Aintree to contest the three-mile, three-furlong Tote Becher Chase. With Tom Jenks back on board, he pulverised a small field coming home a distance clear of Samlee at the very generous odds of 6/1.

A couple of weeks later the gelding ran what Peter Scudamore described as 'the race of his life'. Meeting Suny Bay at level weights in the Edward Hanmer Chase at Haydock, our hero chased the grey all the way to the line, finishing a mere one-and-a-half lengths adrift after three miles on good ground. For a while it seemed as though he had improved again as he approached his eleventh year. However, a disappointing run in the Welsh National at Chepstow in December gave us all food for thought concerning his long-term wellbeing.

He was rested before the 1999 Grand National in which he finished eighth out of thirty-nine starters. The Tommy Carberry trained Bobbyjo triumphed on a mild April day on ground that was far too quick for Earth Summit, though he jumped faultlessly and suffered no ill effects from another four-and-a-half miles around the toughest racecourse in the world.

He returned to Liverpool to defend his Tote Becher crown in November. Carrying top weight of twelve stone, he gave another superb display of jumping, this time in the hands of an ecstatic Jamie Goldstein, finishing sixth to Feels Like Gold, who carried two stone less.

Earth Summit saw out the century by finishing a distant eighth in the 1999 Welsh Grand National, again carrying top weight of eleven stone ten pounds.

On Saturday January 15th 2000, I received a telephone call from Nigel Payne to tell me the sad news that our great champion had suffered a small injury in training and the decision had been taken to retire him immediately. Although I agreed wholeheartedly with the decision, it could not compensate for the awful feeling of sadness that stayed with me throughout the weekend. On Sunday afternoon I watched again the video of all his victories and some defeats, culminating with Aintree on April 4th 1998.

At the end of each race there was always a rush to greet him and the main concern of all remained his wellbeing. As a handicapper he has been penalised for his great success. As the only horse ever to have won all three Nationals – the Martell Grand National and the Welsh and Scottish equivalents – he had a fair amount of weight to carry in his final races.

It has already been decided that he will be given to his most devoted and caring servant, Marcella Bayliss, who has looked after him night and day for eight years. He could have had no better retirement.*

I may own other horses in the future. At this time, I have a half share in a five-year-old gelding by the name of Dmowski and a tenth share in a lovely five-year-old mare who delights in the name of Hannigans Lodger. Dmowski won on his racecourse debut, then suffered an injury that sidelined him for nineteen months. He is now fully fit. Hannigans Lodger has won twice, once over hurdles and recently over the Cheltenham fences.

It is most unlikely that I will ever own or part own a horse like Earth Summit again. His record entitles him to be counted amongst the greatest steeplechasers of all time. Carl Llewellyn described him as 'probably the best jumper of a fence that I've ridden'. Nigel Twiston-Davies echoed the thoughts of all involved when he called him 'a kind, gentle, laid-back type of horse – a nice horse'. In all, Earth Summit raced forty-one times, winning ten races for total prize money of £372 565. How lucky I was – again – to have been just a small part of him.

* Tragically, less than two months after the announcement of Earth Summit's retirement in January 2000, Nigel Payne's wife Liz passed away after a short illness. At the memorial service held at Chalfont St Giles, Nigel and Liz's great friend Peter Earl gave a moving and affectionate address. She is sadly missed.

What is certain is that I will not score an FA Cup goal again. It is likely that I will relive it every now and then when someone like Motty reminds the world that there was a winning goal scored against Newcastle in 1972. Even if they don't, Ronnie Radford's wonderful strike will be shown as long as moving pictures are beamed into millions of homes and the greatest domestic football competition in the world survives the nonsense that deprived it of Manchester United's participation in 1999.

And I will be reminded yet again how lucky I have been.

My fifteen minutes of fame became thirty, but as we all know, fame doesn't necessarily bring happiness. Maybe the short experience and quick return to anonymity makes you appreciate all the more the part that Lady Luck plays.

I hope my memory of it was worth reading.